John Hoole

Jerusalem Delivered

An Heroic Poem

John Hoole

Jerusalem Delivered
An Heroic Poem

ISBN/EAN: 9783742837264

Manufactured in Europe, USA, Canada, Australia, Japa

Cover: Foto ©Andreas Hilbeck / pixelio.de

Manufactured and distributed by brebook publishing software (www.brebook.com)

John Hoole

Jerusalem Delivered

JERUSALEM DELIVERED;

AN

HEROIC POEM:

Translated from the ITALIAN of

TORQUATO TASSO,

By JOHN HOOLE.

IN TWO VOLUMES.

VOL. II.

THE FIFTH EDITION,

WITH NOTES.

LONDON:
Printed for J. Dodsley, in Pall-Mall.

M.DCC.LXXXIII.

THE

ELEVENTH BOOK

OF

JERUSALEM DELIVERED.

Vol. II.   B

THE ARGUMENT.

THE Christians make a solemn procession, and, with public prayers, implore the assistance of heaven. The next morning a general assault is given to the city; and numbers are slain on both sides. A breach is made in the wall; Godfrey, preparing to enter first, is wounded by an arrow from Clorinda, and obliged to retire from the field. The day then seems to change in favour of the Pagans. Solyman and Argantes signalize themselves. In the mean time Godfrey, being conveyed to his tent, is miraculously healed by an angel. He returns to the walls, and renews the attack, till night puts an end to the battle.

THE
ELEVENTH BOOK
OF
JERUSALEM DELIVERED.

THE Christian leader now, with care oppress'd,
    The near assault revolv'd within his breast:
But, while he hastes his vast machines to frame,
Before his presence reverend Peter came;
The hermit sage apart the hero took,   5
And thus sedate with awful words bespoke.
  You, mighty Prince! terrestrial arms prepare,
But first another duty claims your care.
To heav'n your thoughts be turn'd, your vows be paid,
And call the angels and the saints to aid: 10
With public pray'rs their succour seek to gain,
So may your arms the wish'd success obtain.
Then let the priesthood in procession move,
And humbly supplicate the pow'rs above:

And

And you, O chiefs! the vulgar herd inspire, 15
And kindle in their souls devotion's fire.
  Severely thus the holy hermit said;
Th' observant leader his advice obey'd.
O servant, lov'd of JESUS! (he reply'd)
Well pleas'd I follow where thy counsels guide. 20
While I the chieftains of the camp invite,
Call thou the people's pastors to the rite,
William and Ademar, (a reverend pair)
Thine be the sacred pomp, and thine the care!
  Soon as th' ensuing morning's light arose, 25
The hermit with the priests assembled goes,
Where in a vale, to worship sacred made,
The Christians oft their pure devotions paid.
Robes, white as snow, the priestly band enfold;
The pastors shone in mantles rich with gold, 30
That hung divided on their breasts before,
And hallow'd wreaths around their brows they wore.
  First Peter leads, and waves aloft in air
The sign which saints in Paradise revere:

Ver. 25. *Soon as th' ensuing morning's light arose.*] History relates, that before the general assault, the litany was chanted with a solemn religious procession. I have elsewhere observed, and I believe the reader will agree with me, that the following passage, for solemnity of description, is equal to any part of the poem.

Next

Next in two ranks, with solemn steps and slow, 35
The tuneful choir in lengthen'd order go:
Then, side by side, the holy chiefs appear,
William and Ademar, and close the rear:
Next Godfrey comes, like one of high command,
Alone and foremost of his martial band. 40
By two and two the field the leaders tread;
Then, sheath'd in arms, the warrior-host succeed.
Thus from the trenches move the pious train,
Sedate and silent stretching o'er the plain;
Nor clang of arms, nor trumpet's sound is heard, 45
But holy hymns from humble hearts preferr'd.

 Thee, FATHER! first, omnipotent, they sung,
Thee, SON, coequal! from the FATHER sprung:
Thee, SPIRIT! in whose influence both combine;
Thee, Virgin-mother of the man divine! 50
And you, ye leaders! who in heaven above
Th' effulgent bands in triple circles move:
And thee, whose hand baptiz'd th' incarnate God
With the pure stream in Jordan's hallow'd flood.

 Ver. 51. *And you, ye leaders!*—] The angelical orders thus classed by the theological writers of that time, seraphim, cherubim, thrones, dominations, principalities, and powers; virtues, angels, and archangels. Thus Milton:

 Thrones, dominations, princedoms, virtues, powers!

Thee, Peter! they invoke in songs of praise, 55
The rock on which heav'n fix'd, his church to raise;
Where now thy great descendant holds the place,
T' unclose the gates of pardon and of grace:
And all the nunciates of th' ethereal reign,
Who testify'd the glorious death to man: 60
With those, the martyrs for the truth, who stood
To seal the precious doctrine with their blood:
And those, whose words or writings taught the way
To the lost regions of eternal day:
And her, the damsel true, of Christ belov'd, 65
Whose pious choice the better life approv'd;
The virgins chaste, in lonely cells enclos'd,
By mystic rites to heav'n alone espous'd:
With every other name in torments try'd,
Whose zeal the nations and their kings defy'd! 70

Thus chanting hymns devout, the numerous train,
In ample circuit, mov'd along the plain:
Their pensive march to Olivet they frame,
(Fruitful in olives, whence it bears the name;
Eastward it rises from the sacred town, 75
A mount by fame through every region known)
So pass the tuneful bands with cadence sweet,
The hollow vales the lengthen'd notes repeat;

The

The winding caverns and the mountains high
A thousand echoes to the sounds reply.   80

 Meantime, in wonder fix'd, the pagan band
All hush'd and silent on the ramparts stand;
Struck with their solemn pace, their humble tone,
The pomp unusual, and the rites unknown.
But when their wonder ceas'd, th' ungodly crew 85
From impious tongues blaspheming curses threw:
With barb'rous shouts they shake the bulwarks round,
The hills and vallies to the noise resound!
But not their course the Christian powers refrain,
Nor cease their ritual or melodious strain;   90
Fearless they move, nor heed the clamours more
Than cries of birds loquacious on the shore.

 Then on the summit of the hill they rear'd
A splendid altar, for the priest prepar'd;
On either side, refulgent to behold,   95
A beamy lamp was plac'd of burnish'd gold!
There William now, in costlier robes array'd,
His reverend homage at the altar paid;
There, with low voice, his humble suit prefers,
And supplicates with vows and holy prayers.   100

 Ver. 73. *Their pensive march to Olivet they frame.*
  81. —— *the pagan band*
  All hush'd and silent —] All these circumstances are taken from the history.

Devoutly hush'd the near assistants stand;
With eyes intent behold the distant band!
But when compleat the mystic rites were ceas'd,
The sacred fire th' attending train dismiss'd,
And with his priestly hand the squadrons bless'd.

   The pious troops return (this duty o'er)   106
And tread the path their feet had trod before:
'Till, at the vale arriv'd, their ranks they broke,
When to the tents his course the hero took:
With smiles he parted from the vulgar band,   110
But there the captains of his host detain'd
To due repast; and full before him plac'd
Thouloufe's valiant earl with honours grac'd:
The call of thirst and hunger now represt,
The chief of chiefs his leaders thus addrefs'd.   115

   Soon as the morn ascends her early throne,
Rise all in arms t' assault Judæa's town:
Be that the day t' invade our impious foe,
The present hours to needful tasks bestow.

   This said, the chiefs depart; with trumpet's sound
Th' obedient heralds send his mandates round;   121
And bid each ardent warrior rise to fight,
Array'd in armour, with the dawning light.
In different works the tedious day they waste,
And various thoughts revolve in every breast,   125

                                   Till

Till welcome night, that irksome care relieves,
A grateful truce to mortal labour gives.

Aurora still with doubtful lustre gleams,
Scarce has the dawn display'd her orient beams;
No stubborn ploughs the yielding furrows tear, 130
No watchful shepherds to the meads repair;
Each bird secure his peaceful slumber takes;
Nor hound nor horn the silent forest wakes:
When now the trumpet's echoes rouze the morn,
To arms! to arms! the vaulted skies return: 135
To arms! to arms! with universal cry
A hundred legions to the notes reply.
First Godfrey rose, but now neglects to bear
His ponderous cuirass, oft approv'd in war;
A slight defence the fearless hero chose, 140
And o'er his limbs the lighter burthen throws;
Arm'd like the meanest of the martial name;
When aged Raymond to his presence came:
Soon as he view'd the chief, his thoughts divin'd
What deed the leader's secret soul design'd. 145
Where is thy corslet's massy weight (he cry'd)
Where all thy other arms of temper try'd?
What dost thou seek? a private palm to gain,
To scale the walls amongst the vulgar train?

Think

Think not this task a gen'ral's sword demands: 150
Such dangers leave to less important hands.
Resume thy arms: regard thy safety most,
And save a life, the spirit of our host.

 He ceas'd. The gen'rous leader thus reply'd:
When holy Urban girded to my side   155
This sword in Clarmont; and when first 'twas giv'n
To Godfrey's hand to wage the wars of heav'n,
To God I vow'd my social arms to wield,
A private warrior in the dangerous field.
Since I have every duty now display'd   160
As fits a chief by whom the host is led;
It next remains (with justice shalt thou own)
To march in equal arms t' assault the town.
Thus shall I keep the faith to heaven I gave;
His hand shall lead me, and his power shall save. 165

 This said; his brethren soon th' example took;
Each knight of France his heavy arms forsook;
The other chiefs less cumberous harness chose,
And boldly march'd on foot t' invade the foes.

 Ver. 155. *When holy Urban girded to my side*
   This sword in Clarmont —] Pope Urban went in person to the council of Clarmont, a city of France, where he appointed numbers to the crusade, and among the first Godfrey, giving to each adventurer the sacred badge of the expedition.

               Alike

Alike prepar'd the pagan troops afcend 170
Where tow'rds the north the crooked rampares bend;
And where the weft furveys the rifing towers,
Of leaft defence againft the hoftile powers:
For, well fecur'd on ev'ry part befide,
The town th' attempts of all their hoft defy'd. 175
Nor here alone the tyrant's watchful care
Had plac'd the beft and braveft of the war;
But, fummon'd in this utmoft rifque of ftate,
Old age and childhood fhare the toils of fate:
Thefe to the brave fupply (as time requires) 180
Sulphur, and ftones, and darts, and miffile fires.
With vaft machines and arms the walls they ftow,
Whofe rifing height commands the plain below;
There from aloft, the foldan ftrikes the eyes,
In form a giant of ftupendous fize! 185
There on the ramparts, flaming from afar,
The fierce Argantes tow'rs with threatening air:
And where the higheft fort its fummit rears,
The fam'd Clorinda o'er the reft appears,
And ftor'd with darts her deadly quiver bears. 190
Already in her hand the bow fhe tries,
Now ftrains the nerve, and now the fhaft applies.
Eager to ftrike, the lovely archer ftands,
And waits, with longing eyes, the hoftile bands.

So

So feign'd of old, from heaven's ethereal height,
The Delian virgin dealt a feather'd flight. 196

   The hoary king, forgetful of his state,
Within the city moves from gate to gate;
Renews again his orders on the wall,
And breathes a hope and confidence in all; 200
Here adds supplies of men, and there provides
Fresh store of arms, and o'er the whole presides.
But to the fanes the matrons sad repair,
And seek their fabled god with fruitless prayer.

   O! hear our vows! thy righteous arm advance,
And sudden break the Christian robber's lance! 206
And him who dares thy hallow'd name offend,
Now prone beneath the lofty gates extend!

   While thus the city bends her different cares,
The pious chief his arms and troops prepares: 210
And first he leads the foot, a numerous train,
In skilful order marshal'd on the plain:
Then in two squadrons he divides his powers
T' attack, on either side, the hostile towers.
The huge balistæ in the midst appear, 215
And every dreadful implement of war;
Whence on the walls, like thunderbolts, are thrown
Enormous darts, and crags of ponderous stone.

                               The

The heavy arm'd the weaker foot fuſtain;
The lighter horſe are ſent to ſcour the plain.   220
At length the word is giv'n, the ſignals found;
The bows are bent, the ſlings are whirl'd around:
Their deathful rage the mighty engines pour,
And gall the pagans with a rocky ſhower:
Some quit their poſts, and others headlong fall,   225
And thinn'd appear the ranks that guard the wall.

 The Franks, impatient now to prove their force,
More near the walls advance with eager courſe.
Some, ſhield to ſhield in cloſeſt texture laid,
Above their heads an ample covering made: 230
And ſome, beneath machines, in ſafety move,
A ſure defence from falling ſtones above.
And now the foſſe th' advancing ſoldiers gain,
And ſeek the depth to level with the plain.
(The bottom firm a ſafe foundation ſhow'd)   235
This ſoon they fill'd, a late impervious road!
Adraſtus foremoſt of the troop appears,
And 'gainſt the walls a ſcaling-ladder rears:
Boldly he mounts, while round his head they pour
The ſtones and ſulphur in a mingled ſhower: 240
The fierce Helvetian wond'ring crowds ſurvey,
Who now had finiſh'd half his airy way:

           When

When lo! with fury sent, a rugged stone,
With rapid force, as from an engine thrown,
(Sent by the vigour of Circassia's knight)   245
Struck on his helm, and hurl'd him from his height.
Nor wound ensu'd, nor mortal was the stroke,
Yet prone he tumbled, senseless with the shock.
Then thus Argantes with a threatening cry:
Fall'n is the first: who dares the second try?   250
Behold, I fearless stand before your sight,
Why, warriors! drew ye not to open fight?
Think not those sheds can fence your dastard train,
For you, like beasts, shall in your caves be slain!

 He said; yet not for this the Christians stay; 255
But in their coverts still pursue their way:
While others on their fencing bucklers bear
The storm of arrows, and the rattling war.
Now to the walls the battering rams drew nigh,
Enormous engines, dreadful to the eye!   260
Strong iron plates their massy heads compose:
The gates and ramparts fear th' approaching blows.
'Gainst these a hundred hands their aid supply,
And roll vast beams and ruins from on high;   264
The ponderous fragments thunder on the fields;
At once they break the well-compacted shields,
And the crush'd helmet to the fury yields!

            The

The plain is ſtrewn with arms, and cover'd o'er
With ſhatter'd bones, and brains, and mingled gore!
 The fierce aſſailants now, for bolder fight,   270
Forth from their covert ruſh'd to open light:
Some place their ladders, and the height aſcend;
Againſt the ramparts ſome their engines bend.
The rams begin to ſhake the batter'd wall,
The nodding bulwarks threat a ſudden fall.   275
But, watchful, from the town the foes prepare
Each various method of defenſive war:
And where the forceful beams impetuous drove,
A maſs of wool, ſuſpended from above,
Whoſe yielding ſubſtance breaks the dreadful blows,
The wary pagans 'gainſt the ſtorm oppoſe.   281
 While thus, with dauntleſs hearts, the warrior-train
Againſt the walls the bold attack maintain;
Sev'n times her twanging bow Clorinda drew,
As oft her arrow from the bow-ſtring flew;   285
And every ſhaft that to the plain ſhe ſped,
Its ſteel and feathers dy'd with bluſhing red.
The nobleſt warriors drench'd her weapons o'er,
She ſcorn'd to dip their points in vulgar gore.
 The firſt who, 'midſt the tumult of the war,   290
Felt her keen darts, was England's youngeſt care;

Scarce

Scarce from his fence his head appear'd in view,
When, wing'd with speed, the vengeful arrow flew:
Swift thro' his better hand it held its course,
Nor could the steely gauntlet stop the force.   295
Disabled thus, with grief he left the plain,
And deeper groan'd with anger than with pain.
Then, near the fosse, the earl of Amboise fell:
Clotharius mounting found the deadly steel.
That, pierc'd from back to breast, reluctant dy'd:
This headlong fell, transfix'd from side to side. 301
The Flemish chief the battering engine heav'd,
When his left arm the sudden wound receiv'd:
He stay'd, and furious strove to draw the dart,
But left the steel within the wounded part.   305
To reverend Ademar, who, plac'd afar,
Uncautious stood to view the raging war,
The fatal reed arriv'd, his front it found;
He try'd to wrench the weapon from the wound;
Another dart, with equal fury sent,   310
Transfix'd his hand, and thro' his visage went.

He fell, and falling, pour'd a purple flood,
And stain'd the virgin-shaft with holy blood.
As Palamede to scale the bulwarks strove,
In his right eye the fatal arrow drove,   315

Through

Through all the optic nerves its paſſage tore,
And iſſu'd at his nape beſmear'd with gore:
At once he tumbles with a dreadful fall,
And dies beneath the well-conteſted wall!

While thus the virgin round her ſhafts beſtows,
With new devices Godfrey preſs'd his foes: 321
Aſide he brought againſt a portal near,
The largeſt of his huge machines of war;
A tower of wood, ſtupendous to the ſight,
Whoſe top might mate the lofty ramparts height:
Its ample womb could arms and men contain,   326
And, roll'd on wheels, it mov'd along the plain.
Near and more near the bulk enormous drew,
While from within the darts and javelins flew.
But, from the threaten'd walls, the wary foes   330
With ſpears and ſtones th' advancing pile oppoſe:
Againſt the front and ſides their ſtrokes they bend,
And heavy fragments on the wheels they ſend.
So thick, on either ſide, the javelins pour,
The air is darken'd with the miſſile ſhow'r: 335
Cloud meets with cloud; and, claſhing in the ſky,
Back to the ſenders oft the weapons fly.
As from the trees are torn the ſhatter'd leaves,
What time the grove the ſtormy hail receives;

As ripen'd fruit from loaded branches falls: 340
So fell the pagans from the lofty walls;
While others that furviv'd, with deep difmay,
Fled from the huge machine's tremendous fway.
Not fo the foldan; fearlefs he remain'd,
And with him many on the height detain'd. 345
Then fierce Argantes thither bent his courfe,
And feiz'd a beam t'oppofe the hoftile force:
Firm in his hand th' enormous weight he held,
By this his mighty ftrength the tower repell'd
And kept aloof. With thefe the martial * fair 350
Appear'd, their glory and their toils to fhare.
Meanwhile, with fcythes prepar'd, the Franks divide
The cords to which the woolly fence is ty'd;
No more fuftain'd, at once on earth it falls,
And undefended leaves the threaten'd walls. 355
Now from the Chriftian tower more fierce below,
The thundering ram redoubles every blow.
A breach is made: when, fir'd with martial fame,
The mighty Godfrey to the bulwarks came:
His body cover'd with his ampleft fhield, 360
(A weight his arm was feldom wont to wield)
He faw, as round he caft his careful view,
Where from the walls fierce Solyman withdrew,
And fwift to guard the dangerous paffage flew;

* CLORINDA.

While

While still Clorinda and Circassia's knight 365
Maintain'd their station on the rampart's height.
He sees, and instant from Sigero's hands
A lighter buckler and his bow demands.
Myself (he cries) will first the deed essay
Thro' yon disjointed stones to force the way: 370
'Tis time to shew some act that merits praise,
That may to either hoft our glory raise.

Then, changing shields, he scarce the word had said,
When from the wall a vengeful arrow fled:
The destin'd passage in his leg it found, 375
Where strong each nerve, and painful is the wound.
The deadly shaft from thee, Clorinda! came,
To thee alone the world ascribes the fame:
This day, preserv'd by thy unerring bow,
Thy pagan friends to thee their safety owe. 380
But still his troops the dauntless leader fires,
Still o'er the works his daring foot aspires:
'Till now he feels the wound's increasing pains;
No more the leg his sinking bulk sustains:
To noble Guelpho then a sign he made: 385
Behold compell'd I leave the field (he said)
Thou, in my place, a leader's task sustain,
And, in my absence, head my social train.

Soon will I turn, the combat to renew—
He said, and on a courser thence withdrew, 390
Yet not unnoted by the pagan crew.
Thus parts th' unwilling hero from his post,
And with him fortune quits the Christian host:
While on the adverse side their force increas'd,
And hope, rekindling, dawn'd in every breast. 395
In every Christian heart now terrors rose,
And chilling fears their former ardor froze:
Already flew their weapons slow to wound,
And their weak trumpets breath'd a fainter sound.

Now on the ramparts height again appear 400
The bands, so late disperd'd with coward fear.
Incited by Clorinda's glorious fires,
Their country's love the female train inspires:
Eager they run to prove the tasks of war,
With vestments girded and dishevel'd hair: 405
They hurl the dart; nor fear, where danger calls,
T' expose their bosoms for their native walls.
But that which most the Franks with doubts op-
    press'd,
And banish'd fear from every pagan breast,
The mighty Guelpho, 'midst the rage of fight, 410
Fell by a wound, in either army's sight:

Amongst

Amongſt a thouſand fates, on earth o'erthrown,
Sent from afar he felt the miſſile ſtone.
Another ſtone alike on Raymond flew,
And prone to earth the hoary warrior threw. 415
While in the foſſe the brave Euſtatius ſtood,
A weapon deeply drank his gen'rous blood.
This hour (ill fated for the Chriſtian train)
No pagan weapon flies, which flies in vain.
Fir'd with ſucceſs, and ſwell'd to loftier pride, 420
The fierce Circaſſian rais'd his voice and cry'd.

 Not Antioch this; nor now the ſhades extend,
The ſhades of night that Chriſtian frauds befriend!
A wakeful foe ye view, an open light,
Far other forms, far other taſks of fight! 425
No ſparks of glory now your ſoul inflame,
No more ye thirſt for plunder or for fame;
Do ye ſo ſoon from weak attacks refrain?
O! leſs than women, in the ſhape of men!

 He ſpoke, and ſcorn'd, in narrow walls confin'd, 430
To hide the purpoſe of his daring mind:
With eager bounds he ſeeks the wall below,
Where gaping ſtones a dangerous paſſage ſhow.
While dauntleſs there to guard the paſs he flies,
To Solyman, who ſtood beſide, he cries. 435

Lo! Solyman, the place, the deftin'd hour,
In danger's field to prove our martial pow'r:
Why this delay? O! rouze thy noble fire;
Who prizes fame muft here to fame afpire.

He faid: and either warrior's ardor grows: 440
At once they iffue where the combat glows,
And, unexpected, thunder on the foes.
Beneath their arms what numbers prefs the ground,
What broken fhields and helms are fcatter'd round!
What rams and ladders cleft in ruins fall, 445
And raife new ramparts for the fhatter'd wall!

Now thofe, who lately hop'd the town to gain,
Can fcarce in arms the doubtful fight maintain.
At length they yield, and to the furious pair
Refign their engines and machines of war. 450
The pagan chiefs, as native fury fway'd,
With dreadful fhouts invoke the city's aid:
Now here, now there, they call for fiery brands,
And arm with flaming pines their dreadful hands;
Then on th' tower with furious hafte they bend: 455
So from the black Tartarian gates afcend
Pluto's dire minifters, (tremendous names!)
With hiffing ferpents and infernal flames!

Tancred, no lefs with thirft of fame infpir'd,
In other parts his hardy Latians fir'd! 460

When

When now the spreading carnage he beheld,
And saw the torches blazing o'er the field,
He left the walls, and turn'd his rapid course
T' oppose the Saracens' impetuous force:
He comes, he turns the scale of victory; 465
The vanquish'd triumph, and the victors fly!

Thus stood the war, while from the martial band
His lofty tent the wounded leader gain'd,
Baldwin and good Sigero near him stood,
And round of mourning friends a pensive crowd. 470
He strove to draw the shaft with eager speed,
And broke within the flesh the feather'd reed:
Then swift he bade explore the wounded part,
And bare a passage for the barbed dart.
Restore me swift to arms (the hero cries) 475
Ere rising night th' unfinish'd strife surprize.
Now old Erotimus t' assist him stood,
Who drew his birth by Po's imperial flood;
Who well the pow'r of healing simples knew,
The force of plants and every virtuous dew: 480
Dear to the muse; but, pleas'd with lowly fame,
He gain'd by private arts an humbler name.
His skill could mortals from the grave reprieve;
His verse could bid their names for ever live.

All unconcern'd the godlike chief appears, 485
While every pale affiftant melts in tears.
The fage phyfician for the tafk prepares,
He girds his vefture, and his arm he bares;
With lenient med'cine bathes th' afflicted part,
And with a gentle hand attempts the dart; 490
With pincers next the ftubborn fteel he ftrains,
Yet fix'd it ftands, and mocks his utmoft pains.
What means fhall next his baffled art devife,
Since fortune thus her favouring aid denies?
Full foon the chief th' increafing anguifh found, 495
And fleeting life hung doubtful in the wound.
But now the guardian angel, touch'd with grief,
From Ida's fummit brought the wifh'd relief;
A branch of dittany, of wonderous pow'r,
Whofe downy foliage bears a purple flower: 500
By nature taught (th' inftructrefs of their kind)
The mountain goats its fecret virtue find,
What time they feel the winged dart from far,
And in their wounded fides the arrow bear.
With this, tho' diftant thence the region lies, 505
The pitying angel in a moment flies:
Unfeen, with this, the vafe prepar'd he fills,
And odoriferous panacy diftils.

The

The leech anoints the part, and, (strange to tell!)
Loos'd from the wound, the shaft spontaneous fell:
The blood forbore to flow, the anguish ceas'd, 511
And strength, return'd, in every nerve increas'd.
Then thus Erotimus with wonder cries!
No skill of mine thy sudden cure supplies:
A greater power his timely aid extends, 515
Some guardian angel from his heaven descends:
I see celestial hands!—To arms! to arms!
Return, and rouze again the war's alarms!

 He said; and Godfrey, eager for the fight,
Soon o'er his thighs dispos'd the cuishes bright; 520
He shook his ponderous lance, his helmet lac'd,
And his forsaken shield again embrac'd.
He moves; a thousand on his steps attend;
Thence to the town their rapid march they bend,
With clouds of dust the face of heaven is spread, 525
Wide shakes the earth beneath the warrior's tread.
The foes behold the squadron drawing near,
And feel their blood congeal'd with chilling fear.
Thrice on the field his voice the hero rear'd;
Full well the welcome sound his people heard; 530
The sound that oft was wont to chear the fight;
Then, fir'd anew, they rouze their fainting might.

Still

Still at the walls, the haughty pagan pair,
Plac'd in the breach, support the dangerous war;
Firm in the pass a bold defence maintain,   535
'Gainst noble Tancred and his valiant train.

   Now, sheath'd in arms, the glorious chief drew nigh,
Disdain and anger flashing from his eye:
On fierce Argantes all his force he bends,
And 'gainst the foe his lance impatient sends.   540
Not with more noise some stone enormous flies,
Sent by an engine through th' affrighted skies;
Through sounding air its course the jav'lin held;
Argantes, fearless, lifts th' opposing shield:
The riven target to the force gives way,   545
Nor can the corslet's plates the fury stay:
Through shatter'd armour flies the missive wood,
And dips it thirsty point in Pagan blood:
Swift from his side the lance Argantes drew,
And to its lord again the weapon threw;   550
Receive thy own, he cry'd—but, stooping low,
The wary Christian disappoints the foe:
The deadly point the good Sigero found,
Full in his throat he felt the piercing wound:
Yet with a secret joy he sunk in death,   555
Pleas'd in his sovereign's stead to yield his breath.

A craggy flint the raging foldan threw;
Refiftlefs on the Norman chief it flew;
Stunn'd with the dreadful blow he reel'd around,
Then fudden tumbled headlong to the ground. 560
No longer Godfrey now his wrath repell'd,
Grafp'd in his hand the flaming fword he held;
And now to nearer fight his foes defy'd:
What deeds had foon been wrought on either fide!
But night, to check their rage, her veil difplay'd, 565
And wrapt the warring world in peaceful fhade:
Then Godfrey, ceafing, left th' unfinifh'd fray.
So clos'd the dreadful labours of the day!

But, ere the chief retir'd, with pious care,
He bade the wounded from the field to bear: 570
Nor would he leave (a welcome prey) behind
His warlike engines to the foes refign'd.
Safe from the walls he drew the loftieft tower,
Tho' broke and crufh'd with many a horrid fhower.
So feems a fhip from feas and tempefts borne, 575
Her planks all fhatter'd and her canvas torn,
When, 'fcap'd from furious winds and roaring tides,
Within the port fhe fcarce fecurely rides.
The broken wheels no more the tower fuftain,
Heavy and flow it drags along the plain, 580
The weight fupported by th' affifting train.

And

And now the workmen hafte, with ready care,
To fearch the pile, and every breach repair:
So Godfrey bade, who will'd that morning light
Should view the wonderous tower renew'd for fight:
On every fide his watchful thoughts he caft,   586
And guards around the lofty engine plac'd.
But, from the walls, their speech the Pagans hear,
And ftrokes of hammers breaking on the ear:
A thoufand torches gild the dufky air,   590
And all their purpofe and their toils declare.

THE END OF THE ELEVENTH BOOK.

THE TWELFTH BOOK
OF
JERUSALEM DELIVERED.

THE ARGUMENT.

Argantes and Clorinda undertake by night to burn the tower of the Christians. Arsetes, who had brought up Clorinda from her infancy, endeavours to dissuade her from the enterprize, but in vain: he then relates to her the story of her birth. The two adventurers sally from the town, and set fire to the tower: the Christians take arms: Argantes retreats before them, and gains the city in safety; but the gates being suddenly closed, Clorinda is left amongst the enemy. Tancred, not knowing her, pursues her as she is retiring towards the walls. They engage in a dreadful combat: Clorinda is slain, but, before she dies, receives baptism from the hand of Tancred. His grief and lamentation.

THE

TWELFTH BOOK

OF

JERUSALEM DELIVERED.

'TWAS night; but either hoft, with cares op-
    prefs'd,
Reliev'd not yet their toils with balmy reft;
Here, under covert of the gloomy hour,
The bufy Franks repair'd their batter'd tower;
And there the pagans, prefs'd with equal care,   5
Review'd their bulwarks tottering from the war,
And propp'd the walls. Alike on either fide,
The warriors' wounds each fkilful leech employ'd.
Now deeper darknefs brooded on the ground,
And many an eye was clos'd in fleep profound: 10
But not in flumber funk the * martial dame,
Whofe generous bofom ever pants for fame:

        * CLORINDA.

With

With her Argantes join'd the watch partook;
Then thus in secret to her soul she spoke.

 What wonderous praise has Solyman obtain'd! 15
What, by his deeds to-day, Argantes gain'd!
Alone, amidst yon numerous host to go,
And crush the engines of the Christian foe!
While I (how poor the vaunted fame I share!)
Here plac'd aloft maintain'd a distant war: 20
'Tis true my shafts may boast successful aim:
And is this all a woman's hand can claim?
'Twere better far in woods and wilds to chace
And pierce with darts remote the savage race,
Than here, when manly valour braves the field, 25
Appear a maid in feats of arms unskill'd.

 She said; and soon revolving in her breast
Heroic deeds, Argantes thus addres'd.

 Long has my soul unusual ardor prov'd,
And various thoughts this restless bosom mov'd: 30
I know not whether God th' attempt inspires,
Or man can form a God of his desires.
See! from yon vale the Christians' glimmering light—
My mind impels me, this auspicious night
To burn their tower; at least the deed be try'd, 35
And for th' event let heaven alone provide.

         But

But should it chance (the fate of war unknown)
The foes forbid me to regain the town;
I leave my damsel-train thy care to prove,
And one that loves me with a father's love: 40
Protect them, chief! and safe to Egypt send
My mourning virgins, and my aged friend:
O grant my prayer!—This duty from thy hands
Those claim by sex, and this by age demands.

With wonder fill'd, Argantes heard the dame, 45
And caught the kindling sparks of generous flame,
Then shalt thou go, and leave me here behind,
Despis'd (he cry'd) among th' ignoble kind?
Think'st thou I shall behold with joyful eyes,
Secur'd, afar the curling flames arise? 50
No—if in arms I ever grac'd thy side,
Still let me here thy doubtful chance divide,
I too can boast a heart despising death,
That prizes honour, cheaply bought with breath!

O generous chief! (reply'd the fearless maid) 55
In such resolves thy virtue stands display'd:
Yet here permit me to depart alone,
A loss like mine shall ne'er distress the town:
But (Heaven avert the omen!) should'st thou fall,
What hand shall longer guard Judæa's wall? 60

In vain is each pretence (the knight rejoin'd)
For fix'd remains the purpose of my mind:
Behold I tread the path thy feet shall lead,
But if refus'd, myself will dare the deed.

    This said, they sought the careful king, who sate 65
In nightly council for the public state:
There midst the brave and wise (an awful train)
They came, and first Clorinda thus began.

    Vouchsafe a while, O king! to bend thy ear,
And what we proffer with acceptance hear: 70
Argantes vows (nor vainly boasts the power)
With vengeful flames to burn yon hostile tower:
Myself will aid—our course alone we stay,
Till added toil the foes in slumber lay.

    To heaven his trembling hands the monarch rears,
His wrinkled cheeks are wet with joyful tears: 76
All praise to thee, O guardian power! (he cries)
Who still thy people view'st with gracious eyes!
Long wilt thou yet preserve my threaten'd reign,
When souls like these the town's defence maintain. 80
For you, ye pair! what praises can I find?
What gifts to equal your heroic mind?
Fame shall to distant times your worth proclaim,
And earth aloud repeat each glorious name.

                                     Your

Your deed be your reward—to this receive 85
Such recompence as fits a king to give.

Thus Aladine; and, as he spoke, he prefs'd,
Now this, now that, with transport to his breaft.
No more the liftening foldan could controul
The generous emulation in his foul: 90
Think not (he cry'd) in vain this fword I wear,
This hand with you fhall every labour bear.
Then let us iffue all (the maid rejoin'd)
Should'ft thou depart, who dares remain behind?
And now, with envy fill'd and jealous pride, 95
Argantes his confent had here deny'd;
But ftrait the word Judæa's monarch took,
And mildly thus the chief of Nice befpoke.

Intrepid warrior! whom no dangers fright,
Nor toil can weary in the day of fight: 100
Full well I deem that, iffuing on the foe,
Thy deeds would worthy of thy courage fhow:
But much unmeet it feems, that, parting all,
None, fam'd in arms, remain within the wall.
Nor would I thefe permit th' attempt to dare, 105
(So high their fafety and their lives I bear)
Were this a work of lefs important kind,
Or meaner hands could act the part defign'd.

D 2 But

But since, so well 'gainst ev'ry chance dispos'd,
The lofty tower is round with guards enclos'd, 110
No little force can hope the pass to gain;
Nor must we issue with a numerous train;
Let these who claim the task, this valiant pair,
Oft prov'd before in every risk of war,
Let these alone depart, in happy hour, 115
Whose strength is equal to a legion's power;
While thou, as best befits thy regal state,
Here with the rest remain within the gate.
And when (so fate succeed the glorious aim)
These shall return, and wide have spread the flame,
If chance a hostile band pursue their course, 121
Then haste and guard them from superior force.

 So spoke the king; nor aught the Turk rejoin'd,
Though discontent lay rankling in his mind.

 Then thus Ismeno: You who boldly dare 125
Th' adventurous task, awhile th' attempt forbear;
'Till various mixtures, cull'd with art, I frame,
To burn the hostile tower with sudden flame;
Perchance the guards, that now the pile surround,
May then be lost, in friendly slumbers drown'd. 130

 To this they yield; and each, apart retir'd,
Expects the season for the deed desir'd.

And now Clorinda threw her vest aside,
With silver wrought; her helmet's crested pride:
For these (ill omen !) sable arms she wore, 135
And sable casque that no plum'd honours bore.
She deem'd it easier, thus disguis'd to go,
And pierce the watchful squadrons of the foe.
The eunuch, old Arsetes, near her stay'd,
Who from her childhood bred the warrior-maid; 140
Who all her steps with faithful age pursu'd,
And near her now a trusty guardian stood.
He saw the virgin change her wonted arms;
Her rash design his anxious breast alarms:
He weeps, adjures her oft with earnest prayers, 145
By his long service, by his silver hairs,
By the dear mem'ry of his former pains,
To cease th' attempt; but she unmov'd remains.
To whom he said: Since, bent on future ill,
Thou stand'st resolv'd thy purpose to fulfil; 150
Since neither helpless age, nor love like mine,
Nor tears, nor prayers, can change thy dire design,
Attend—my tongue shall wondrous things reveal,
Nor longer now thy former state conceal.
That done, no more I strive thy thoughts to shake;
Resume thy purpose, or my counsel take. 156

He said; with eyes intent the virgin stood,
While thus the hoary sire his speech pursu'd.

In Ethiopia once Senapus reign'd,
(And still perchance he rules the happy land)   160
Who kept the precepts giv'n by Mary's Son,
Where yet the sable race his doctrines own.
There I, a pagan liv'd, remov'd from man,
The Queen's attendant midst the female train;
Though native gloom was o'er her features spread, 165
Her beauty triumph'd through the dusky shade.
Her husband lov'd—but ah! was doom'd to prove
At once th' extremes of jealousy and love:
He kept her close, secluded from mankind,
Within a lonely deep recess confin'd;   170
While the sage matron mild submission pay'd,
And, what her lord decreed, with joy obey'd.

Her pictur'd room a sacred story shows,
Where, rich with life, each mimic figure glows:

Ver. 173. —— *a sacred story shows.*] This alludes to the fabulous legend of Saint George, to which the poet here seems to give a mystical sense. Thus Ariosto, Orlando Furioso, Canto xv. speaking of the spurs given by Sanfonetto to Astolpho.

 Believ'd the champion's once, whose valiant deed,
 The holy virgin from the dragon freed. Ver. 716.

There, white as snow, appears a beauteous maid, 175
And near a dragon's hideous form display'd.
A champion through the beast a javelin sends,
And in his blood the monster's bulk extends.

 Here oft the Queen her secret faults confess'd,
And prostrate here her humble vows address'd. 180
At length her womb disburthen'd gave to view
(Her offspring thou) a child of snowy hue.
Struck with th' unusual birth, with looks amaz'd,
As on some strange portent, the matron gaz'd:
She knew what fears possess'd her husband's mind, 185
And hence to hide thee from his sight design'd,
And, as her own, expose to public view
A new-born infant like herself in hue:
And since the tower, in which she then remain'd,
Alone her damsels and myself contain'd; 190

Ver. 182. —— *a child of snowy hue.*] This fiction is apparently taken from the famous romance of Heliodorus, called Theagenes and Chariclea, where Persina lying with her husband, in a chamber painted with the story of Perseus delivering Andromeda from the monster, was delivered of a daughter of a white complexion, afterwards called Chariclea, which, fearful of incurring the jealousy of her husband, she exposed in the same manner as is here related of the mother of Clorinda.

To me, who lov'd her with a faithful mind,
Her infant charge she unbaptiz'd consign'd,
With tears and sighs she gave thee to my care,
Remote from thence the precious pledge to bear!
What tongues her sorrows and her plaints can tell, 195
How oft she press'd thee with a last farewell!
With streaming tears each tender kiss is drown'd,
While frequent sighs her faltering words confound;
At length with lifted eyes—O GOD! (she cry'd)
By whom the secrets of my breast are try'd; 200
If still my thoughts have undefil'd remain'd,
And still my heart its constancy maintain'd;
(Not for myself I ask thy pitying grace,
A thousand sins, alas! my soul deface!)
O! keep this harmless babe, to whom, distress'd, 205
A mother thus denies her kindly breast:
Give her from me her spotless life to frame,
But copy in her fate some happier name!
Thou, heavenly chief! whose arm the serpent brav'd,
And from his ravenous jaws the virgin sav'd: 210
If e'er I tapers burn'd with rites divine,
Or offer'd gold and incense at thy shrine;

Ver. 192. —*unbaptiz'd*—] According to the custom of that country, the males could not be baptized till the age of fourteen, and the females till the age of sixteen.

For her I pray, that she, thy faithful maid,
On thee, in every chance, may call for aid.

She ceas'd; her heart convulsive anguish wrung,
And on her face a mortal sorrow hung. 216

With tears I took thee, and with care bestow'd
Within a chest, with leaves and flowers o'erstrow'd,
And bore thee thence conceal'd a pleasing load!
At length remote, my lonely footsteps stray'd 220
Amidst a forest thick with horrid shade;
When lo! a tigress drawing near I view'd,
Her threatening eyes suffus'd with rage and blood:
Wild with affright I left thee on the ground,
And climb'd a tree, and thence my safety found: 225
The furious beast now cast her eyes aside,
And thee deserted on the herbage spy'd;
Intent she seem'd to gaze, and milder grew,
'Till all the fiercenefs from her looks withdrew:
Approaching nigh, she fawn'd in wanton play, 230
And lick'd your infant members as you lay;
While you secure the savage form carefs'd,
And strok'd with harmless hand her dreadful crest;
She offer'd then her teats, and (strange to view!)
Thy willing lips the milky moisture drew. 235
With anxious fear and wonder I beheld
A sight so new, that all belief excell'd.

Soon

Soon as she found thee sated with the food,
The beast departed, and regain'd the wood.
Then hastening down to where on earth you lay, 240
I with my charge resum'd my former way:
'Till midst a village my retreat I made,
In secret there thy infancy was bred:
And there I dwelt, 'till coursing round, the moon
Had sixteen changing months to mortals shown; 245
'Till thy young feet began their steps to frame,
And from thy tongue imperfect accents came.
But sinking now, as middle life declin'd,
To hoary age, the winter of mankind;
Enrich'd with gold, which with a bounteous hand 250
The Queen had giv'n me when I left the land,
I loath'd this irksome life, with wandering tir'd,
And to review my native soil desir'd;
There midst my friends to pass my latter days,
And chear my evenings with a social blaze. 255
To Egypt then I turn'd, my natal shore,
And thee the partner of my journey bore.
When, lo! a flood we gain—there thieves enclose
My doubtful pass, and here the current flows.
What should I do, reluctant to forego 260
My dearest charge, or trust the barbarous foe?

I take

I take the flood; one hand the torrent braves;
And one fuſtains thee while I plough the waves.
Swift was the ſtream, and in its midmoſt courſe,
A circling eddy whirl'd with rapid force: 265
There round and round, with giddy motion toſt,
Sudden I ſunk, in depth of waters loſt;
Thee ſoon I miſs'd; but thee the waters bore,
And winds propitious wafted to the ſhore.
Breathleſs and faint at length I reach'd the land, 270
And there, with joy, my deareſt pledge regain'd.

But now what time to duſky ſhade conſign'd,
Night ſpreads her veil of ſilence o'er mankind,
Behold a warrior in my dream appear'd,
And o'er my head a naked falchion rear'd.   275
Hear my command! (he cry'd with threatening air)
What once a mother truſted to thy care,
Thy infant charge with ſacred rites baptize;
Belov'd of Heaven, with me her ſafety lies:
For her to ravenous beaſts I pity gave,   .   280
And breath'd a living ſpirit in the wave.
Oh! wretched thou! if, ſuch a warning given,
Thou dar'ſt to ſlight the meſſenger of Heaven!

He ceas'd; I wak'd, and then reſum'd my way,
Soon as the morn reveal'd her early ray.   285

But,

But, partial to my faith, I kept thee still,
Nor would thy mother's last commands fulfil:
I heeded not the visions of the night,
But bred thy youth in every pagan rite.
Mature in years now shone thy dauntless mind   290
Above thy sex, the rival of mankind!
In many a fight thy deeds have glory won;
Thy fortune since full well to thee is known.
In me thou still hast prov'd, in peace or war,
A servant's duty and a parent's care.   295
As yester-morn my mind, with thought oppress'd,
Lay senseless in a deep, a death-like rest,
The phantom-warrior came with fiercer look,
And dreadful with a louder accent spoke.
Lo, wretch! th' appointed hour at hand (he cry'd)
That must Clorinda from this life divide.   301
In thy despite the virgin shall be mine,
And thee to tears and anguish I resign.

He said; and vanish'd swift to fleeting air:
Then hear, my best belov'd! my tenderest care! 305
For thee these threatening visions Heaven has sent;
To thee, alas! foretels some dire event;
Perchance displeas'd by me to see thee train'd
In rites unpractis'd in thy natal land;

Remote

Remote perhaps from truth.—O! yet forbear; 310
Confent, no longer now thofe arms to wear:
Supprefs thy daring, and relieve my care.

   He ceas'd, and wept: In deep fufpenfe fhe ftay'd,
A dream, like his, her troubled foul difmay'd: 314
At length her looks fhe clear'd, and thus reply'd:
That faith, which feems the truth, be ftill my guide;
The faith I learn'd from thee in early years,
Which now thou feek'ft to fhake with caufelefs fears:
Nor will I (noble minds fuch thoughts difdain)
Forego thefe arms, or from th' attempt refrain; 320
Tho' death, in every fhape that mortals fear,
Should undifguis'd before my eyes appear.

   So fpoke the generous maid, and gently ftrove
To calm his anguifh, and his doubts remove.
Now came the feafon for the deed defign'd, 325
When parting thence th' expecting * knight fhe
    join'd;
Ifmeno, with his words, their zeal infpir'd,
(But no incitement either breaft requir'd)
And to their hands two fulphurous balls confign'd,
With fecret fire in hollow reeds confin'd. 330

   Now through the night their filent march they bend,
Now leave the city, and the hill defcend:

        * ARGANTES.

                          Till

Till near the place arriv'd, where towering high,
The hostile engine rises to the sky;
No longer can their daring souls restrain   335
The warmth that breathes in every glowing vein.
Too eager now, their quicken'd pace alarms
The watchful guard, who call aloud to arms.
No more conceal'd remain the generous pair,
But boldly rushing forth provoke the war.   340
As missile stones from battering engines fly,
As forky thunders rend the troubled sky;
One instant sees them, with resistless hand,
Attack, disperse, and penetrate the band.
'Midst clashing spears and hissing darts they flew,
And unrepuls'd their glorious task pursue: 346
Now, held in fight, the ready fires they raise:
Now near the pile the threatening vapours blaze;
'Till on the tower the dreadful pest they bend;
On every side the curling flames ascend;   350
Heavy and thick the smoky volumes rise,
And shade with sable clouds the starry skies,
Flash follows flash, the mingled blaze aspires,
'Till all the ether glows with ruddy fires!
Fann'd by the wind, the flame more furious grows:
Down falls the pile, the terror of the foes,   356
And one short hour the wondrous work o'erthrows!

Meanwhile

Meanwhile with speed two Christian squadrons
  came,
Who from the field had seen the rising flame:
To these the bold Argantes turn'd, and vow'd 360
To quench the burning ruins with their blood:
Yet, with Clorinda join'd, retreating still,
By slow degrees he gain'd the neighbouring hill;
While, like a flood by sounding rains increas'd,
Behind their steps the eager Christians press'd. 365
  Soon was the gate unbarr'd, where ready stands
The king, surrounded by his numerous bands,
To welcome back (if fate th' attempt succeed)
The pair triumphant from the glorious deed.
Now near the town the knight and virgin drew, 370
And swift behind the troop of Franks pursue;
These Solyman dispers'd: the portal clos'd,
But left Clorinda to the foe expos'd;
Alone expos'd; for while the hasty bands
Shut fast the sounding gate with ready hands, 375
She follow'd Arimon, by fury driven,
T'avenge the wound his luckless arm had given:
His life she took: nor yet Argantes knew
That she, ill-fated! from the walls withdrew.
All cares were lost, the tumult of the fight 380
Amaz'd the senses midst the gloom of night.

At

At length, her rage allay'd with hostile blood,
The maid at leisure all her peril view'd:
The numbers round, and clos'd the friendly gate,
She deem'd her life a prey to certain fate. 385
But when she finds no Christian eye descries
The hostile warrior in the dark disguise,
New schemes of safety in her mind arise.
Herself securely midst the ranks she throws,
And undiscover'd mingles with the foes. 390
Then, as the wolf retires besmear'd with blood,
And seeks the shelter of the distant wood;
So, favour'd by the tumult of the night,
The dame, departing, shunn'd the prying sight.
Tancred alone perceiv'd, with heedful view, 395
Some pagan foe as near the place he drew.
He came what time she Arimon had slain,
Then mark'd her course, and follow'd o'er the plain:
Eager he burn'd to prove her force in fight,
Esteem'd a warrior worthy of his might, 400
Her sex unknown. And now the virgin went
A winding way along the hill's ascent:
Impetuous he pursu'd, but ere he came,
His clashing armour rouz'd th' unwary dame.

Then

Then turning swift—What bring'st thou here? (she
    cry'd)   405
Lo! war and death I bring!—(the chief reply'd)
Then war and death (the virgin said) I give;
What thou to me would'st bring, from me receive!
Intrepid then she stay'd; the knight drew near;
But when he saw the foe on foot appear,   410
He left his steed to meet in equal war.

  Now with drawn swords they rush the fight to
    wage:
With fury thus two jealous bulls engage.
What glorious deeds on either part were done,
That claim'd an open field and conscious sun! 415
Thou, night! whose envious veil with dark disguise,
Conceal'd the warrior's acts from human eyes,
Permit me from thy gloom to snatch their fame,
And give to future times each mighty name:
So shall they shine, from age to age display'd,   420
For glories won beneath thy sable shade!
All art in fight the dusky hour denies,
And fury now the place of skill supplies.
The meeting swords with horrid clangor sound;
Each whirls the falchion, each maintains the ground:
Alternate furies either breast inflame,   426
Alternate vengeance and alternate shame.

No paufe, no reft, th'impatient warriors know,
But rage to rage, and blow fucceeds to blow:
Still more and more the combat feems to rife, 430
That fcarce their weapons can their wrath fuffice:
Till grappling fierce, in nearer ftrife they clofe,
And helm to helm, and fhield to fhield oppofe.
Thrice in his nervous arms he held the maid;
And thrice elufive from his grafp fhe fled. 435
Again with threatening fwords refum'd they ftood,
And dy'd again the fteel with mutual blood:
Till, fpent with labour, each awhile retir'd,
And faint and breathlefs from the fight refpir'd.

Now fhines the lateft ftar with fainter ray, 440
And ruddy ftreaks proclaim the dawning day:
Each views the foe; while, bending on the plain
The fwords revers'd their finking bulks fuftain.
Then Tancred marks the blood that drains his foe,
But fees his own with lefs effufion flow. 445
He fees with joy:—O! mortals blind to fate,
Too foon with Fortune's fav'ring wind elate!
Ah! wretch! rejoice not — Thou too foon fhalt
    mourn!
Thy boaft and triumph fhall to forrow turn!
Soon fhall thy eyes diftil a briny flood, 450
For all thofe purple drops of precious blood!

Thus

Thus for a while the weary warriors stay'd,
And speechless each the other's wounds survey'd.
At length the silence gallant Tancred broke,
Besought her name, and mildly thus bespoke. 455

Hard is our fate to prove our mutual might,
When darkness veils our deeds from ev'ry fight:
But since ill fortune envies valour's praise,
And not a witness here our strife surveys;
If prayers from foes can e'er acceptance claim, 460
To me reveal thy lineage and thy name:
So shall I know, whate'er th' event be found,
Who makes my conquest or my death renown'd.

Thou seek'st in vain (the haughty maid reply'd)
To fathom what my soul resolves to hide. 465
Yet, one of those thou see'st (whate'er my name)
Who gave thy boasted engine to the flame.

At this with rage indignant Tancred burn'd:
In hapless hour thou speak'st (he thus return'd)
Alike thy speech, alike thy silence proves, 470
And either, wretch! my arm to vengeance moves.

With rest refresh'd, with wrath inflam'd anew,
Again transported to the fight they flew.
What dreadful wounds on either side are giv'n!
Thro' arms and flesh the ruthless swords are driv'n.

Tho' faint with blood effus'd from every vein, 476
Their staggering limbs can scarce their weight sustain,
Yet still they live, and still maintain the strife,
Disdain and rage with-hold their fleeting life.
So seems th' Egean sea, the tempest past, 480
That here and there its troubled waters cast;
It still preserves the fury gain'd before,
And rolls the sounding billows to the shore.

But now behold the mournful hour at hand,
In which the fates Clorinda's life demand. 485
Full at her bosom Tancred aim'd the sword;
The thirsty steel her lovely bosom gor'd:
The sanguine current stain'd with blushing red
Th' embroider'd vest that o'er her arms was spread.
She feels approaching death in every vein; 490
Her trembling knees no more her weight sustain:
But still the Christian knight pursues the blow,
And threats and presses close his vanquish'd foe:
She, as she falls, her voice, unhappy! rears,
And her last suit with moving tone prefers. 495
Some pitying angel form'd her last desire,
Where faith, and hope, and charity conspire!
On the fair rebel Heaven such grace bestow'd,
And now in death requir'd the faith she ow'd.

'Tis

'Tis thine, my friend!—I pardon thee the stroke—
O! let me pardon too from thee invoke!—   501
Not for this mortal frame I urge my prayer,
For this I know no fear, and ask no care:
No, for my soul alone I pity crave;
O! cleanse my follies in the sacred wave!   505

Feebly she spoke; the mournful sounds impart
A tender feeling to the victor's heart;
His wrath subsides, while softer passions rise,
And call the tear of pity from his eyes.
Not far from thence, adown the mossy hill   510
In gentle murmurs roll'd a crystal rill:
There in his casque the limpid stream he took;
Then sad and pensive hasten'd from the brook.
His hands now trembled, while her helm he rear'd,
Ere yet the features of his foe appear'd;—   515
He sees!— he knows! — and senseless stands the knight!
O fatal knowledge—O distracting sight!
Yet still he lives, and rouz'd with holy zeal,
Prepares the last sad duty to fulfil.
While from his lips he gave the words of grace,
A smile of transport brighten'd in her face: 521
Rejoic'd in death, she seem'd her joy to tell,
And bade for heaven the empty world farewell.

E 3   A lovely

A lovely palenefs o'er her features flew;
As vi'lets mix'd with lilies blend their hue. 525
Her eyes to heaven the dying virgin rais'd;
The heavens and fun with kindly pity gaz'd;
Her clay-cold hand, the pledge of lafting peace,
She gave the chief; her lips their mufic ceafe.
So life departing left her lovely breaft; 530
So feem'd the virgin lull'd to filent reft!

Soon as he found her gentle fpirit fled,
His firmnefs vanifh'd o'er the fenfelefs dead.
Wild with his fate, and frantic with his pain,
To raging grief he now refigns the rein. 535
No more the fpirits fortify the heart,
A mortal coldnefs freezes every part.
Speechlefs and pale like her the warrior lay,
And look'd a bloody corfe of lifelefs clay!
Then had his foul purfu'd the fleeting fair, 540
Whofe gentle fpirit hover'd yet in air:
But here it chanc'd a band of Chriftians came
In fearch of water from the cryftal ftream:
Full foon their leader, with a diftant view,
Well by his arms the Latian hero knew: 545
With him the breathlefs virgin he beheld,
And wept the fortune of fo dire a field:

Nor

Nor would he leave (tho' deem'd of pagan kind)
Her lovely limbs to hungry wolves consign'd:
But either burden, on their shoulders laid, 550
To Tancred's tent the mournful troop convey'd.
Thus step by step their gentle march they took,
Nor yet the warrior from his trance awoke:
Yet oft he groan'd, and shew'd that fleeting life
Still in his breast maintain'd a doubtful strife: 555
While hush'd and motionless, the damsel show'd
Her spirit parted from its mortal load.
Thus either body to the camp they bear,
And there apart dispose with pious care.

With every duteous rite, on either hand, 560
Around the wounded prince th'assistants stand.
And now by slow degrees he lifts his sight,
Before his eyes appears a glimmering light;
He feels the helping hand, the speech perceives,
Yet, scarce recovering, doubts if yet he lives: 565
Amaz'd he gazes round: at length he knows
The place, his friends, and thus laments his woes.

And do I live!—and do I yet survey
The hated beams of this unhappy day!
Ah! coward hand! to righteous vengeance slow! 570
Though deeply vers'd in every murd'rous blow!

Dar'st thou not, impious minister of death!
Transfix this heart, and stop this guilty breath?
But haply us'd to deeds of horrid strain,
Thou deem'st it mercy to conclude my pain.   575
Still, still 'tis mine with grief and shame to rove,
A dire example of disastrous love!
While keen remorse for ever breaks my rest,
And raging furies haunt my conscious breast,
The lonely shades with terror must I view,   580
The shades shall every dreadful thought renew:
The rising sun shall equal horrors yield,
The sun that first the dire event reveal'd!
Still must I view myself with hateful eye,
And seek, though vainly, from myself to fly!—   585
But ah! unhappy wretch! what place contains
Of that ill-fated fair the chaste remains?
All that escap'd my rage, my brutal power,
Perhaps the natives of the woods devour!
Ah! hapless maid! 'gainst whom alike conspire   590
The woodland savage and the hostile ire!
O! let me join the dead on yonder plain,
(If still her beauteous limbs untouch'd remain)
Me too those greedy jaws alike shall tear,
Me too the monster in his paunch shall bear.   595

         O! happy

O! happy envy'd hour! (if such my doom)
That gives us both in death an equal tomb.

  And now he heard that near his tent was laid
The lifeless body of his much-lov'd maid.
At this awhile his mournful look he clears: 600
(So through the clouds a transient gleam appears)
And from the couch his wounded limbs he rears.
With faltering steps he thither bends his way,
Where plac'd apart the hapless virgin lay:
But when arriv'd he saw the wound impress'd, 605
With which his hand had pierc'd her tender breast;
And deadly pale, yet calm as evening's shade,
Beheld her face, with every rose decay'd;
His trembling knees had sunk beneath their load,
But here his circling friends their aid bestow'd, 610
Till thus again he vents his plaints aloud:
O! sight! that e'en to death can sweetness give,
But cannot now, alas! my grief relieve!
O! thou dear hand, that once to mine was press'd,
The pledge of amity and peace confess'd; 615
What art thou now? alas! how chang'd in death!
And what am I, that still prolong my breath?
Behold those lovely limbs in ruin laid,
The dreadful work my impious rage has made!

                                             This

This hand, thefe eyes alike are cruel found; 620
That gave the ftroke, and thefe furvey the wound!
Tearlefs furvey!—fince tears are here deny'd,
My guilty blood fhall pour the vital tide!

 He ceas'd; and groaning with his inmoft breath,
Fix'd in defpair and refolute on death, 625
Each bandage ftrait with frantic paffion tore:
Forth gufh'd from every wound the fpouting gore:
But here excefs of grief his will deceiv'd,
His fenfes fetter'd, and his life repriev'd.

 Then to his bed again the knight was borne; 630
His fpirits to their hated home return.
And foon around the tongues of fame relate
The hero's forrow, and his haplefs fate.
Now Godfrey fought his tent; and with him came
Each noble chief, a friend to Tancred's name. 635
But nor reproof nor foothing yields relief,
And words are vain to calm his rage of grief.
So when fome limb a mortal wound receives,
Each probing hand increafing anguifh gives.
But reverend Peter's care the reft tranfcends, 640
(A fhepherd thus his fickly charge attends)
With awful words the lover's breaft he moves,
And wifely thus his wandering thought reproves.
Unhappy

Unhappy prince! why thus indulge thy shame,
Why thus forgetful of thy former fame? 645
Why thus obscure thy eye, and deaf thy ear?—
View honour's charms, and virtue's summons hear,
Thy lord recalls thee to thy former post,
And shows the path thy erring feet have lost!
New tasks await thee in the field of fight, 650
The glorious station of a Christian knight!
Which thou hast left, by fatal love betray'd,
Lost in wild passion for a pagan maid!
To thee this chastening is in mercy giv'n,
And thou, dost thou reject the grace of Heaven? 655
Think where thy errors tend; thy state survey,
To senseless sorrow a regardless prey!
Thy feet are tottering on the brink of death,
Behold th' eternal gulph that gapes beneath!
Think, Tancred, think! this impious grief control,
That in a twofold death involves thy soul! 661

He ceas'd; nor here in vain the youth assail'd;
The fear of second death o'er all prevail'd.
His yielding heart confess'd the kind relief;
Returning reason calm'd his raging grief: 665
Yet still the frequent sighs his sorrow speak;
Still from his tongue the mournful accents break:

With

With tender found his lips invoke the fair,
Who lent perchance from heaven a pitying ear.
On her, when sets the sun, and when returns, 670
He calls inceffant, and inceffant mourns.
So fares the nightingale, with anguish stung,
When some rude swain purloins her callow young,
Torn from the nest; all helpless and alone, 674
Each night she fills the woods with plaintive moan.
At length one morn, as sleep his eyes oppress'd,
And o'er his sorrows shed the dews of rest;
Lo! in a dream, with starry robes array'd,
With heavenly charms appear'd the warrior maid:
She seem'd to view him with a pitying look, 680
And dry'd his tears, and gently thus bespoke.

 Behold what glories round my person shine!
Then weep no more, thy faithful grief resign:
Such as I am, to thee my state I owe,
Who freed me from the vale of sin below: 685
Who made me worthy, midst the saints above,
To dwell with GOD in realms of endless love.
There wrapt in heavenly bliss, and crown'd with
   grace,
My hopes prepare for thee an equal place:
Where thou shalt stand before th' eternal throne, 690
Partake my glories, and enjoy thy own!

Unless

Unless thyself reject the mercy given,
Or sensual follies spurn the grace of Heaven:
Then live!—and know thou hast Clorinda's love, 694
As far as earthly thoughts can souls immortal move.

So speaking, from her eyes the lightening came,
And all her features glow'd with holy flame:
Then, lost in rays, she vanish'd from his sight,
And breath'd new comfort in the mourning knight.
Consol'd he wak'd; and with a temperate mind 700
To skilful hands his wounded limbs consign'd.
And next he bade t'inhume, with pious care,
The last dear relics of the breathless fair.
Though for the tomb no costly marbles came,
Nor hand Dædalean wrought the sculptur'd frame:
Yet, as the time allow'd, the stone they chose, 706
And o'er the grave the figur'd structure rose.
With funeral pomp the troops the corse convey'd,
While torches round their solemn light display'd:
High on the naked pine her arms were plac'd, 710
And every rite the martial virgin grac'd.

Now Tancred sought the tomb, his vows to pay,
Where, cold in death, her precious relics lay:
Soon as he reach'd the pile, in which enshrin'd,
Repos'd the treasure of his tortur'd mind; 715

All

All pale and speechless for a time he stood,
Awhile, with eyes unmov'd, the marble view'd;
At length releas'd, the gushing torrents broke,
He drew a length of sighs, and thus he spoke.

 O tomb rever'd! where all my hopes are laid; 720
O'er which my eyes such copious sorrows shed;
Thou bear'st not in thy womb a lifeless frame,
There love still dwells, and lights his wonted flame!
Still, still that form ador'd my breast inspires,
With not less ardent, but more painful fires! 725
O give these kisses, give these mournful sighs
To that lov'd form that in thy bosom lies.
Should e'er her looks her blameless spirit turn,
Where sleep these relics in the silent urn;
Would she thy pity or my tears reprove? 730
Can scorn or anger touch the blest above?
Ah! may she then my hapless crime forgive,
In that dear hope my soul consents to live:
She knows my erring hand the deed has wrought,
My heart was guiltless of so dire a thought: 735
Nor will she scorn that he who owns his flame,
Should still, while life endures, adore her name;
Till death shall bid me here no longer rove,
But join us both in mutual peace above.

Then in one tomb our mortal parts may reſt! 740
And in one heaven our ſpirits may be bleſt.
So ſhall I dead enjoy what life deny'd,
O happy change! if fate ſuch bliſs provide!

   Thus he: but now the dreadful tidings flew,
And ſpread in whiſpers thro' the hoſtile crew: 745
At length, the certain tale divulg'd around,
With cries and female ſhrieks the walls reſound,
As if the foes had every fortreſs won,
And one vaſt blaze involv'd the ruin'd town.

   But chief Arſetes every eye demands, 750
He o'er the reſt in grief ſuperior ſtands;
No tears from him, like common ſorrows flow,
Too deep his boſom feels the frantic woe.
With ſordid duſt he ſtains his hoary hairs,
He ſtrikes his aged breaſt, his cheeks he tears. 755
While fix'd on him the vulgar bend their look,
Thus in the midſt the fierce Argantes ſpoke.

   When firſt I heard the city gates were clos'd,
And midſt the foes the glorious dame expos'd,
Fain would I then have iſſu'd to her aid, 760
And ſhar'd one fortune with the hapleſs maid!
In vain I pray'd!—the king's command reſtrain'd,
And me reluctant in the town detain'd.

                                    O! had

O! had I issu'd then, this faithful sword
Had safe the virgin to these walls restor'd; 765
Or, where her blood now stains the purple ground,
My days had run their race, with glory crown'd!
What could I more? what means remain'd untry'd?
But men and Gods alike my suit deny'd!
Pale lies she now, in fatal conflict slain; 770
Then hear what duties for this arm remain!
Hear, all Jerusalem! my purpose hear!
And conscious Heaven be witness whilst I swear!
I vow dire vengeance on the Christian's head:
And if I fail, on me thy bolts be shed! 775
The task be mine the murderer's life to take;
Ne'er shall this trusty sword my side forsake,
Till deep in Tancred's heart it finds a way,
And leaves his corse to ravenous fowls a prey!

He spoke: well pleas'd his speech the Syrians hear,
And loud applauses rend the sounding air. 781
The hopes of vengeance all their pains relieve;
Each calms his sorrow, and forgets to grieve.
O empty words! O Heaven in vain adjur'd!
Far other end disposing fate ensur'd! 785
For soon subdu'd the pagan boaster dies
By him who now in thought beneath his prowess lies!

THE END OF THE TWELFTH BOOK.

THE THIRTEENTH BOOK OF JERUSALEM DELIVERED.

THE ARGUMENT.

Ismeno, by his enchantments, raises the Demons, and appoints them to guard the wood which supplied the Christians with timbers to carry on the siege. The workmen being sent to fell the trees are terrified, and return to the camp. Several of the chiefs successively attempt the adventure, but in vain. Tancred then undertakes it, and penetrates into the wood; but at length retires, deceived by new illusions. The Christian army is afflicted with a drought, by which it is reduced to the utmost extremity. A disaffection spreads amongst the troops, several of whom withdraw themselves under favour of the night. Godfrey invokes the assistance of Heaven, and the camp is relieved by a seasonable shower.

THE THIRTEENTH BOOK OF JERUSALEM DELIVERED.

BUT scarce consum'd in smouldering ashes falls
Th' enormous pile that shook the Pagan walls;
When other schemes Ismeno's arts compose,
To save the ramparts from th' invading foes:
He bends his thought to guard the woodland shade,
From which the Franks their mighty beams con-
  vey'd;   6
That thus their engines they no more may rear,
Nor Sion more the threatening fury fear.
 Not far from where encamp'd the Christian bands,
Midst lonely vales, an aged forest stands: 10
Here, when the day with purest beams is bright,
The branches scarce admit a gloomy light;
Such as we view from morning's doubtful ray,
Or the faint glimmerings of departing day.

But when the sun beneath the earth descends,   15
Here mournful night her deeper vale extends;
Infernal darkness broods o'er every sight,
And chilling terrors every breast affright.
No shepherd here his flock to pasture drives;
No village swain, with lowing herd, arrives: 20
No pilgrim dares approach; but struck with dread
In distant prospect shows the dreary shade.
Here, with their minions, midnight hags repair,
Convey'd on flitting clouds through yielding air:
While one a dragon's fiery image bears;   25
And one a goat's mishapen likeness wears.
And here they celebrate, with impious rite,
The feasts profane and orgies of the night.
Thus went the fame: untouch'd the forest stood;
No hand presum'd to violate the wood;   30
Till now the fearless Franks the trees invade,
From these alone their vast machines they made.

  Here the magician came; the hour he chose,
When night around her deepest silence throws;
Close to his loins he girt his flowing vest,   35
Then form'd his circle, and his signs impress'd:
With one foot bare, within the magic round
He stood, and mutter'd many a potent sound.

                                Thrice

Thrice turning to the east his face was shewn;
Thrice to the regions of the setting sun;   40
And thrice he shook the wand, whose wondrous force
Could from the tomb recall the bury'd corse:
As oft with naked foot the soil he struck,
Then thus aloud with dreadful accents spoke.

 Hear you! who once by vengeful lightening driv'n,
Fell headlong from the starry plains of heav'n!   46
Ye powers who guide the storms and wintry war,
The wandering rulers of the middle air!
And you, the ministers of endless woe
To sinful spirits in the shades below!   50
Inhabitants of hell! your aid I claim,
And thine, dire Monarch of the realms of flame!
Attend my will; these woods in charge receive;
To you consign'd each fatal plant I leave,
As human bodies human souls contain,   55
So you inshrin'd within these trees remain.
Thus shall the Christians fly, at least forbear
To fell this forest, and your anger fear.

 He said; and added many an impious spell,
Dreadful to hear, and horrible to tell.   60
While thus he murmur'd, from the face of night
Th' affrighted stars withdrew their glittering light;

The moon, disturb'd, no more her beams reveal'd,
But, wrapt in clouds, her silver horns conceal'd.

Now, fill'd with wrath, he rais'd his voice again:
Why are ye thus, ye fiends! invok'd in vain? 66
Why this delay? or do you wait to hear
More potent words and accents more severe?
Though long difus'd, my memory yet retains
Each deeper art that every power constrains: 70
These lips can sound that name with terror heard,
That awful name by every demon fear'd;
The name that startles hell's tremendous reign,
And calls forth Pluto from his own domain.
Hear! and attend!—no more th' enchanter said, 75
The spell was ended, and the fiends obey'd.

Unnumber'd spirits to the grove repair,
Of those that wander through the fields of air;
Of those that deep in earth's foundations lie,
In seats far distant from the chearful sky. 80
Still in their mind they bear the high command,
That late, from fields of fight, their host restrain'd;
Yet each compell'd the direful charge receives,
Invades the trunk, or lurks beneath the leaves.

The Sorc'rer now, his impious purpose wrought,
Without delay the Monarch's presence sought. 86
O king!

O king! difmifs thy doubts (he thus begun)
Behold fecur'd thy walls and regal throne!
No more the Chriftians, as their thoughts intend,
Can bid their towers againft the town afcend. 90
He faid; and to the liftening prince difclos'd
The various fpells by magic power compos'd;
Then thus purfu'd—To what my lips have told,
As grateful tidings let me now unfold.
Know Mars and Sol will foon their force combine,
To dart their mutual beams from Leo's fign: 96
No favouring winds fhall cool the burning ray,
No fhowers or dews refrefh the fultry day.
Yet may we here the parching feafon bear,
Reliev'd with pleafing fhade and gentle air: 100
This town fuch fhelter yields and plenteous ftreams,
And gentle gales to check the fcorching beams:
While on the barren earth the Franks fhall lie,
And feel the fury of th' inclement fky.
Thus, firft fubdu'd by Heaven, th' Egyptian train 105
Shall o'er their hoft an eafy conqueft gain.
So fhall the foes, without thy labour, yield:
Then tempt no more the fortune of the field.
But if too high Argantes' courage grows,
To bear, what prudence wills, a fhort repofe: 110

F 4   If

If ſtill, as wont, he urge thee to the fight,
The care be thine to curb th' impetuous knight:
For ſoon will Heaven on thee its peace beſtow,
And whelm in ruin yon flagitious foe!

   With joy the king theſe welcome tidings heard, 115
The engines of the foes no longer fear'd:
But not for this he ceas'd his watchful care,
The walls to view, and every breach repair:
Alike the citizens the toils divide,
And various throngs the works inceſſant ply'd. 120

   Meanwhile the pious chief, their labours known,
Reſolv'd no more t' attempt the ſacred town,
Till once again his lofty tower he rear'd,
And every engine for th' attack prepar'd.
Where midſt the wood the living timbers grew, 125
The workmen ſwift he ſent the trees to hew;
Theſe reach'd, at early dawn, the gloomy ſhade,
But ſudden fears their trembling ſouls diſmay'd.

   As ſimple children dread the hours of night,
When fabled ſpectres fill their minds with fright: 130
So theſe were ſeiz'd with dread: yet ſcarce they knew
From what new cauſe th' unwonted terrors grew,
But fancy form'd perhaps a numerous train
Of empty ſpinxes and chimeras vain!

                                    Back

Back from the wood with speed the camp they sought,
And wild reports, and tales uncertain brought. 136
The Christian warriors scorn'd their dastard fears,
And heard their words with unbelieving ears.
Then Godfrey next dispatch'd a squadron try'd,
A valiant troop that every chance defy'd, 140
To succour those, and urge their fainting hands
To act with courage what their chief commands.
Now near they came, where midst the horrid shade
The fiends conceal'd their impious dwelling made.
Soon as their eyes their dreary seats behold, 145
Each beating heart is numb'd with freezing cold.
Yet on they move, while looks of boldness hide
Th' ignoble thoughts that every breast divide.
Arriv'd at length within the vale they stood,
And reach'd the entrance of th' enchanted wood. 150
When sudden issu'd forth a rumbling sound,
As when an earthquake rocks the trembling ground;
A hollow noise, like murmuring winds, they hear,
Or dashing billows breaking on their ear:
There serpents seem to hiss, and lions roar, 155
To howl the wolf, to grunt the tusky boar:
The trumpet's clangor sounds, the thunders roll,
And mingled clamours echo to the pole!

At

At once their bloodless cheeks their thoughts dis-
    play'd;
A thousand signs their timorous hearts betray'd: 160
No more could discipline their ranks sustain,
A secret power dismay'd the routed train:
At length they fled: when one with looks confus'd,
To pious Godfrey thus their flight excus'd:

  No more we boast, O chief! those woods to fell,
Impervious woods secur'd by hidden spell!   166
Infernal furies midst the gloom resort,
And Pluto there has fix'd his horrid court!
Of triple adamant his heart is made,
Who unappall'd beholds the fatal shade: 170
And more than mortal he, who free from fear,
Can the dire howlings and the thunders hear.

  He said; and while he thus his tale pursu'd,
Amongst the listening chiefs Alcastus stood;
A man of courage rash, whose daring mind   175
Scorn'd every monster dreadful to mankind;
Nor storms nor earthquakes could his fear excite,
Nor aught that fills the world with pale affright.

  He shook his head, and smiling thus reply'd;
By me this arduous task shall soon be try'd!   180
Alone I go yon dreaded woods to fell,
Where visionary shapes and terrors dwell!

                                                    No

No ghastly spectres shall this hand restrain,
And fiends shall howl, and thunders roar in vain:
Behold my soul each threatening pow'r defies, 185
Though hell's dire passage gape before my eyes!

   Boastful he spoke: the leader gave consent:
From thence with daring steps the warrior went.
At length the forest to his sight appear'd,
And from within the mingled noise was heard. 190
But still the knight pursu'd his course unmov'd;
No terrors yet his dauntless bosom prov'd.
Now had his feet the soil forbidden trod,
When lo! a rising fire his steps withstood.
Wide and more wide it spread, and seem'd to frame
Huge lofty walls and battlements of flame! 196
The wondrous fence around the wood extends,
And from the sounding axe its trees defends.
What monsters arm'd upon the ramparts stand!
What horrid forms compose the grisly band! 200
With threatening eyes some view him from afar,
And some, with clashing arms, the champion dare.
At length he flies, but with a tardy flight,
So parts a lion yielding in the fight.
Surpriz'd, his conscious heart the doubts confess'd,
And own'd the fears that struggled in his breast. 206

                                       Then,

Then, to the camp return'd, with humbled pride,
From every eye he fought the shame to hide:
Nor longer durst, his face with grief o'erspread,
Among the warriors lift his haughty head.　　210

　By Godfrey summon'd now, awhile he stay'd,
And with excuses vain the time delay'd:
Slowly at length he came, unwilling spoke,
And from his lips imperfect accents broke.
Full well the leader saw his troubled mind,　　215
And, by his looks, the boaster's flight divin'd.

　What may (he cries) these strange events portend?
What tales are these that nature's laws transcend?
Is there a man who, fill'd with glorious heat,
Dares yet explore the forest's dark retreat?　　220
Now let his courage yonder feats invade,
Or bring more certain tidings from the shade.

　So spoke the chief: and three succeeding days
The boldest warriors, urg'd by thirst of praise,
Assay'd the dreary wood: but, struck with dread,　　225
Each knight by turns the threatening terrors fled.

　Now in her tomb has noble Tancred laid
The honour'd relics of his much-lov'd maid:
Pale are his looks, his languid limbs appear
Too weak the cuirass or the shield to bear.　　230
　　　　　　　　　　　　　　　　　　　But,

But, since the Christian cause his sword requires,
Nor toil nor danger damps his generous fires;
Heroic ardors all his soul inflame,
And give new vigour to his feeble frame.
With native firmness arm'd, he hastes to prove 235
The secret perils of the magic grove.
Unmov'd his eyes the gloomy shade behold:
In vain the earthquakes rock'd, the thunders roll'd:
At first a transient doubt assail'd his breast,
But each unworthy thought was soon repress'd. 240
Still on he pass'd, till full before his eyes
The burning walls and flaming ramparts rise.
At this awhile his hasty course he stay'd:
What here can arms avail? (the warrior said)
Shall I, where yon devouring furies wait, 245
Amidst the flames attempt a desperate fate?
Ne'er would I fly from death in glory's strife,
When fame, when public good, demands my life.
From useless perils yet the brave refrain;
The warrior's courage here were spent in vain: 250
Yet how will yonder camp my flight receive?
What other forest can their want relieve?
By Godfrey then the task will sure be try'd;
These fires perhaps may vanish when defy'd.

But

But be it as it may! th' attempt I claim!— 255
He said: and fearless rush'd amidst the flame,
At once he leapt, and press'd unhurt the ground,
Nor fire nor heat th' intrepid hero found:
At once the visionary flames were fled,
And all around a dismal darkness spread: 260
Tempests and clouds arose: but soon anew
The storms were vanish'd, and the clouds withdrew!
Surpriz'd, but dauntless, noble Tancred stood,
And when the skies thus clear'd the warrior view'd,
With steps secure he pierc'd th' unhallow'd glade,
And trac'd each secret winding of the shade. 266
No wondrous phantoms now his course oppos'd,
No burning towers the guarded wood enclos'd:
But oft the trees, with tangled bows entwin'd,
Perplex'd his passage, and his fight confin'd, 270
At length a sylvan theatre he found;
Nor plant nor tree within the verdant round;
Save in the midst a stately cypress rose,
And high in air advanc'd its spreading boughs.
To this the knight his wandering steps address'd, 275
And saw the trunk with various marks impress'd:
Like those (ere men were vers'd in scriptur'd lore)
Mysterious Egypt us'd in days of yore.

Amidst the signs unknown he chanc'd to find
These words engrav'd conspicuous on the rind. 280
 O! valiant knight! whose feet have dar'd to tread
These mansions sacred to the silent dead:
If pity e'er thy dauntless breast could move,
Forbear to violate this fatal grove.
Revere the souls depriv'd of vital air,   285
Nor with the dead an impious war declare.

 These lines the knight perus'd, and lost in thought,
He long in vain the secret meaning sought.
Now thro' the leaves a whispering breeze he hears,
And human voices murmuring in his ears;   290
That various passions in his heart instil;
Soft pity, grief, and awe, his bosom fill.

 At length, resolv'd, his shining steel he drew,
And struck the tree, when (dreadful to his view!)
The wounded bark a sanguine current shed,   295
And stain'd the grassy turf with streaming red.
With horror fill'd, yet fix'd th' event to know,
Again his arm renew'd the forceful blow:
When from the trunk was heard a human groan,
And plaintive accents in a female tone.   300

 Too much on me before thy rage was bent,
O! cruel Tancred! cease—at last relent!

               By

By thee from life's delightful feat I fell,
Driv'n from the breast where once I us'd to dwell.
Why do'st thou still pursue with ruthless hate, 305
This trunk, to which I now am fix'd by fate?
Ah! cruel!—shall not death th' unhappy save?
And would'st thou reach thy foes within the grave?
Clorinda once was I!—nor here confin'd,
My soul alone informs a rugged rind: 310
The like mysterious fortune waits on all
Who sink in fight beneath yon lofty wall;
By strange enchantment here (relentless doom!)
They find in sylvan forms a living tomb:
These trunks and branches human sense endows, 315
Nor canst thou, guiltless, lop the vital boughs.

 As one distemper'd, to whose sleeping eyes
A dragon or chimera seems to rise,
Attempts to fly, while yet he scarce believes
The monstrous phantom that his sense deceives: 320
So far'd the lover, doubting what he heard;
Yet, midst his doubts, he yielded and he fear'd.
A thousand tender thoughts his bosom pain'd,
No more his trembling hand the sword retain'd.
Now in his mind he views th' offended fair 325
With all the sighs and tumults of despair:

          Nor

Nor longer can he bear, with pitying eyes,
To view the ſtreaming bark, or hear the mournful cries!
Thus he, whoſe courage every deed had try'd,
And all the various forms of death defy'd,   330
Submits his reaſon to deluſive charms,
And love's all-powerful name his breaſt diſarms.

A whirlwind now aroſe with ſudden roar,
Which from the wood his fallen falchion bore.
The warrior thus ſubdu'd, no longer ſtrove,   335
But left th' attempt, and iſſu'd from the grove.
His ſword regaining, to the chief he came,
And thus at length began his tale to frame.

Unthought-of truths, O prince! I ſhall reveal,
Wonderous to know, incredible to tell!   340
I heard the dreadful ſounds, the fire I view'd
That, ſudden riſing, in my paſſage ſtood;
Like walls and battlements the flames were rear'd,
Where armed monſters for defence appear'd.
Yet free from heat I paſs'd the burning towers,   345
Nor found my path oppos'd by hoſtile powers:
To this ſucceeded clouds, and ſtorms, and night,
But ſoon again return'd the chearful light.
More ſhall I ſpeak?—A human ſpirit lives
In every tree, and ſenſe and reaſon gives   350

To every plant—deep groans affail'd my ear,
And ftill I feem the mournful founds to hear.
Each parted trunk pours forth a purple ftream,
Like fanguine currents from a wounded limb!
I own myfelf fubdu'd—no more I dare   355
A branch diffever, or a fapling tear.

 While Tancred thus his wondrous tidings brought,
The leader waver'd, loft in anxious thought:
Uncertain if himfelf th' attempt to prove,
And try the dangers of th' enchanted grove;   360
Or feek what other diftant wood might yield
The planks to frame his engines for the field;
But from his doubts the hermit foon relieves
The penfive chief, and thus his counfel gives.

 Forego thy fchemes, nor think the wood t' invade,
Another hand muft pierce the fatal fhade.   366
Now, now, the veffel gains the diftant ftrand,
She furls her fails, fhe cuts the yielding fand!
See! where at length th' expected hero breaks
His fhameful bondage, and the fhore forfakes!   370
Full foon will Heaven yon towering walls o'erthrow,
And quell the numbers of th' Egyptian foe!
While thus he fpoke, inflam'd his looks appear'd;
With more than mortal found his voice was heard.

The

The pious Godfrey, still with cares oppress'd, 375
New plans revolv'd within his thoughtful breast.
But now, receiv'd in Cancer's fiery sign,
The sun, with scorching rays, began to shine:
A direful drought succeeds: the martial train
No more the labours of the field sustain. 380
Each gentle star has quench'd its kindly beam;
From sullen skies malignant planets gleam;
Their baneful influence on the earth they shed,
And wide through air infectious vapours spread.
To dreadful day more dreadful night succeeds, 385
And each new morn increasing terror breeds.
The sun ne'er rises chearful to the sight,
But sanguine spots distain his sacred light:
Pale hovering mists around his forehead play,
The sad forerunners of a fatal day! 390
His setting orb in crimson seems to mourn,
Denouncing greater woes at his return;
And adds new horrors to the present doom,
By certain fear of evils yet to come!

Ver. 377. *But now, receiv'd in Cancer's fiery sign,*] This drought with which the Christian army was afflicted, is mentioned in the history. In the particulars of the description the poet has made great use of Lucretius.

All nature pants beneath the burning sky: 395
The earth is cleft, the lessening streams are dry;
The barren clouds, like streaky flames, divide,
Dispers'd and broken through the sultry void.
No chearful object for the sight remains;
Each gentle gale its grateful breath retains; 400
Alone the wind from Libya's sands respires,
And burns each warrior's breast with secret fires.
Nocturnal meteors blaze in dusky air,
Thick light'nings flash, and livid comets glare!
No pleasing moisture nature's face renews: 405
The moon no longer sheds her pearly dews
To chear the mourning earth: the plants and flowers
In vain require the soft and vital showers!
Sweet slumber flies from every restless night,
In vain would men his balmy power invite; 410
Sleepless they lie: but, far above the rest,
The rage of thirst their fainting souls oppress'd.
For, vers'd in guile, Judæa's impious king
With poisonous juice had tainted every spring;
Whose currents now with dire pollution flow, 415
Like Styx and Acheron in realms below;
The slender stream, where Siloa's gentle wave
Once to the Christians draughts untainted gave,

          Now

Now scarcely murmurs, in his channels dry,
And yields their fainting host a small supply. 420
But not the Po, when most his waters swell,
Would seem too vast their raging thirst to quell:
Nor mighty Ganges, nor the seven-mouth'd Nile,
That with his deluge glads th' Egyptian soil.
If e'er their eyes, in happier times, have view'd, 425
Begirt with grassy turf, some crystal flood:
Or living waters foam from Alpine hills,
Or through soft herbage purl the limpid rills:
Such flattering scenes again their fancies frame,
And add new fuel to increase their flame. 430
Still in the mind the wish'd idea reigns:
But still the fervor rages in the veins!
Then might you see on earth the warriors lie,
Whose limbs robust could every toil defy;
Inur'd the weight of ponderous arms to bear, 435
Inur'd in fields the hostile steel to dare:
Deep in their veins the hidden furies prey,
And eat, by slow degrees, their lives away.

 The courser, late with generous pride indu'd,
Now loaths the grass, his once delightful food: 440
With feeble steps he scarcely seems to tread,
And prone to earth is hung his languid head.

No mem'ry now of ancient fame remains,
No thirst of glory on the dusty plains:
The conquer'd spoils and trappings once bestow'd,
His joy so late, are now a painful load! 446

 Now pines the faithful dog, nor heeds the board,
Nor heeds the service of his dearer lord!
Out-stretch'd he lies, and as he pants for breath,
Receives at every gasp new draughts of death. 450

 In vain has nature's law the air assign'd
T' allay the inward heat of human kind:
What here, alas! can air mankind avail,
When fevers float on every burning gale!

 Thus droop'd the earth, and every glory lost, 455
Dire prospects terrify'd the faithful host:
Complaints aloud resound from every band,
And words, like these, are heard on either hand.

 What next can Godfrey hope? Why longer stay
Till one sad fate sweep all our camp away? 460
Still can he think yon lofty walls to gain,
What force is left, what engines now remain?
And sees not he, of all the host alone,
The wrath of God by every signal shown?
A thousand signs and prodigies declare 465
His will oppos'd against this fatal war.

What scorching rays the sickening land invade!
Nor Ind nor Libya asks a cooler shade!
Then thinks our leader no regard we claim,
And views us as a vile, a worthless name! 470
That souls like ours to death must tamely yield,
So he may still th' imperial sceptre wield!
Behold! the boasted chief, the pious nam'd,
For acts of mercy and for goodness fam'd,
Forgets his people's weal, his power to raise, 475
And on their ruin builds destructive praise!
While thus we mourn each spring and fountain dry'd,
From Jordan's stream his thirst is well supply'd;
Amidst his festive friends the prince reclines,
And mixes cooling draughts with Cretan wines. 480
  Thus said the Franks; but louder far complain'd
The Grecian chief, who Godfrey's sway disdain'd;
Who with reluctance long his rule obey'd:
Why should I tamely perish here? (he said)
And why with me on mine shall ruin wait? 485
If Godfrey blindly rush on certain fate,
On him and on his Franks th' event be thrown,
Nor let us fall for follies not our own.

Thus said the chief; nor bade the host adieu,
But, with his train, at evening's close withdrew. 490
Soon as the morn beheld his squadron fled,
On other troops the quick contagion spread.
Those that in battle Ademar obey'd,
And brave Clothareus, now in silence laid,
(Since death, which all dissolves, had burst the bands
That held them subject to their lords commands) 496
Already meditate their secret flight,
And some depart beneath the favouring night.

All this full well observant Godfrey knew,
Nor yet his soul would rigorous means pursue 500
T' oppose the ill; resolv'd the faith to prove,
That rapid streams can stay, and rocks remove;
The Ruler of the world with prayers t' implore
The sacred fountains of his grace to pour.
With hands conjoin'd, and eyes with zeal on flame,
He thus aloud invok'd th' eternal name. 506

Ver. 490. — *with his train, at evening's close withdrew.*] History mentions, that in the famine which the Christians suffered before Antioch, the Grecian commander departed, under pretence of seeking assistance from the emperor at Constantinople, and that he returned no more. The poet feigns this circumstance to have happened before the walls of Jerusalem.

O king!

O King! and Father! if thy pitying hand
E'er shed thy manna in the desert land;
If e'er thy will to man such virtue gave,
From veins of rock to draw the gushing wave! 510
Be now for these thy wondrous power display'd:
But if their merits less can claim thy aid,
O! let thy grace, to veil their faults, be given,
Still may thy warriors feel the care of Heaven!

These righteous prayers, in humble words express'd,
On eagle wings to heaven their flight address'd; 516
There full before the throne of GOD appear'd:
Th' Eternal Father with complacence heard:
His awful eyes he bent on Syria's lands,
And view'd the labours of his faithful bands: 520
He saw their sufferings with a gracious look,
Then thus, with mild benevolence, he spoke.

Lo! to this hour, on earth my camp belov'd
Has various woes and dreadful perils prov'd!
The world, in arms, resists their glorious toils, 525
And hell obstructs their course with all its wiles.
Now, chang'd the scene, a happier fate attends:
From favouring clouds the friendly shower descends:
Their matchless hero comes t' exalt their name,
And Egypt's host arrives to crown their fame. 530

Th'

Th' Almighty ceas'd: heaven trembled as he
    spoke;
The stars and every wandering planet shook;
The air was hush'd, the sea was calm'd to rest,
And every hill and cave its awe confess'd.
Swift to the left the lightening's blaze appear'd; 535
At once aloft the thunder's noise was heard.
The troops transported view the lowring skies,
And hail the rolling sound with joyful cries.
Now thickening clouds their gloomy veil extend;
Not these in vapours from the earth ascend   540
By Phœbus' warmth; but heaven the deluge pours,
And opens all the sluices of its stores.
The torrents fall impetuous from the skies;
Above their banks the foamy rivers rise.
As on the shore, when heats have parch'd the plain,
The cackling breed expect the kindly rain;   546
Then greet the moisture with expanded wings,
And sport and plunge beneath the cooling springs:
The Christians thus salute with joyful cry
The grateful deluge from the pitying sky.   550
These on their locks or vests the stream receive;
From helms or vases those their thirst relieve:
Some hold their hands beneath the cooling wave;
Their faces some, and some their temples lave:

While earth, that late her gaping rifts difclos'd, 555
And fainting lay to parching heat expos'd,
Receives and minifters the vital fhowers
To fading herbs, to plants, to trees and flowers:
Her fever thus allay'd, new health returns,
No more the flame within her bofom burns; 560
Again new beauties grace her gladden'd foil,
Again renew'd her hills and vallies fmile.

Now ceas'd the rain; the fun reftor'd the day,
And fhed with grateful warmth a temper'd ray:
As when his beams benign their influence bring 565
T' unlock, with genial power, the welcome fpring.
O wondrous faith! that, trufting Heaven above,
Can purge the air, and every ill remove:
Can change the feafons, and reverfe their ftate,
And quench the fury of impending fate! 570

THE END OF THE THIRTEENTH BOOK.

THE FOURTEENTH BOOK OF JERUSALEM DELIVERED.

THE ARGUMENT.

GODFREY is admonished in a dream to recall Rinaldo to the camp. Guelpho pleads for his nephew's return, and Godfrey consents to it. Ubald and Charles the Dane are appointed the messengers for that purpose: these, by the directions of Peter, proceed to Ascalon, where they are entertained by a Christian magician, who shews them many wonders. He gives them a particular relation of the manner in which Rinaldo was ensnared by Armida, and then instructs them fully how to deliver him from the power of the enchantress.

THE
FOURTEENTH BOOK
OF
JERUSALEM DELIVERED.

NOW from her mother's antient lap arose
　　Indulgent night, befriending sweet repose;
Soft breezes in her train attendant flew,
While from her robe she shook the pearly dew:
The fluttering Zephyrs breath'd a grateful wind,　5
And sooth'd the balmy slumbers of mankind.
　Now, every thought forgot, the peaceful host
Their cares and labours in oblivion lost:
But, ever watchful o'er his creatures' state,
In light eternal Heaven's Almighty sate:　　　10
His looks he turn'd, and view'd, from upper skies,
The Christian leader with benignant eyes:
To him, with speed, he sent a mystic dream,
To speak the purpose of the will supreme.

　　　　　　　　　　　　　　　　　Not

Not far from where the sun, with eastern ray, 15
Through golden portals pours the beamy day,
A cryſtal gate there ſtands, whoſe valves unfold
Ere yet the ſkies the dawning light behold.
From thence the dreams ariſe, which heavenly pow'r
To pious mortals ſends in gracious hour. 20
From thence to Godfrey's tent the viſion fled,
And o'er the chief his radiant pinions ſpread.
No ſlumber e'er ſuch pleaſing ſcenes diſplay'd,
As now the hero, in a trance, ſurvey'd:
That brought the ſtarry manſions to his eyes, 25
And open'd all the ſecrets of the ſkies:
Then full reflected to his ſenſe was ſhown
The happy ſtate, by righteous ſpirits known.

He ſeem'd aloft to realms of glory rais'd, 29
Where beams on beams with mingled luſtre blaz'd.
There, while he, wondering, view'd the ſeats around,
And heard the ſacred choir their hymns reſound,
Begirt with rays, and cloath'd with lambent flame,
Full in his ſight a graceful warrior came.
His tuneful voice no ſounds can reach below, 35
And from his lips theſe gentle accents flow:
Then will not Godfrey own this face again,
And is thy friend, thy Hugo, ſeen in vain?

To whom the chief reply'd: That form divine,
Where circling beams of dazzling glory shine, 40
So far my feeble mortal sense obscur'd,
That scarely yet my mem'ry stands assur'd.
He said; and thrice with eager arms essay'd
With pious love to clasp the friendly shade:
And thrice the phantom mock'd his fruitless care, 45
And fled like empty dreams or fleeting air.

  Think not (the vision cry'd) thy eyes behold
A mortal substance of terrestrial mould:
A naked spirit stands before thy sight,
A citizen of this celestial light. 50
Behold God's temple! here his warriors rest,
With these shalt thou reside, for ever blest.
When comes that happy hour? (the chief replies)
Ah! now release my soul from earthly ties!

  Soon shalt thou (Hugo thus return'd again) 55
Partake the triumphs of th' immortal train:
But first thy warfare claims new toils below;
In fields of fight thy courage yet must glow.
'Tis thine to free from impious pagan bands
The sacred empire of Judæa's lands; 60
And, firmly fix'd, the Christian throne to place,
The seat thy brother is decreed to grace.

But, that thy breast may feel a holier fire,
And purer pleasures purer thoughts inspire;
Contemplate well this place, these starry rays, 65
Where Heaven's Almighty pours the boundless blaze!
Hark! how th' angelic choir their hymns prolong,
And warble to the lyre celestial song!
Now cast thy sight to yonder globe below,
See! all that earth on mortals can bestow! 70
Behold what vileness there obscures mankind;
Say, what rewards can there the virtuous find?
A naked solitude, a narrow space
Confines the senseless pride of human race.
Earth, like an isle, is round with waves embrac'd: 75
Survey yon sea, the mighty and the vast!
Which here can no such glorious titles claim,
A pool unnoted, and a worthless name!

 He said; and Godfrey downward bent his eyes,
And view'd the earth with pity and surprize: 80
He smil'd to see the numerous nations' boast,
Lands, floods, and oceans, in an atom lost;
Amaz'd that man, with sensual follies blind,
Should there, immers'd in smoke, in gloom confin'd,
Pursue vain empire, and an airy name, 85
Nor heed the call of Heaven, and virtue's lasting fame.
          Then

Then thus he said: Since 'tis not GOD's decree,
From mortal prison yet my soul to free;
O! be my guide! Vouchsafe the path to show,
Amidst the errors of the world below. 90
    The path before thee (Hugo then reply'd)
Pursue, nor from the track remove aside.
This only counsel from thy friend receive;
From exile brave Bertoldo's son reprieve.
For if to thee th' Almighty King of heaven 95
The sovereign guidance of the host has given;
'Tis his decree no less, th' intrepid knight
Should execute thy high commands in fight:
'Tis thine the foremost duties to sustain,
To him the second honours must remain: 100
To him alone 'tis giv'n the woods to fell,
So deeply guarded by the fiends of hell;
From him the troops, that seem a lifeless host,
Their numbers weaken'd, and their courage lost;
That inly meditate a shameful flight, 105
Shall gain new vigour for th' approaching fight:
So shall they teach yon haughty walls to yield,
And rout the eastern armies in the field.
    He said, and ceas'd; when Godfrey made reply:
The knight's return would fill my breast with joy:

Thou know'st (and thou my secret thought canst
    prove)   111
That in my soul he meets a brother's love.
But say, what offers must I make? and where
To seek him shall the messengers repair?
How suits it with my state, the youth to greet, 115
T' exact obedience, or with prayer entreat?
To whom the shade: Th' Eternal King, whose grace
To thee has given on earth a leader's place,
Decrees that those o'er whom he gave thee sway,
To thee, their head, should rightful homage pay: 120
Request not then—(thou can'st not, void of blame,
With servile prayers debase a general's name)
But when thy friends beseech, thy ears incline;
The part be theirs t' entreat, to yield be thine:
To thee, inspir'd by Heaven, shall Guelpho plead, 125
And ask forgiveness for Rinaldo's deed.
Though now far distant from th' abandon'd host,
He lives, in love and ease inglorious lost;
A few short days will bring the youth again,
To shine in arms amidst his social train: 130
For holy Peter can thy envoys send
Where certain tidings shall thy search attend:
They shall be taught the arts, and given the power,
The knight to free, and to the camp restore.
                                                                Thus

Thus all thy wandering partners of the war   135
Shall Heav'n at length reduce beneath thy care.
Yet, ere I ceafe, one truth I fhall reveal,
Which well I know thy breaft with joy fhall fill:
His blood fhall mix with thine, and thence a race
Of glorious names fucceeding times fhall grace! 140

He ended here; and pafs'd like fmoke away,
Or fleeting clouds before the folar ray.
Then fleep, departing, left the hero's breaft
At once with wonder and with joy poffefs'd.
The pious chief th' advancing morn furvey'd,   145
And ftrait his limbs in weighty arms array'd.
Soon in his tent th' attending leaders met,
In daily council where conven'd they fate;
There every future act they weigh with care,
And every labour of the war prepare.   150

Then noble Guelpho, who, by Heaven opprefs'd,
New thoughts revolv'd within his careful breaft,
Firft turn'd to Godfrey midft the warrior-train:
O! prince! for mercy fam'd (he thus began)

Ver. 151. *Then noble Guelpho*—] The poet here, as in the fifth book, admirably preferves the decorum of Godfrey's character, by making the requeft for his recall come from Guelpho.

H 3   I come

I come t'implore thy grace; thy grace difpenfe, 155
Though rafh the deed, though recent be th'offence;
Hence may it feem too boldly here I ftand,
And immaturely urge the fond demand.
But when I think to Godfrey's friendly ear,
For brave Rinaldo I my fuit prefer; 160
Or view myfelf, of no ignoble ftrain,
That intercedes thy favouring grace to gain:
I truft thou wilt not fuch a boon deny,
Which all will here receive with equal joy.
Ah! let the youth return, retrieve his name, 165
And lave, in fields of blood, his fully'd fame.
What hand but his intrepid fhall invade
The foreft-gloom, and bare the fatal fhade?
Who more adventurous in the field to dare,
Defpifing death, amidft the ranks of war? 170
Behold he fhakes the walls, the gates o'erthrows,
Or foremoft fcales the ramparts of the foes!
Reftore him to the camp!—O chief! reftore
The hope of battle, and the foldiers' power.
Reftore to me a nephew well-belov'd, 175
A champion to thyfelf, in arms approv'd:
Nor let him in ignoble floth remain,
But give him to his rank and fame again,

         Thy

Thy conquering banners let him still pursue,
So may the gazing world his virtues view: 180
Great deeds he then shall shew in open light,
While thou, his leader, rul'st the field of fight.

He ended here; and, while his suit he press'd,
All join'd, with favouring murmurs, his request:
And Godfrey now (each inward thought conceal'd)
Seem'd to his reasons and his suit to yield. 186
Can I (he cry'd) refuse the grace requir'd,
By all expected, and by all desir'd?
Here rigour ends—enough your counsel moves;
Then be it as the public voice approves. 190
Let young Rinaldo view the camp again,
But learn henceforth his anger to restrain:
May he, with actions equal to your praise,
Fulfil your wishes, and his glory raise!
Him to recall, O Guelpho! be thy care: 195
(And grateful sure the tidings to his ear!)
'Tis thine the trusty envoy to select,
And where the youth resides, his steps direct.

He ceas'd; when, rising, thus the Dane began:
An envoy if you seek, behold the man! 200
Nor length of way, nor perils I decline,
To him this honour'd weapon to resign.

So spoke the knight, with generous ardor mov'd,
And noble Guelpho his desire approv'd;
And join'd with him, the labours to divide, 205
Ubald, in ev'ry art of wisdom try'd.
Ubald, in youth, had many regions seen,
Explor'd the customs and the ways of men;
And wander'd long, with unremitted toil,
From polar cold to Libya's burning soil: 210
From different nations different arts he drew;
Their laws, their manners, and their speech he knew:
In age mature him Guelpho now caress'd,
His much-lov'd friend, and partner of his breast.

Such were the men, selected midst the host, 215
From exile to recall the champion lost:
These Guelpho now instructs their course to bend
Where mighty Bæmond's regal walls ascend:
Since all (for thus the public fame was blown)
Had fix'd the knight's retreat in Antioch's town: 220
But here the word the reverend hermit took,
And interposing, on their converse broke.

Ye warriors brave! attend my words (he said)
Nor be by voice of vulgar fame misled;
But haste to Ascalon, and seek the shores 225
Where to the sea a stream its tribute pours:

There

There shall a sage, the Christians' friend, appear;
Attend his dictates, and his counsel hear:
Full well he knows, long since foretold by me,
Of this your journey, fix'd by GOD's decree: 230
'Tis his your steps to guide; from him receive
Such welcome as a faithful heart can give.

The hermit said: and, as his words requir'd,
The ready knights obey'd what Heaven infpir'd.
Direct to Afcalon they bent their way, 235
Where breaks against the land the neighbouring sea.
Their ears perceive not yet the hollow roar
Of dashing billows sounding on the shore:
When now the chiefs a rapid stream beheld,
With sudden rains and rushing torrents swell'd: 240
The banks no more confine its headlong course;
Swift as a shaft it drives with furious force.

Ver. 235. *Direct to Afcalon they bent their way.*]
438. *But soon be heard the stream* —] Here begins the narrative of the wonders met with by these knights, in their embassy to recall Rinaldo, and the description of the enchantments of Armida; and I have little doubt, notwithstanding the severity, and perhaps pedantry, of classical criticism, but every poetical reader will call these the finest passages of the JERUSALEM. The reader will see what use our admirable Spenser has made of these, xivth, xvth, and xvith books.

While

While in suspense they stand, a sage appears,
Of reverend aspect and experienc'd years.
An oaken wreath surrounds his aged brows; 245
In lengthen'd folds his snowy vesture flows;
A wand he shakes; secure he treads the waves,
And with his feet unbath'd the torrent braves.

So, near the freezing pole, the village-swains
(When winter binds the floods in icy chains) 250
Oft o'er the Rhine in fearless numbers glide
With hissing sound, and skim the solid tide.

Now came the sage to where, in deep surprise,
On him the silent warriors fix'd their eyes;
Then thus: O friends! you 'tempt an arduous task,
Your high designs uncommon guidance ask. 256
What toils what dangers still attend your way,
What seas to pass, what regions to survey!
Far must your search, where other suns ascend,
Beyond the limits of our world extend. 260
But first vouchsafe to view my homely cell,
The hidden mansion where retir'd I dwell:
There shall my lips such wondrous truths declare,
As well befits your purpose now to hear.

He ceas'd; and bade the stream a passage yield; 265
Th' obedient stream a sudden path reveal'd;

Full

Full in the midſt the parting waves divide,
A liquid mountain roſe on either ſide.
Then by the hand he ſeiz'd the knights, and led
Within the winding river's ſecret bed.   270
There doubtful day ſcarce glimmers to their ſight;
As when pale Cynthia through the groves, by night,
Sheds from her ſlender horns a trembling light.
There caverns huge they view; from theſe ariſe
The watery ſtores that yield the earth ſupplies, 275
To run in rills, in guſhing ſprings aſcend,
To flow in rivers, or in lakes extend.
There might they ſee whence Po and Iſter came,
Hydaſpes, Ganges, and Euphrates' ſtream:
Whence mighty Tanaïs firſt derives his courſe; 280
And Nilus there reveals his ſecret ſource.
Deep underneath they next a flood behold,
Where ſulphur, mix'd with living ſilver, roll'd:
Till theſe, by Sol's enlivening rays refin'd,
In ſolid gold or lucid cryſtal ſhin'd.   285
Along the banks they ſaw, on either ſide,
Unnumber'd jewels deck the wealthy tide:
From theſe by fits, a flaſhing ſplendor play'd,
And chac'd the horrors of the duſky ſhade.
There ſhines the ſapphire gay with azure bright, 290
And there the jacynth gives a pleaſing light:

There flames the ruby; there the di'mond beams:
And milder there the verdant emerald gleams!

 The warriors still pursu'd their reverend guide;
These wondrous scenes in deep amazement ty'd 295
Each various sense; till prudent Ubald broke
The silence first, and thus the sage bespoke.
Say, Father! what the place we now behold?
Where do'st thou lead? and what thy state, unfold?
Scarce can I tell, bewilder'd with surprise, 300
If truth I view, or dreams deceive my eyes!

 Then he: Lo! here the spacious womb of earth,
Where all productions first receive their birth:
Nor could you thus her entrails dark explore,
Without my guidance and superior power: 305
Now to my palace I your steps convey
(My palace shining with resplendent day.)
A Pagan was I born, but gracious Heav'n
A second life by cleansing streams has giv'n.
Think not these wonders, that confound your thought,
By influence of the Stygian angels wrought. 311
Heaven shield I should invoke Cocytus' shore,
Or Phlegethon with impious arts implore;
But well my knowledge from its source reveals
The virtue every plant or spring conceals: 315

        I meditate

I meditate the ſtars, explore the cauſe
Of nature's works, and trace her ſecret laws.
Yet deem not, ever diſtant from the ſkies,
In ſubterranean ſeats my dwelling lies.
For oft on Lebanon or Carmel's brow   320
I make abode, and view the world below.
There Mars and Venus to my ſearching eyes,
Without a cloud, in all their aſpects riſe.
Each ſtar I know, of ſwift or lingering courſe,
Of mild appearance, or malignant force: 325
Beneath my feet the vapours I ſurvey,
Now dark, and now with Iris' colours gay.
What exhalations rains and dews compoſe
I mark, and how the wind obliquely blows:
What fires the lightning, how the bolt deſcends, 330
And through the air a dreadful paſſage rends.
There, near at hand, I ſee the meteors ſtream,
And wandering comets dart a fiery gleam!
Elate with pride, I deem'd my art could ſoar
To every height, and fathom heavenly pow'r. 335
But when your Peter, in the ſacred flood,
With myſtic rites my ſinful ſoul renew'd;
I rais'd my thoughts, and own'd my wiſdom's boaſt,
Without a guide divine, in darkneſs loſt!

The minds of men, in truth's immortal ray, 340
Appear like birds of night before the day!
Inly I smil'd my follies paft to view,
From which fo late my empty pride I drew:
Yet (fo your pious hermit gave command)
I ftill my former magic arts retain'd: 345
But all my knowledge now obeys his word,
'Tis his to bid, my teacher and my lord!
He now vouchfafes with me (a worthlefs name!)
T' entruft a tafk more righteous hands might claim:
To me he gives to call from diftant lands 350
Th' unconquer'd hero to his focial bands:
Long have I ftay'd, your coming to behold;
For this event the holy fage foretold.

Thus fpoke the fire; and now the knights he fhow'd
Where in the lonely rock he made abode: 355
The manfion like an ample cave was feen,
And halls and ftately rooms appear'd within.
There fhone whate'er th' all-breeding earth contains
Of riches nourifh'd in her fruitful veins:
There native fplendor dwells in every part, 360
And nature rifes o'er the works of art!
An hundred duteous flaves obfequious ftand
T' attend the guefts, and wait their lord's command;

Magnificent

Magnificent the plenteous board is plac'd,
With vases huge of gold and crystal grac'd.   365
At length, the rage of thirst and hunger fled,
The wise magician to the warriors said,

   'Tis time, what most imports, should now be shown;
To you in part Armida's arts are known:
How to the camp she came, and thence convey'd   370
The bravest champions, by her wiles betray'd.
Full well you know that these, in bonds restrain'd,
Th' insidious dame within her tower detain'd;
And sent them guarded thence to Gaza's land,
When fortune, in the way, releas'd their band.   375
It now remains for me th' events to tell
(As yet unknown) which since that time befel.

   Soon as th' enchantress saw her prisoners lost,
Her schemes defeated, and her labours crofs'd;
Opprefs'd with sudden grief, her hands she wrung,
And thus exclaim'd, with raging fury stung: 381

   Then shall he live to boast th' audacious deed,
My guards defeated, and my captives freed!
No—if his arms to others freedom give,
Let him in pains and shameful bondage live: 385
Nor he alone my just revenge shall claim,
My rage shall burst on all the Christian name!

                              Furious

Furious she spoke, and as she spoke design'd
A new device within her fraudful mind:
She sought the plain, where late Rinaldo's might 390
Her warriors vanquish'd, and dispers'd in fight,
The battle o'er, his mail the chief unbrac'd,
And on his limbs a pagan's armour lac'd.
Perchance he sought to veil his glorious name,
Conceal'd in humbler dress unknown to fame. 395
His arms th' enchantress took, in these enclos'd
A headless trunk, and near a stream expos'd;
Here well she knew that, charg'd with daily care,
A band of Franks would from the camp repair.
And fast beside she stationed in the shade 400
A crafty slave in shepherd's garb array'd,
Instructed well suspicion's bane to spread:
He first amongst your troops th' infection shed;
That, wide diffusing, scatter'd discord far,
And threaten'd direful rage and civil war. 405
Thus, as her arts design'd, the Christian train
Believ'd by Godfrey brave Rinaldo slain.

Ver. 396. *His arms th' enchantress took—*] The following passage explains fully the account given in the viiith book to Godfrey by Aliprando, of the supposed death of Rinaldo. See ver. 343 of that book.

Till

Till soon to all confess'd the truth appear'd,
And jealous doubts from every breast were clear'd.
Behold the first device Armida try'd; 410
Now, mark what next her wily thoughts employ'd.
The sorc'ress stay'd by fam'd Orontes' stream,
Till near the banks the young Rinaldo came;
Where from the main a parting riv'let glides,
And forms an island in the limpid tides. 415
There by the shore a little bark appear'd,
A marble pillar close beside was rear'd;
On this, as in suspense, awhile he stood,
Engrav'd in gold these words the hero view'd.

" O thou! whoe'er thou art, whose steps are led, 420
" By choice or fate, these lonely shores to tread;
" No greater wonders east and west can boast,
" Than yon small island on its pleasing coast.
" If e'er thy sight would blissful scenes explore,
" This current pass, and seek the further shore." 425
Th' uncautious warrior with th' advice comply'd,
And curious turn'd, resolv'd to cross the tide;
But, for the bark could only one contain,
Alone he pass'd, and bade his squires remain.
Now, to the land th' impatient hero brought, 430
With eager looks, the promis'd wonders sought;

VOL. II.   I   Yet

Yet nought beheld save meadows deck'd with flowers,
Clear waters, cooling caves, and leafy bowers.
Th' enticing scenes awhile the youth delay'd;
He stretch'd his weary limbs beneath the shade; 435
Then from the massy helm his brows reliev'd,
And in his face the freshening breeze receiv'd.

But soon he heard the stream, with bubbling noise,
Remurmuring soft, and thither turn'd his eyes:
When midst the flood the circling waves he spy'd, 440
That form'd an eddy in the whirling tide:
Whence, rising slow, dishevell'd locks appear'd,
And female features o'er the water rear'd;
The snowy neck, and gently swelling breast;
A crystal veil beneath conceal'd the rest. 445
So from the parting stage is seen to rise
A nymph or goddess to the gazer's eyes.
This, though her form a Syren's charms display'd,
Was but a semblance and delusive shade;
Yet one of those she seem'd, who wont of yore, 450
In faithless seas, t' infest the Tyrrhene shore.
Sweet as her looks, so sweet her tuneful voice;
And thus she sings, while winds and skies rejoice.

O happy man! when youth reigns o'er your hours,
And strows the paths of life with smiling flowers; 455
Ah!

Ah! let not virtue with fallacious ray,
Or glory, lead your tender mind aftray.
Who learns the fruit each feafon yields to prize,
Who follows pleafure, he alone is wife.
Know, this is nature's voice:—Will you withftand
Her facred laws, and flight her high command? 461
Infenfate he who waftes his bloomy prime,
Nor takes the tranfient gifts of fleeting time.
Whate'er the world may worth or valour deem,
Is but a phantom, and delufive dream! 465
Say, what is fame, that idol of the brave,
Whofe charms can thus deceiv'd mankind enflave?
An echo—or a fhade—to none confin'd;
A fhifting cloud, difpers'd with every wind!
Then reft fecure; in every offer'd joy 470
Indulge your fenfes, and your foul employ.
Paft woes forget; nor antedate your doom
By vain prefage of evils yet to come.
Let thunders roll, and nimble lightenings fly;
Yet heed not you the terrors of the fky. 475
This, this is wifdom; hence each bleffing flows;
This nature bids, and this the path fhe fhows.

Thus impious fhe: The foothing accents creep,
And lull the liftening knight to balmy fleep:

I 2 In

In vain the thunder's noise had rent the skies, 480
So deep entranc'd in death-like rest he lies.

  Now fir'd with vengeance, issuing from the wood,
The false enchantress o'er the warrior stood:
But, when she view'd intent his manly face,
His features glowing with celestial grace, 485
Rapt in suspense, beside the youth she sate,
And, as she view'd, forgot her former hate.
Low-bending o'er his charms she hangs amaz'd;
So once Narcissus in the fountain gaz'd.
Now from his cheeks she wipes the dews away; 490
Now bids the fanning breeze around him play:
Now through the meads, that smil'd with various flowers,
She stray'd, and wanton cropt the fragrant stores;
The rose and lily, with her artful hands
Together join'd, she forms in pleasing bands; 495

  Ver. 488. *Low-bending o'er his charms* —] See the passage in Spenser where Acrasia is described with the knight in the bower of bliss.

    And all the while right over him she hong,
    With her false eyes fast fixed in his sight,
    As seeking medicine, whence she was stung,
    Or greedily depasturing delight, &c.
              FAIRY QUEEN, B. ii. c. 12. st. 73.

With these the warrior's arms and legs enfolds,
And gently thus in flowery fetters holds!
Then, while in soft repose he senseless lies,
She lays him on her car, and cuts the skies.
Nor seeks she to regain Damascus' lands,   500
Or where, with waves enclos'd, her castle stands;
But, jealous of her prize, and fill'd with shame,
In ocean's vast profound she hides her flame;
Where from our coast no bark the billow ploughs;
There midst circumfluent tides an isle she chose; 505
Then to a mountain's lofty summit flies,
Forlorn and wild, expos'd to stormy skies:
She clothes the foot and sides with dreary snows,
While on the brow eternal verdure grows.
There, rear'd by spells, and more than mortal hands,
Beside a lake her spacious palace stands;   511
Where, in unfailing spring, and shameful ease,
Th' imprison'd champion leads his amorous days.
'Tis yours the jealous sorc'ress' guards to quell,
That watch th' ascent, and near the palace dwell. 515
Nor shall you want a guide your course to lead;
Nor arms t' assist you in th' adventurous deed.
Soon as you quit my stream, your eyes shall view
A dame, tho' old in years, of youthful hue;

I 3   Known

Known by the locks that o'er her forehead play, 520
And changeful robes, with various colours gay;
'Tis hers to guide you to the task decreed,
With more than eagle's wings or lightening's speed;
'Tis hers to waft you o'er the watery plain,
And safe return you from the roaring main. 525
The mount ascending, on whose tow'ring height
Th' enchantress dwells, remote from human sight;
Then shall you numerous savage forms behold:
There Pythons hiss, in dreadful volumes roll'd:
With horrid bristles stands the foaming boar; 530
With gaping jaws the bear and lion roar!
Then sudden shake this potent wand around,

And

Ver. 532. —— *this potent wand* —] The palmer that accompanies Sir Guyon in Spenser, has a staff of the like virtue. Speaking of the wild beasts that attacked Sir Guyon and his guide on their coming to the bower of Acrasia, the poet thus beautifully enlarges on the fiction of the Italian author.

> But soon as they approach'd, with deadly threat,
> The palmer over them his staff upheld;
> His mighty staff, that could all charms defeat:
> Eftsoons their stubborn courages are quell'd,
> And high advanced crests down meekly fell'd:
> Instead of fraying, they themselves did fear,
> And trembled, as them passing they beheld:

Such

And all with fear shall fly the hissing sound.
But when your feet the steepy summit gain,
Yet greater perils in your way remain: 535
A fountain rises there, whose streams invite
Th' admiring stranger, and the thirst excite;

> Such wondrous power did in that staff appear,
> All monsters to subdue to him that did it bear!
>
> Of that same wood it fram'd was cunningly,
> Of which Caduceus whilom was made;
> Caduceus, the rod of Mercury,
> With which he wonts the Stygian realms invade,
> Through ghastly horror and eternal shade:
> Th' infernal fiends with it he can assuage,
> And Orcus tame, whom nothing can persuade,
> And rule the Furies, when they most do rage:
> Such virtue in his staff had eke this palmer sage.
>
> FAIRY QUEEN, B. ii. c. 12. st. 40.

Ver. 536. *A fountain rises there, whose streams invite Th' admiring stranger.* —] Pomponius Mela writes thus of such a fountain in the Fortunate Islands: " Contra fortunatæ insulæ abundant sua sponte genitis " et subinde aliis superaliis innascentibus; nihil sollicitos " alunt beatius, quam aliæ urbes excultæ. Una singulari " duorum fontium ingenio maxime insignis, alterum qui " potavere risu solvuntur in mortem." Petrarch likewise speaks of two fountains in the Fortunate Islands.

> Fuor tutti i nostri lidi
> Nel' isole famose di fortuna
> Due fonti ha, chi dell' una
> Bee muor ridendo.

But, deep within, th'alluring cryſtal hides
A ſecret venom in its treacherous tides:
One fatal draught can ſtrange effects diſpenſe,   540
And fill with dire delight the madding ſenſe:
Unbidden laughter ſwells the panting breath,
Till lo! the dread convulſion ends in death!
But far! ah, far from thence with ſpeed remove,
Nor let your lips the deadly waters prove: 545
Nor let the banks, with taſteful viands grac'd,
Invite your ſenſes to the rich repaſt:
Nor heed th'inticing dames, whoſe voice decoys,
Whoſe beauty poiſons, and whoſe ſmile deſtroys:
O! fly their looks, their guileful words deſpiſe;   550
And enter where the lofty gates ariſe.
Within, high walls with winding paths ſurround
The ſecret dwelling, and the ſearch confound:
Maze within maze diſtracts the doubtful ſight:
A map ſhall guide your wandering ſteps aright.   555
Amidſt the labyrinth lies the magic grove,
Where every leaf impregnate ſeems with love.
There ſhall you view, beneath th'embowering ſhade,
Th'enamour'd champion and the damſel laid.
But when awhile th'enchantreſs ſhall depart,   560
And leave behind the partner of her heart;

         Then

Then sudden issue forth, to light reveal'd,
And show the knight my adamantine shield:
There shall he see, reflected to his eyes,
His own resemblance, and obscure disguise: 565
Th' ignoble sight his generous wrath shall move,
And banish from his breast inglorious love.
No more remains to tell; 'tis yours alone,
To take secure the path my words have shown;
Safe through the winding maze to bend your course,
Nor fear th' opposing spells of magic force: 571
Not ev'n Armida (such is Heaven's decree)
Can your arrival, by her arts, foresee.
Nor less, returning from th' enchanted seat,
Propitious powers shall favour your retreat. 575
But now the wasting hours to sleep invite,
The morn must see you rise with dawning light.

 Thus spoke the reverend sage; and speaking led
The knights to slumber on a downy bed:
There, fill'd with joy and wonder, either guest 580
He left: and thence himself retir'd to rest.

THE END OF THE FOURTEENTH BOOK.

THE

FIFTEENTH BOOK

OF

JERUSALEM DELIVERED.

THE ARGUMENT.

The two knights take their leave of the hermit, and embark on a vessel steered by a female pilot. Their voyage along the Mediterranean described. They pass the straits, and proceed to the Fortunate Islands. Their conversation with the pilot during the voyage. They arrive at the Island of Armida, where the knights land, who overcome all the obstacles they meet with in ascending the mountain, and afterwards withstand all the various allurements of pleasure offered to their senses.

THE
FIFTEENTH BOOK
OF
JERUSALEM DELIVERED.

NOW rose the ruddy morn with gladsome ray,
And waken'd mortals to the toils of day;
When to the knights the sage the buckler bore,
The map and golden wand of wondrous power:
Prepare t' attempt your arduous way (he cries)   5
Ere yonder sun advances o'er the skies.
These are my promis'd gifts, and these your arms,
To quell th' enchantress, and dissolve her charms.
  At once the warriors rose, and eager round
Their limbs robust the shining armour bound.   10
Thence, as the hermit led, they bent their way
Through paths ne'er lighted by the cheerful day;
Again their former steps returning tread:
But when they reach'd the river's sacred bed,

I now

I now difmifs you from my care (he cry'd): 15
Farewel! and profperous fortune be your guide!
  Soon as they came where ftill the parted flood
On either fide a cryftal mountain ftood,
The waters clos'd, and from the depth upbore
The knights, and left them on the flowery fhore. 20
So, from the branch by winds autumnal torn,
Light on the tide the fcatter'd leaves are borne.
Now from the bank their eyes around they threw,
And foon beheld the promis'd guide in view.
Amidft the ftream a little bark appear'd, 25
A virgin, at the ftern, the veffel fteer'd:
Depending ringlets o'er her forehead ftray,
And mild benevolence her looks difplay:
Her lovely features beams effulgent fhed,
And heavenly glories blaze around her head. 30
Her vefture gay a thoufand colours fhows,
Now flames with red, and now with azure glows:
At every turn it fhifts the tranfient light,
And cheats with momentary hues the fight!
Such various grace the billing dove affumes, 35
Whofe gentle neck is cloth'd with glofly plumes;
For ever new the vary'd feathers play,
Reflecting every tint of every ray;
                          While,

While, as they move, succeffive beauties rife,
And fill with ftrange delight the gazer's eyes! 40
  Favour'd of Heaven! afcend this bark (fhe cry'd)
In which fecure I plough the fwelling tide:
The ftormy winds their wonted rage reftrain,
While fafe in this each freight may pafs the main:
From him, whofe fovereign mercies wide extend, 45
I come, at once your pilot and your friend!
  So fpoke the dame; and, haftening to the land,
The crooked keel divides the yielding ftrand.
Soon as her bark the noble pair receives,
She quits the fhore, and fwift the water cleaves; 50
Then gives the fpreading canvas to the wind,
And guides the veffel from the helm behind.
So wide, fo deep, the river fwells its tide,
That lofty fhips might there fecurely ride;
Though now a fhallow ftream could well fuffice, 55
So light the pinnace o'er the furface flies!
Now, rifing from the land, th' infpiring gales
With profperous breath diftend the bellying fails:
The foaming ftream is white with froth before,
Behind the ftern the parted waters roar. 60
At length they came where, midft its mightier waves,
The fea's vaft gulph the river's ftore receives.
                                                Soon

Soon as the vessel gains the briny tides,
The winds are hush'd, the angry surge subsides:
The clouds disperse, the south forgets to blow, 65
That threaten'd tempests to the world below:
Light Zephyrs only brush along the main,
And scarcely curl the smooth cerulean plain.
By Ascalon they pass'd; to left they veer'd,
And tow'rd the west the rapid vessel steer'd. 70
Then gliding swift, to Gaza next they came,
An ancient harbour, not unknown to fame,
But now, from many a neighbouring ruin great,
An ample city, and a potent state!
The warriors, from the bark, beheld the shore 75
With tents of various nations cover'd o'er:
There horse and foot, along the crowded way,
Swarm thick between the city and the sea.
There loaded camels move in solemn state,
And the huge elephant's unwieldy weight. 80
Safe in the port they see the vessels ride,
Or floating loose, or at their anchors ty'd.
Some hoist their spreading sails, while others sweep,
With level strokes, the surface of the deep.
Then thus the guiding maid—Though here we view
The thronging numbers of this impious crew; 86

Yet

Yet these, that fill the seas and line the shore,
Compose not all the mighty tyrant's power.
These Egypt and the neighbouring lands supply:
But other aids he waits, that distant lie.   90
Far to the east extends his ample sway,
To realms that burn beneath the southern ray;
And hence I trust our swift return to make,
Ere these, departing, shall their tents forsake.

While thus she spoke, as through th' aerial space
An eagle towers above the feather'd race;   96
Till, soaring in the sun, the sharpest eye
No more can trace his progress through the sky:
So midst the ships the bark its passage cleaves,
And far behind the lessening navy leaves.   100
Now, quick as thought, by Paphia's towers they sail,
(The town that first Egyptian pilots hail
On Syria's land) then near the shore they fly,
And Rhinocera's barren sands espy.
Not far from thence a mountain, crown'd with wood,
Casts a brown shadow o'er the subject flood;   106

Ver. 101. *Now, quick as thought, by Paphia's towers they sail.*] I have elsewhere observed, in my notes to Ariosto, that this voyage of Charles and Ubald through the Mediterranean, seems to be imitated from the voyage of Astolpho from the Indies to the Persian Gulph.

Around its rocky foot the billows rave;
There hapless Pompey's bones obtain'd a grave.
Fair Damiata next the eye surveys,
Where ancient Nile his sacred tribute pays   110
Through seven wide mouths, and many a stream beside,
His waters mingling with the briny tide.
They pass the city rais'd by him *, whose name
To latest times shall bear the Grecian fame.
By Pharos then they glide, an isle no more,   115
An isthmus now projecting from the shore.
Nor Rhodes, nor Crete, they to the north survey,
But near the climes of Afric speed their way.
Fruitful her coast: but, more remote, her lands
Are fill'd with monsters dire and burning sands.   120
By Marmarique they steer'd, and now they pass'd
Where five fair cities fam'd Cyrene grac'd.
Here Ptolemais stands, and here they view
Whence his slow stream the fabled Lethe drew.
The greater Syrtes next (the sailors' fear)   125
They leave aloof, and far to seaward veer:
And now Judeca's cape behind them stood;
And now they left the mouth of Magra's flood;

---

* ALEXANDER the GREAT.

Now

Now Tripoly's high rising towers espy'd,
Now Malta scarcely o'er the waves descry'd. 130
The Syrtes past; Alzerbé they beheld,
Where once the race that fed on Lotos dwell'd.
Tunis they see, whose crooked shores display,
With circumjacent arms, a spacious bay:
Tunis the rich, a place well known to fame, 135
No Libyan city boasts a greater name.
Near this Sicilia's fertile lands are spread;
There Lilybæum rears its lofty head.

Now to the knights the damsel-pilot show'd
The spot where once imperial Carthage stood. 140
Ill-fated Carthage! scarce, amidst the plains,
A trace of all her ruin'd pomp remains!
Proud cities vanish, states and realms decay,
The world's unstable glories fade away!
Yet mortals dare of certain fate complain; 145
O impious folly of presuming man!

From thence they see Biserta's spires arise;
Far to the right Sardinia's island lies:
They view, where once the rude Numidian swain
Pursu'd a wandering life from plain to plain. 150
Algiers and Bugia then they reach, the seat
Of impious corsairs; next Oran they greet;

And now by Mauritania's strand proceed,
Where elephants and hungry lions breed:
Morocco here and Fez their cities rear; 155
To these oppos'd Granada's lands appear.
At length they came where, press'd in narrow bounds,
Between the capes, the boiling deep resounds.
'Tis feign'd, that first Alcides forc'd a way,
And gave this passage to th' indignant sea. 160
And here perchance a lengthen'd tract of land
With one continu'd mound the flood restrain'd;
But now the furious main, with rushing tides,
From towering Calpè Abyla divides;
A strait 'twixt Libya now and Spain appears, 165
Such is the force of time and change of years!

Four times the east had seen the rising sun,
Since first the vessel had its course begun:
Nor sheltering bays, nor ports its speed delay,
It shoots the strait, and leaves the midland sea. 170
But what are seas to ocean's vast profound,
Whose circling arms the spacious earth surround?

Soon from the sight, amid the waves, are lost
The fertile Gades, and each neighbouring coast.
Behind, the lessening shores retreating fly; 175
Sky bounds the ocean, ocean bounds the sky.

Then

Then Ubald thus began: Say, thou! whose power
Gives us these endless waters to explore;
Did ever prow before these seas divide,
Do mortals here in distant worlds reside? 180
He ceas'd; the virgin pilot thus reply'd.

When great Alcides had the monsters slain,
That wasted Libya and the realms of Spain;
Your lands subdu'd, at yonder strait he stay'd;
Nor durst old Ocean's surgy gulphs invade. 185
He fix'd his pillars there, in vain design'd
To curb the searching spirit of mankind:
Urg'd by desire new regions to explore,
Ulysses scorn'd the confines of the shore:
He pass'd the bound'ry, loosening to the gales, 190
Amidst the wider flood, his daring sails:
But all his skill in naval arts was vain,
He sunk entomb'd beneath the roaring main.
And those, by tempests forc'd amidst the waves,
Have ne'er return'd, or found untimely graves. 195
Hence undiscover'd still the seas remain,
That numerous isles and mighty states contain.
Inhabitants abound on many a coast;
The lands, like yours, their fertile produce boast;
Where, not ungrateful to the labourer's toil, 200
The sun prolific warms the pregnant soil.

Then Ubald—Of those climes, remov'd afar,
The manners and religious rites declare.
Various their lives (the virgin thus rejoin'd)
Their speech, their customs, are of various kind: 205
Some worship beasts, the stars, or solar power;
And earth, the common parent, some adore.
There are who stain their feasts with human blood,
And load their dreadful board with horrid food;
And every land, from Calpè's towering heights, 210
Is nurs'd in impious faith and cruel rites!

Will then that pitying GOD (the knight reply'd)
Who came with heavenly truths mankind to guide,
Leave, far excluded from the sacred light,
So large a portion of the world in night? 215

O no! the faith of CHRIST shall there be spread,
(She cry'd) and science rear her laurel'd head.
Think not this length of ocean's whelming tide
Shall from your future search those climes divide:
The time shall come, when sailors, yet unborn, 220
Shall name Alcides' narrow bounds in scorn:
Lands now unknown, and seas without a name,
Shall then through all your realms extend their fame:
Perils untry'd succeeding ships shall brave,
And cut, with daring course, the distant wave; 225

Through

Through all the flood's unfathom'd currents run,
Gird the vaſt globe, and emulate the ſun.
From fair Liguria ſee th' adventurer riſe,
Whoſe courage firſt the threatening paſſage tries.
Nor raging ſeas, by furious whirlwinds toſt,   230
Nor doubtful proſpects of th' uncertain coaſt,
Shall, in the ſtraits of Abyla confin'd,
Detain the ardour of his dauntleſs mind!
'Tis thou, Columbus, to another pole
Shalt rear the maſt, and o'er the ſurges roll;   235
While, with a thouſand wings, and thouſand eyes,
Fame ſcarce purſues thy veſſel as it flies!
Let Bacchus or Alcides claim her praiſe,
Thy worth, in future time, her trump ſhall raiſe:
Thy deeds ſhall laſt in ſtoried annals long,   240
The copious ſubject of ſome poet's ſong.

 She ſaid, and weſtward ſteer'd before the wind,
Then gently tow'rds the ſouth her ſails inclin'd.
Now in their front they ſee the ſun deſcend,
And now the morn behind her beams extend: 245
But when Aurora, from her radiant head,
Had all around her pearly moiſture ſhed;
Before their eyes a mountain huge appear'd,
That midſt the clouds its lofty ſummit rear'd.

Near as they came, the fleeting clouds withdrew, 250
And like a pyramid it show'd to view:
From whence black curling smoke was seen to rise;
As where 'tis feign'd th' * Ætnean giant lies
Transfix'd, and breathes eruptions to the skies.
By day thick vapours from the mouth aspire, 255
By night terrific flames of ruddy fire.

   Then other islands midst the main they 'spy'd,
And lands less steepy rising o'er the tide.
Delightful isles, renown'd of ancient date,
And styl'd, by tuneful bards, The Fortunate. 260
'Twas said, that Heaven to these such grace allow'd,
No shining share the sable furrows plough'd.
The lands untill'd could plenteous crops produce;
And vines, unprun'd, supply nectareous juice.
Here olives bloom'd with never-fading green; 265
From hollow oaks was liquid honey seen.
The rivers murmuring from the hills above,
With crystal streams renew'd the vernal grove.
No sultry heat oppress'd the grateful day;
Soft dews and Zephyrs cool'd the solar ray. 270
And here were feign'd the mansions of the blest,
Th' Elysian seats of everlasting rest.

      * ENCELADUS.

To these her course the damsel-pilot bore:
Behold, (she cry'd) our destin'd voyage o'er:
The Isles of Fortune to your sight appear, 275
Whose fame, though doubtful, yet has reach'd your
  ear:
Fair is their soil; but fame each wonder swells,
And every truth, with added fiction, tells.
While thus she spoke, along the main they flew,
Till near the foremost isle their vessel drew. 280
Then Charles began—O ever sacred dame!
If this the cause permits for which we came:
Grant that our feet a while may tread the shore,
To view a race and land unknown before;
T' observe their rites, and mark with curious eyes
Whate'er may claim th' attention of the wise: 286
So shall our lips declare, in future time,
The wonders witness'd in this foreign clime.

Your suit demands my praise, (the maid replies)
But Heaven's decree the bold request denies. 290
The time arrives not yet, by God design'd,
To give the great discovery to mankind:
Nor must you, back from ocean's bosom borne,
With certain tidings to your world return.
To you, beyond the sailor's art, 'tis given 295
To pass these billows, by the will of Heaven;

To

To rouze your champion from his fatal sleep,
And safe convey him o'er the watery deep:
Let this suffice—with prouder thoughts elate,
'Twere impious folly to contend with fate. 300
   Thus while she spoke, the foremost isle withdrew,
And soon the second gain'd upon the view:
She shew'd the warriors how the islands lay,
In order rang'd against the rising day.
The lands with equal space the sea divides, 305
And rolls between the shores its beating tides.
In sev'n are seen the marks of human care,
Where cultur'd fields and rural cots appear:
But three a barren desert soil reveal,
Where savage beasts in woods and mountains dwell.
   Amidst these isles a lone recess they found, 311
Where circling shores the subject flood surround,
And, far within, a spacious bay enclose;
Sharp rocks, without, the rushing surge oppose:
Two lofty cliffs before the entrance rise, 315
A welcome sign to future sailors' eyes:
Within, the waves repose in peace serene;
Black forests nod above, a sylvan scene!
A grotto opens in the living stone,
With verdant moss and ivy-leaves o'ergrown; 320

The grateful shade a gentle murmur fills,
While o'er the pavement glide the lucid rills.
No cables need the floating ships secure,
No bearded anchors here the vessels moor.
To this retreat her course the pilot bore, 325
And, entering, furl'd her sails, and reach'd the shore.

   Behold (she cry'd) where yonder structure stands
Rais'd on the mountain, and the isle commands!
There, lost in festive sloth, in folly lost,
Slumbers the champion of the Christian host. 330
'Tis yours, when next the sun forsakes the deep,
With labouring feet t' ascend the threatening steep:
Meanwhile this short delay with ease be borne;
All times are luckless save the hour of morn:
But to the mountain's foot pursue your way, 335
While yet remains the light of parting day.

   Thus she; the word th' impatient warriors took,
And, leaping from the bark, the strand forsook.
With ready steps a pleasing road they cross'd,
And all their toils in sweet delusion lost. 340
At length th' expected hill's broad base they gain,
(The sun yet hovering o'er the western main)
From hence their eyes the arduous height survey,
The pendent ruins and the rocky way.

Inclement

Inclement frost the mountain's sides deforms, 345
And all around is white with wintry storms.
The lofty summit yields a milder scene,
With budding flowers and groves for ever green!
There ends the frozen clime; there lilies blow,
There roses blush upon the bordering snow. 350
There youthful spring, and hoary winter here;
Such power has magic o'er the changing year!

Now at the mountain's foot the heroes stay'd,
And slept secure beneath a cavern's shade.
But when the sun (eternal fount of day!) 355
Spread o'er the laughing skies his golden ray:
At once they rose, at once their course renew'd,
And up the steep ascent the way pursu'd.
When lo! a serpent, rushing from his cell,
Oppos'd their passage, horrible and fell! 360

Ver. 359. *When, lo! a serpent* ——] Virgil and Milton have both excelled in describing the motion of this animal.

    ——Rapit orbes pro humum. VIRG.

    ——He leading swiftly roll'd
    In tangles—— MILTON.

But the commentator on Milton, thinks that Tasso has surpassed both in the above passage, the beauty of which can scarcely be rendered into English.

    Hor rientra in se stessa, hor le nodose
    Ruote distende e se dopo se tira.

               Aloft

Aloft his head and squalid breast he held
Bestreak'd with gold; his neck with anger swell'd;
Fire fill'd his eyes; he hid the path beneath;
And smoke and poison issu'd with his breath.
Now in thick curls his scaly length he wound; 365
Now trail'd his opening folds along the ground.
Such was the dreadful guardian of the place,
Yet on the heroes press'd with fearless pace.
The Dane his falchion draws, and eager flies
T' assail the snake, when sudden Ubald cries: 370
Forbear! can arms like these our foes repel?
And think'st thou thus the monster's rage to quell?

 He said; and shook the golden wand around;
The serpent fled, astonish'd at the sound.
The knights proceed; a lion fierce descends, 375
And, roaring loud, the dangerous pass defends;
He rolls his fiery eyes, his mane he rears,
Wide as a gulph his gaping mouth appears;
His lashing tail his slumbering wrath awakes:
But, when his potent rod the warrior shakes, 380
Unusual fears the dreadful beast surprise,
Sunk is his rage, he trembles, and he flies!

 Still on they pass'd; but soon a numerous host
Of monsters dire their daring passage cross'd.

In

In various shapes the ghastly troops appear, 385
With various yells they rend the startled ear.
Each savage form that roves the burning sands,
From distant Nilus to the Libyan lands,
Here seem'd to dwell, with all the beasts that roam
Hyrcania's woods, or deep Hircinia's gloom! 390
But not their numbers could the chiefs detain;
The powerful wand made all their fury vain.
These dangers past; the conquering pair ascend;
Now near the brow their eager steps they bend;
Yet, as they tread the cliffs, the sinking snows 395
And slippery ice awhile their course oppose.
But when at length they reach'd the rocky height,
A spacious level opens to their sight.
There youthful spring salutes th' enraptur'd eye,
Unfading verdure, and a gladsome sky; 400
Eternal Zephyrs through the groves prevail,
And incense breathes in every balmy gale;
No irksome change th' unvaried climate knows
Of heat alternate, and alternate snows:
A genial power the tender herbage feeds, 405
And decks with every sweet the smiling meads;
Diffuses soft perfumes from every flower,
And clothes with lasting shade each rural bower:
There,

There, rear'd aloft, a stately palace stands,
Whose prospect wide the hills and seas commands.

 The warriors, weary'd with the steep ascent, 411
More slowly o'er th' enamel'd meadow went;
Oft looking back, their former toils review'd,
Now paus'd awhile, and now their course pursu'd.
When sudden, falling from the rocky heights, 415
A copious stream the traveller's thirst excites;
From hence a thousand rills dispersing flow,
And trickle through the grassy vale below:
At length, uniting all their different tides,
In verdant banks a gentle river glides, 420
With murmuring sound a bowery gloom pervades,
And rolls its sable waves through pendent shades:
A cool retreat! the flowery border shows
A pleasing couch, inviting soft repose.
Behold the fatal spring where laughter dwells, 425
Dire poison lurking in its secret cells!
Here let us guard our thoughts, our passions rein,
And every loose desire in bonds detain:
A deafen'd ear to dulcet music lend,
Nor dare the Syren's impious lays attend. 430

 The knights advanc'd till, from their narrow bed,
Wide in a lake the running waters spread.

There

There on the banks a fumptuous banquet plac'd,
With coftly viands feem'd t' allure the tafte.
Two blooming damfels in the water lave, 435
And laugh and plunge beneath the lucid wave.

Ver. 435. *Two blooming damfels* ——] All this beautiful paffage is imitated, or rather tranflated, by our Spenfer, in his Fairy Queen, where Guyon is defcribed with the palmer, entering the bower of blifs.

>Two naked damfels he therein efpy'd,
>Which therein bathing feemed to contend,
>And wreftle wantonly, ne car'd to hide
>Their dainty parts from view of any which them ey'd.

>As that fair ftar, the meffenger of morn,
>His dewy face out of the fea does rear;
>Or as the Cyprian Goddefs, newly born
>Of th' Ocean's fruitful froth, did firft appear;
>Such feemed they, and fo their yellow hair
>Cryftalline humour dropped down apace.

>With that, the other likewife arofe,
>And her fair locks, which formerly were bound
>Up in one knot, fhe low adown did loofe;
>Which flowing long and thick her cloath'd around,
>And th' ivory in golden mantle gound;
>So that fair fpectacle from him was reft,
>Yet that which reft it, no lefs fair was found:
>So hid in locks and waves from looker's theft,
>Nought but her lovely face fhe for his looking left.
>FAIRY QUEEN, B. ii. c. 12. ft. 65, 67.

Now round in sport they dash the sprinkling tide;
And now with nimble strokes the stream divide:
Now, sunk at once, they vanish from the eyes;
And now again above the surface rise! 440

The naked wantons, with enticing charms,
Each warrior's bosom fill'd with soft alarms:
Awhile they stay'd their steps, and silent view'd,
As those their pastime unconcern'd pursu'd,
Till one erect in open light appear'd, 445
And o'er the stream her ivory bosom rear'd;
Her upward beauties to the sight reveal'd:
The rest, beneath, the crystal scarce conceal'd.

As when the morning star, with gentle ray,
From seas emerging leads the purple day: 450
As when, ascending from the genial flood,
The queen of love on ocean's bosom stood:
So seems the damsel, so her locks diffuse
The pearly liquid in descending dews!
Till on th' approaching chiefs she turn'd her eyes,
Then feign'd, with mimic fear, a coy surprise: 456
Swift from her head she loos'd, with eager haste,
The yellow curls in artful fillets lac'd;
The falling tresses o'er her limbs display'd,
Wrapt all her beauties in a golden shade! 460

Thus hid in locks, and circled by the flood,
With side-long glance, o'erjoy'd, the knights she
 view'd.
Her smiles amid her blushes lovelier show;
Amid her smiles, her blushes lovelier glow!
At length she rais'd her voice with melting art, 465
Whose magic strains might pierce the firmest heart.

 O happy strangers! to whose feet 'tis given
To reach these blissful seats, this earthly heaven!
Here are those rapturous scenes so fam'd of old,
When early mortals view'd an age of gold. 470
No longer bear the helm, the falchion wield,
The cumbrous corslet, or the weighty shield;
Here hang your useless arms amidst the grove,
The warriors now of peace-inspiring love!
Our field of battle is the downy bed, 475
Or flowery turf amid the smiling mead.
Then let us lead you to our sovereign's eyes,
From whose diffusive power our blessings rise.
She shall amongst those few your names receive,
Elected here in endless joys to live. 480
But first refresh your limbs beneath the tide,
And taste the viands which our cares provide.

 She ceas'd; her lovely partner join'd her prayer,
With looks persuasive, and enticing air,

         So,

So, in the scene, the active dancers bound, 485
And move responsive to the tuneful sound.
But firmly steel'd was either champion's heart,
Against their fraudful strains and soothing art.
Or, if forbidden thoughts a wish inspire,
And wake the slumbering seeds of wild desire; 490
Soon to their aid assisting reason came,
And quench'd the infant sparks of kindled flame.

  Their arts in vain the vanquish'd damsels view'd;
The warriors thence their fated way pursu'd:
These seek the palace; those indignant hide 495
Their shameful heads beneath the whelming tide.

THE END OF THE FIFTEENTH BOOK.

THE

SIXTEENTH BOOK

OF

JERUSALEM DELIVERED.

THE ARGUMENT.

CHARLES and Ubald enter the palace of Armida. The gardens are described. Rinaldo is seen with his mistress. At the departure of Armida, the two knights discover themselves; and Ubald reproves Rinaldo for his sloth and effeminacy. The youthful hero, filled with shame, abandons those seats of pleasure, and follows the guidance of his deliverers. Armida pursues him, and makes use of every argument to move him, but in vain: He endeavours to pacify her: she then breaks out into bitter reproaches, till, her strength being exhausted, she falls into a swoon. The three warriors go on board their vessel, and set sail for Palestine. Armida, recovering, finds her lover gone: She then gives herself up to rage, and, resolving on revenge, destroys her enchanted palace, and takes her flight to Egypt.

THE SIXTEENTH BOOK OF JERUSALEM DELIVERED.

ROUND was the form in which the palace rose;
   Deep in the midst the circling walls enclose
A sumptuous garden, whose delightful scene
Eclips'd the fairest works of mortal men.
The fiends had bent their skill a pile to raise,   5
Perplex'd with walks in many a devious maze;
And in the centre lay the magic bowers,
Impervious to the search of human powers.
  Now through the loftiest gate the warriors pass'd,
(A hundred gates the spacious structure grac'd)   10
With sculptur'd silver, glorious to behold,
The valves on hinges hung of burnish'd gold!
Surpris'd they saw, excell'd in every part,
The rich materials, by the sculptor's art.

In all but speech alive the figures rise;   15
Nor speech they seem to want to wondering eyes!
   In female converse there (inglorious state!)
Alcides midst Mœonia's damsels sate.
There he who propp'd the stars, and hell subdu'd,
The distaff bore; while Love beside him stood,   20
And with exulting smiles his conquest view'd.
There Iolè was seen, whose feeble hand
With pride the hero's ponderous club sustain'd:
The lion's hide conceal'd the beauteous dame,
Too rough a covering for so soft a frame!   25
   To this oppos'd, the chiefs a sea beheld;
Its azure field with frothy billows swell'd.
There, in the midst, two hostile navies ride;
Their arms in lightening flash from side to side.
Augustus o'er his Romans here commands: 30
There Anthony conducts from eastern lands
His Indian, Arab, and Egyptian bands.
Thou would'st have thought the Cyclades uptorn,
And hills with hills in horrid conflict borne!
So fierce the shock, when, joining ship with ship, 35
The navies meet amidst the roaring deep!
Firebrands and javelins fly from foe to foe;
Unusual slaughter stains the flood below.

             Behold

Behold (while doubtful yet remains the fight)
Behold where Cleopatra takes her flight.   40
See! Anthony, of fame forgetful, flies,
No more his hopes to glorious empire rife.
Yet o'er his foul no fervile fear prevails;
Her flight alone impels his yielding fails.
Contending paffions all his foul inflame,   45
Difdain and rage, and love and confcious fhame:
While, with alternate gaze, he views from far
Her parting veffel, and the dubious war.
Now Nile receives him on his watery breaft;
There, in his miftrefs' arms, he finks to reft;   50
There feems, refign'd, the threatening hour to wait,
And foften, with her fmiles, the ftroke of fate.

   With ftory'd labours thus the portals grac'd,
The heroes view'd, and thence intrepid pafs'd.
And now they try'd the labyrinth's winding maze: 55
As fam'd Meander moves a thoufand ways;
Now rolls direct, now takes a devious courfe,
Now feems to feek again his native fource:
The frequent turnings fo their eyes deceiv'd:
But foon the faithful map their doubts reliev'd;   60
Difplay'd each various paffage to their fight,
And led through paths oblique their fteps aright.

                                              The

The garden then unfolds a beauteous scene,
With flowers adorn'd and ever-living green.
There silver lakes reflect the beaming day; 65
Here cryſtal ſtreams in gurgling fountains play:
Cool vales deſcend, and ſunny hills ariſe,
And groves, and caves, and grottoes, ſtrike the eyes.
Art ſhew'd her utmoſt power; but art conceal'd,
With greater charms the pleas'd attention held. 70
It ſeem'd as Nature play'd a ſportive part,
And ſtrove to mock the mimic works of art!
By powerful magic breathes the vernal air,
And fragrant trees eternal bloſſoms bear:
Eternal fruits on every branch endure; 75
Thoſe ſwelling from their buds, and theſe mature.
There, on one parent ſtock, the leaves among,
With ripen'd figs, the figs unripen'd hung.
Depending apples here the boughs unfold;
Thoſe green in youth, theſe mellow'd into gold. 80
The vine luxuriant rears her arms on high,
And curls her tendrils to the genial ſky:
There the crude grapes no grateful ſweet produce,
And here impurpled yield nectareous juice.
The joyous birds, conceal'd in every grove, 85
With gentle ſtrife prolong the notes of love.

Soft

Soft Zephyrs breathe on woods and waters round;
The woods and waters yield a murm'ring sound:
When cease the tuneful choir, the wind replies;
But, when they sing, in gentle whispers dies: 90
By turns they sink, by turns their music raise,
And blend, with equal skill, harmonious lays.

Amongst the rest, with plumes of various dyes,
And purple beak, a lovely songster flies;
Wondrous to tell, with human speech indu'd, 95
He fills with vocal strains the blisful wood:
The birds attentive close their silent wings,
While thus the fair, the soothing charmer sings.

Behold how lovely blooms the vernal rose,
When scarce the leaves her early bud disclose: 100
When,

Ver. 99. *Behold how lovely blooms the vernal rose.*] This song is closely translated by Spenser; but, as it has been observed very well, our poet has judiciously omitted the fanciful circumstance of a bird singing these words, which has been the subject of Voltaire's ridicule.

> Ah! see the virgin rose, how sweetly she
> Dost first peep forth with bashful modesty,
> That fairer seems, the less you see her may;
> Lo! see soon after, how more bold and free
> Her bared bosom she doth broad display;
> Lo! see soon after, how she fades and falls away.

So

When, half inwrapt, and half to view reveal'd,
She gives new pleasure from her charms conceal'd.
But when she shows her bosom wide display'd,
How soon her sweets exhale, her beauties fade!
No more she seems the flower so lately lov'd, 105
By virgins cherish'd, and by youths approv'd!
So, swiftly fleeting with the transient day,
Passes the flower of mortal life away!
In vain the spring returns, the spring no more
Can waining youth to former prime restore: 110
Then crop the morning rose, the time improve,
And, while to love 'tis given, indulge in love!

He ceas'd: th' approving choir with joy renew
Their rapturous music, and their loves pursue.

> So passeth, in the passing of a day,
> Of mortal life, the leaf, the bud, the flower,
> Ne more doth flourish after first decay,
> That earst was sought to deck both bed and bower,
> Of many a lady and many a paramour:
> Gather therefore the rose, whilst yet in prime,
> For soon comes age, that will her pride deflower:
> Gather the rose of love, whilst yet in time,
> Whilst loving thou may'st loved be with equal crime.

> He ceast, and then 'gan all the quire of birds
> Their diverse notes t' attune unto his lay,
> As in approvance, &c.

Again

Again in pairs the cooing turtles bill; 115
The feather'd nations take their amorous fill.
The oak, the chaster laurel seems to yield,
And all the leafy tenants of the field:
The earth and streams one soul appears to move,
All seem impregnate with the seeds of love. 120
 Through these alluring scenes of magic power
The virtuous warriors pass'd, and pass'd secure:
When 'twixt the quivering boughs they cast their sight,
And see the damsel and the Christian knight.
There sate Armida on a flowery bed; 125
Her wanton lap sustain'd the hero's head:
Her opening veil her ivory bosom show'd;
Loose to the fanning breeze her tresses flow'd;
A languor seem'd diffus'd o'er all her frame,
And every feature glow'd with amorous flame. 130
The pearly moisture on her beauteous face
Improv'd the blush, and heighten'd every grace:

> Ver. 127. *Her opening veil*———] See Spenser.
>   Her snowy breast was bare to ready spoil
>   Of hungry eyes, which n'ote therewith be fill'd:
>   And yet through languor of her late sweet toil,
>   Few drops, more clear than nectar, forth distill'd,
>   That like pure orient pearls adown it trill'd, &c.

Her wandering eyes confefs'd a pleafing fire,
And fhot the trembling beams of foft defire.
Now, fondly hanging o'er, with head declin'd, 135
Clofe to his cheek her lovely cheek fhe join'd.
While o'er her charms he taught his looks to rove,
And drank, with eager thirft, new draughts of love.
Now, bending down, enraptur'd as he lies,
She kifs'd his vermil lips and fwimming eyes: 140
Till from his inmoft heart he heav'd a figh,
As if to hers his parting foul would fly!

All this the warriors from the fhade furvey,
And mark, conceal'd, the lovers' amorous play.
Dependent from his fide (unufual fight!) 145
Appear'd a polifh'd mirror, beamy bright:
This in his hand th' enamour'd champion rais'd;
On this, with fmiles, the fair Armida gaz'd.
She in the glafs her form reflected 'fpies:
And he confults the mirror of her eyes: 150
One proud to rule, one prouder to obey;
He blefs'd in her, and fhe in beauty's fway.
Ah! turn thofe eyes on me (exclaims the knight)
Thofe eyes that blefs me with their heavenly light!
For know, the power that every lover warms, 155
In this fond breaft Armida's image forms.

Since

Since I, alas! am scorn'd! here turn thy sight,
And view thy native graces with delight:
Here on that face thy ravish'd looks employ,
Where springs eternal love, eternal joy; 160
Or rather range through yon celestial spheres,
And view thy likeness in the radiant stars.

 The lover ceas'd; the fair Armida smil'd,
And still with wanton play the time beguil'd.
Now in a braid she bound her flowing hair; 165
Now smooth'd the roving locks with decent care.
Part, with her hand, in shining curls she roll'd,
And deck'd with azure flowers the waving gold.
Her veil compos'd, with roses sweet she dress'd
The native lilies of her fragrant breast. 170
Not half so proud, of glorious plumage vain,
The peacock sets to view his glittering train:
Not Iris shews so fair, when dewy skies
Reflect the changeful light with various dyes.
But o'er the rest her wondrous cestus shin'd, 175
Whose mystic round her tender waist confin'd.

            Here

Ver. 175. —— *her wondrous cestus* —] The idea of this girdle is from the cestus of Homer, which Juno borrows of Venus.

  In this was every art, and every charm,
   To win the wisest, and the coldest warm:
            Fond

Here unembody'd spells th' enchantress mix'd,
By potent arts, and in a girdle fix'd:
Repulses sweet, soft speech, and gay desires,
And tender scorn that fans the lover's fires; 180
Engaging smiles, short sighs of mutual bliss,
The tear of transport, and the melting kiss.
All these she join'd, her powerful work to frame,
And artful temper'd in th' annealing flame.

Now with a kiss, the balmy pledge of love, 185
She left her knight, and issu'd from the grove.
Each day, awhile apart, the dame review'd
Her magic labours, and her charms renew'd;
While he deep-musing, in her absence stray'd,
A lonely lover midst the conscious shade. 190
But when the silent glooms of friendly night
To mutual bliss th' enamour'd pair invite;
Beneath one roof, amid the bowers they lay,
And lov'd, entranc'd, the fleeting hours away.

Soon as Armida (so her arts requir'd) 195
From gentle love to other cares retir'd:

> Fond love, the gentle vow, the gay desire,
> The kind deceit, the still-reviving fire,
> Persuasive speech, and more persuasive sighs,
> Silence that spoke, and eloquence of eyes.
> POPE's ILIAD, B. xiv. ver. 247.

The warriors, from their covert, rush'd to fight,
In radiant arms that cast a gleamy light.

  As when, from martial toil, the generous steed
Releas'd, is given to range the verdant mead;   200
Forgetful of his former fame, he roves,
And wooes in slothful ease his dappled loves:
If chance the trumpet's sound invade his ears,
Or glittering steel before his sight appears,
He neighs aloud, and, furious, pants to bear   205
The valiant chief, and pierce the files of war!
So fares Rinaldo, when the knights he 'spies:
When their bright armour lightens in his eyes:
At once the glorious beams his soul inspire;
His breast rekindles with a martial fire.   210
Then sudden, forth advancing, Ubald held
Before the youth his adamantine shield:
To this he turn'd, in this at once survey'd
His own resemblance full to view display'd:
His sweeping robes he saw, his flowing hair   215
With odours breathing, his luxuriant air.
His sword, the only mark of warlike pride,
Estrang'd from fight, hung idly at his side;
And, wreath'd with flowers, seem'd worn for empty
    show;
No dreadful weapon 'gainst a valiant foe.   220

As one, whom long lethargic slumber ties,
Recovers from his sleep with wild surprise:
So from his trance awakes the Christian knight,
Himself beholds, and sickens at the sight;
And wishes opening earth his shame would hide, 225
Or ocean veil him in its whelming tide.

Then Ubald thus began—All Europe arms,
And Asia's kingdoms catch the loud alarms.
Now all that cherish fame, or CHRIST adore,
In shining armour press the Syrian shore: 230
While thee, Bertoldo's son! from glory's plains,
A narrow isle in shameful rest detains;
Alone regardless of the voice of fame,
Th' ignoble champion of a wanton dame!
What fatal power can thus thy sense control? 235
What sloth suppress the virtues of thy soul?
Rise! rise!—thee Godfrey, thee the camp incites:
'Tis fortune calls, and victory invites!
Come, fated warrior! bid the fight succeed;
And crush those foes thou oft hast made to bleed; 240
Now let each impious sect thy vengeance feel,
And fall extinct beneath thy conquering steel.

He ceas'd: awhile the youth in silence mus'd,
All motionless he stood, with looks confus'd:

Till shame gave way, and stronger anger rose;   245
(A generous anger, that from reason flows)
O'er all his face a noble ardor flies,
Flames on his cheek, and sparkles from his eyes.
  Now, hastening from the bower, their way they hold,
And safely pass the labyrinth's winding fold.   250
Meanwhile Armida view'd, with deep dismay,
Where, breathless at the gate, the keeper lay:
Then first suspicion in her bosom grew;
And soon her lover's flight too well she knew;
Herself beheld the darling hero fly: 255
O direful prospect to a lover's eye!
  Where wouldst thou go, and leave me here alone?—
She strove to say; but, with a rising groan,
Too mighty grief her feeble words suppress'd,
Which deep remurmur'd in her tortur'd breast.   260
Ah wretched fair! a greater power disarms,
A greater wisdom mocks thy frustrate charms!

Ver. 252. *Where, breathless at the gate, the keeper lay.*] There is an obscurity in this passage, for no mention has been made before by the poet of such a circumstance.

> In tanto Armida de la regal porta
> Mirò giacere il fier custode estinto.

This sees the dame, who every art applies
To stay his flight: in vain each art she tries.
Whate'er the witches of Thessalia's strain 265
E'er mutter'd to the shades with lips profane,
That could the planets in their spheres control,
Or call from prisons drear the parted soul,
Full well she knew; but all in vain essay'd;
No hell, responsive, her commands obey'd. 270
Abandon'd thus, she next resolv'd to prove
If suppliant beauty more than spells could move.
See! where, regardless of her former fame,
All wild with anguish runs the furious dame.
She who so late the laws of love despis'd, 275
Who scorn'd the lover, tho' the love she priz'd;
Whose conquering eyes could every heart subdue;
Behold her now a lover's steps pursue!
With soft persuasive grief her look she arms,
And bathes with tears her now neglected charms. 280
O'er rocks and snows her tender feet she plies,
And sends her voice before her as she flies.

 O thou! who bear'st away my yielding heart,
Who robb'st me of my best, my dearest part,
O! give me death—or once again restore 285
My murder'd peace—thy hasty flight give o'er!

           Hear

Hear my laſt words—I aſk no parting kiſs;
For happier lips reſerve that mighty bliſs:
What canſt thou fear, ah cruel! to comply,
Since ſtill with thee remains the power to fly? 290

Then Ubald thus—Awhile thy ſpeed forbear,
And lend her woes, O Prince! a courteous ear:
The praiſe be thine thy virtue to retain,
And hear unmov'd the vanquiſh'd Syren's ſtrain:
So Reaſon ſhall extend her ſacred ſway, 295
And teach the ſubject paſſions to obey.

He ſaid; Rinaldo ſtay'd; and ſudden came,
Breathleſs, o'erſpent with haſte, the hapleſs dame.
Deep ſorrow ſpread o'er all her languid air;
Yet ſweet in woe and beauteous in deſpair: 300
Silent on him her eager look ſhe bent;
Diſdain, and fear, and ſhame her ſpeech prevent;
While from her eyes the knight abaſh'd withdrew,
Or ſnatch'd, with wary glance, a tranſient view.

As fam'd muſicians, ere the notes they raiſe 305
To charm the liſtening ear with tuneful lays,
With accents low, in prelude ſoft, prepare
The rapt attention for the promis'd air:
So ſhe, yet mindful of her fraudful art,
Would ſoften, ere ſhe ſpoke, the hearer's heart; 310

First breath'd a sigh to melt the tender breast;
Then thus, at length, these plaintive words address'd,
  Ah cruel! think not now I come to prove
The prayers that lovers might to lovers move!
Such once we were!—But if thou scorn'st the name,
Yet grant the pity foes from foes may claim.   316
If me thy hate pursues, enjoy thy hate;
I seek not to disturb thy happy state!
A Pagan born, I every means employ'd
T' oppress the Christians and their power divide.   320
Thee I pursu'd, and thee secluded far,
In distant climates, from the sound of war.
But more, which deeper seems thy scorn to move,
Add how I since deceiv'd thee to my love.
O foul deceit!—to yield my virgin flower,   325
To give my beauties to another's power!
To let one favour'd youth that gift obtain,
Which thousands fondly sought, but sought in vain!
These are my frauds; let these thy wrath engage;
Such crimes may well demand a lover's rage!   330
So may'st thou part without one tender thought,
And be these dear abodes at once forgot!
Haste!—pass the seas!—thy flying sails employ,
Go, wage the combat, and our faith destroy!—

Our

Our faith, alas!—Ah, no!—*my* faith no more; 335
I worship thee, and thee alone adore!
Yet hence with thee deceiv'd Armida bear;
The vanquish'd still attends the victor's car:
Let me be shown, to all the camp display'd,
The proud betrayer by thy guile betray'd. 340
Wretch as I am! shall still these locks be worn,
These locks that now are grown a lover's scorn?
These hands shall cut the tresses from my head,
And o'er my limbs a servile habit spread:
Thee will I follow midst surrounding foes, 345
When all the fury of the battle glows.
I want not soul, so far at least to dare
To lead thy courser, or thy javelin bear.
Let me sustain, or be myself thy shield;
Still will I guard thee in the dangerous field. 350
No hostile hand so savage can be found,
Through my poor limbs thy dearer life to wound:
Soft mercy even may fell revenge restrain,
And these neglected charms some pity gain—
Ah, wretch! and dare I still of beauty boast, 355
My prayers rejected, and my empire lost!

   More had she said; but grief her words withstood,
Fast from her eyes distill'd the trickling flood:

With suppliant act she sought to grasp his hand,
She held his robe; unmov'd the chief remain'd: 360
Love found no more an entrance in his breast,
And firm resolves the starting tears suppress'd,
Yet pity soften'd soon his generous soul;
Scarce could he now the tender dew control:
But still he strove his secret thoughts to hide, 365
Compos'd his looks, and thus at length reply'd.

Armida! thy distress with grief I see;
O! could I now thy labouring bosom free
From this ill-omen'd love!—Ah! hapless fair!
No scorn I harbour, and no hatred bear: 370
I seek no vengeance; no offence I know;
Nor canst thou be my slave, nor art my foe.
On either side I fear thy thoughts have stray'd,
As love deceiv'd thee, or as anger sway'd.
But human frailties human pity claim; 375
Thy faith, thy sex, thy years, acquit thy fame.
I too have err'd: and shall I dare reprove
Thy tender bosom with the faults of love?
Hence ever shall thy dear remembrance rest,
In joy and grief the partner of my breast! 380
Still must I be thy champion—thine as far
As Christian faith permits, and Asia's war.

But

But ah! let here our mutual weakneſs end;
No farther now our mutual ſhame extend:
Here from the world, on this extremeſt coaſt, 385
Be all our follies in oblivion loſt!
Midſt all my deeds in Europe's clime reveal'd!
O! ſtill be theſe, and theſe alone, conceal'd!
Then let no raſh ignoble thoughts diſgrace
Thy worth, thy beauty, and thy royal race. 390
With me thou ſeek'ſt in vain to quit the land;
Superior powers thy fond deſire withſtand.
Remain; or ſeek ſome happier place of reſt,
And in thy wiſdom calm thy troubled breaſt.

As thus the warrior ſpoke, the haughty dame 395
Scarce held her rage, now kindling to a flame;
Awhile ſhe view'd him with a ſcornful look,
Then from her lips theſe furious accents broke.

Boaſt not Bertoldo's nor Sophia's blood!
Thou ſprung'ſt relentleſs from the ſtormy flood: 400
Thy infant years th' Hyrcanian tigreſs fed;
On frozen Caucaſus thy youth was bred!—
See! if he deigns one tender tear beſtow,
Or pay one ſigh in pity to my woe!
What ſhall I ſay, or whither ſhall I turn? 405
He calls me his!—yet leaves me here in ſcorn.

See

See how his foe the generous victor leaves,
Forgets her error, and her crime forgives!
Hear how sedate, how sage, his counsels prove;
This rigid cool Zenocrates in love!   410
O Heaven!—O Gods!—and shall this impious race
Your temples ravage, and your shrines deface?
Go, wretch—Such peace attend thy tortur'd mind
As I, forsaken here, am doom'd to find!
Fly hence!—be gone!—but soon expect to view 415
My vengeful ghost thy traiterous flight pursue:
A fury arm'd with snakes and torch I'll prove,
With terrors equal to my former love!
If fate decrees thee safe to pass the main,
Escap'd from rocks, to view th' embattled plain, 420
There shalt thou, sinking in the fatal strife,
Appease my vengeance with thy dearest life:
Oft shalt thou then by name Armida call
In dying groans, while I enjoy thy fall!

 She could no more; as these last words she spoke,
Scarce from her lips the sounds imperfect broke. 426
She faints! she sinks! all breathless pale she lies
In chilly sweats, and shuts her languid eyes.
Dost thou, Armida! now thy eyelids close?
Heaven envies sure one comfort to thy woes.   430
          Ah!

Ah! raife thy fight; behold thy deadly foe:
See down his cheek the kindly forrows flow.
O! could'ft thou now, ill-fated lover! hear
His fighs foft breaking on thy raptur'd ear!
What fate permits (but this thou canft not view) 435
He gives, and pitying takes the laft adieu.
What fhould he do?—thus leave her on the coaft,
'Twixt life and death her ftruggling fenfes loft?
Compaffion pleads, and courtefy detains;
But dire neceffity his flight conftrains. 440
He parts:—and now a friendly breeze prevails,
(The pilot's treffes waving in the gales)
The golden fail o'er furging ocean fpeeds,
And from the fight the flying fhore recedes.

But when, recover'd from her trance, fhe ftood,
And all around the land forfaken view'd: 446
And is he gone?—Has then the traitor fled?
Left me in life's extremeft need? (fhe faid)
Would he not to my haplefs ftate difpenfe
One moment's ftay, or wait returning fenfe? 450
And do I love him ftill? ftill here remain,
And unreveng'd in empty words complain?
What then avail thefe tears, thefe female arms!
Far other arts are mine, and ftronger charms.

I will

I will purſue—nor hell th' ingrate ſhall ſhield, 455
Nor heav'n ſhall ſafety from my fury yield:
Now! now I ſeize him! now his heart I tear,
And ſcatter round his mangled limbs in air.
He knows each various art of torture well,
In his own arts the traitor I'll excel!— 460
But ah! I wander!—O! untimely boaſt!
Unbleſs'd Armida, whither art thou toſt?
Then ſhould'ſt thou to thy rage have given the rein,
When he lay captive in thy powerful chain.
Then did the wretch no leſs thy hatred claim; 465
Too late thy rage now kindles to a flame!
O beauty ſcorn'd! ſince you th' offence ſuſtain'd,
Be yours the due revenge your wrongs demand.
Lo! with my perſon ſhall his worth be paid,
Who from the battle brings that hated head. 470
Ye gallant youths! whom faithful love inſpires,
A dangerous, glorious taſk my ſoul requires!
Ev'n I, to whom Damaſcus' realms ſhall bow,
The price of vengeance with myſelf beſtow.
But, if, contemn'd, I muſt not this obtain, 475
Then nature gave theſe boaſted charms in vain:
Take back th' unhappy gift!—myſelf I hate,
My birth, my being, and my regal ſtate.

              One

One soothing hope alone can comfort give;
For sweet revenge I still consent to live!   480
  Thus with wild grief she ran her frenzy o'er,
Then turn'd her footsteps from the desert shore:
Her fiery looks her stormy passions show;
Loose in the wind her locks dishevell'd flow;
And in her eyes the flashing sparkles glow!   485
  Now, at her dome, she calls with hideous yell,
Three hundred deities from deepest hell:
Soon murky clouds o'er all the skies are spread;
Th' eternal planet hides his sickening head.
On mountain-tops the furious whirlwinds blow; 490
Deep rocks the ground; Avernus groans below.
Through all the palace mingled cries resound;
Loud hissings, howls, and screams are heard around.
Thick glooms, more black than night, the walls enclose,
Where not a ray its friendly light bestows!   495
Save that, by fits, sulphureous lightenings stream,
And dart through sullen shades a dreadful gleam!
At length the night difpers'd; and faintly shone,
With scarce recover'd looks, the doubtful sun:
No longer now the stately walls appear'd;   500
No trace remain'd where once the pile was rear'd.

Like

Like cloudy vapours of the changing skies,
Where towers and battlements in semblance rise,
That flit before the winds or solar beam,
Like idle phantoms of a sick-man's dream: 505
So vanish'd all the pile, and nought remain'd
But native horrors midst a rocky land!

 Then swift th' enchantress mounts her ready car,
And, girt with tempests, cleaves the fields of air.
Declining from the pole, where distant lie 510
Nations unknown beneath the eastern sky;
Alcides' pillars now she journeys o'er;
Nor seeks Hesperia's strand, nor Afric's shore;
But o'er the subject seas suspended flies,
Till Syria's borders to her view arise. 515

 She seeks not then Damascus' regal dome,
But shuns her once-lov'd seats and native home:
And guides her chariot to the fatal lands,
Where, midst Asphaltus' waves, her castle stands.
There, from her menial train and damsels' eyes, 520
All pensive, in a lone retreat she lies:
A war of thought her troubled breast assails;
But soon her shame subsides, and wrath prevails.

 Hence will I haste, (she cry'd) ere Egypt's king
To Sion's plains his numerous force can bring: 525

Try every art, in every form áppear,
Bend the tough bow, and shake the missile spear.
My charms shall every leader's soul inspire,
And every breast with emulation fire.
O let the sweet revenge I seek be mine, 530
And virgin honour I with joy resign!
Nor thou, stern guardian, now my conduct blame:
Thine are my deeds, to thee belongs the shame:
Thy counsel first impell'd my tender mind
To acts that ill beseem'd the female kind. 535
Then all be thine, whate'er my errors prove,
What now I give to rage, as once to love!

   She said; and thus resolv'd, she calls in haste
Knights, squires, and damsels in her service plac'd,
A splendid train in duteous order wait; 540
All richly clad, attendant on her state.
With these, impatient, on her way she goes:
Nor sun, nor moon beholds her take repose;
Till near she comes to where the friendly bands
Lie wide encamp'd on Gaza's sultry sands. 545

THE END OF THE SIXTEENTH BOOK.

THE

SEVENTEENTH BOOK

OF

JERUSALEM DELIVERED.

THE ARGUMENT.

The Egyptian troops and auxiliaries are muſtered before the Caliph, ſeated on his throne. Armida unexpectedly appears with her forces: ſhe enflames the leaders of the army with her beauty, and proffers her hand in marriage to any champion that ſhall kill Rinaldo. A conteſt, thereupon, enſues between Adraſtus and Tiſaphernes; but the Caliph, interpoſing, puts a ſtop to it. Rinaldo and the two knights return to Paleſtine. On their landing, they are met by the hermit, who had before entertained Charles and Ubald: he gives Rinaldo counſel for his future conduct, preſents him with a ſuit of armour, and explains to him the actions of his anceſtors that are repreſented in the ſhield. He then conducts the three warriors within ſight of the camp, and diſmiſſes them.

THE SEVENTEENTH BOOK OF JERUSALEM DELIVERED.

PLAC'D where Judæa's utmost bounds extend
Tow'rds fair Pelusium, Gaza's walls ascend:
Fast by the breezy shore the city stands,
Amid unbounded plains of barren sands,
Which high in air the furious whirlwinds sweep, 5
Like mountain billows of the stormy deep;
That scarce th' affrighted trav'ller, spent with toil,
Escapes the tempest of th' unstable soil.
  Th' Egyptian monarch holds this frontier town,
Which from the Turkish powers of old he won: 10
Since opportunely near the plains it lies,
To which he bends his mighty enterprize;
He left awhile his court and ancient state,
And hither now transferr'd his regal seat;

And hither brought, encamp'd along the coast, 15
From various provinces a countless host.

Say, muse! what arms he us'd, what lands he sway'd,
What nations fear'd him, and what powers obey'd:
How from the south he mov'd the realms afar,
And call'd the natives of the east to war! 20
Thou only canst disclose the dire alarms,
The bands and chiefs of half the world in arms.

When Egypt 'gainst the Grecian sway rebell'd,
The faith forsaking which her fathers held,
A warrior, sprung from Macon, seiz'd the throne, 25
And fix'd his seat in Cairo's stately town,
A Caliph call'd; from him each prince who wears
Th' Egyptian crown the name of Caliph bears.
Thus Nile beheld succeeding Pharaohs shine,
And Ptolemies enroll'd from line to line. 30

And now revolving years their course pursu'd,
And well secur'd the empire's basis stood,
O'er Libya wide and Asia spread its power,
From far Cyrene to the Syrian shore;
Where sev'n-fold Nile o'erflows the fatten'd land, 35
And where Syenna's sun-burnt dwellings stand;
Where proud Euphrates laves Assyria's fields;
Her spicy stores where rich Maremma yields:

And far beyond extends the potent sway,
To climes that nearer greet the rising day, 40
 Vast in itself the mighty kingdom show'd,
But added glories now its Lord bestow'd :
Of blood illustrious, and by virtues known,
The arts of peace and war were all his own!
Against the Turks' and Persians' force engag'd, 45
With various fortune mighty wars he wag'd;
Success and loss by turns ordain'd to meet,
In conquest great, but greater in defeat!
At length, with creeping age his strength decay'd,
Reluctant at his side he sheath'd the blade : 50
For yet his soul retain'd the martial flame,
The thirst of empire and the lust of fame.
His chiefs, abroad, their sovereign's wars maintain'd,
While he, at home, in regal splendor reign'd.
His name the realms of Afric trembling heard, 55
And furthest Ind his distant rule rever'd :
Some sent their martial bands, a willing aid,
And some, with gold and gems, their tribute paid.
 Such was the man who drew his various force
From climes remote, t' oppose the Christians' course:
Armida hither came, in happy hour, 61
What time the king review'd his numerous power.

High on a stately throne himself was plac'd,
Th' ascent a hundred steps of ivory grac'd:
A silver canopy o'erspread his seat,   65
And gold and purple lay beneath his feet:
Around his head the snow-white linen roll'd,
His turban form'd of many a winding fold:
The sceptre in his better hand was seen,
His beard was white, and awful was his mien.   70
His thoughtful brow sedate experience shows,
Yet in his eye-balls youthful ardor glows.
Alike maintain'd, in every act, appears
The pomp of power, or dignity of years.
So when or Phydias' or Apelles' art   75
To lifeless forms could seeming life impart;
In such a shape they show'd to mortal eyes
Majestic Jove when thundering from the skies.
Beside the Caliph, waits on either hand
A mighty peer, the noblest of the land;   80
This holds the seal, ministrant near the throne,
And bends his cares to civil rule alone:
But greater that the sword of justice bears,
And, prince of armies, guides the course of wars.

 Beneath, with thronging spears, a circling band,
In deep array his bold Circassians stand: 86

The

The cuirass-plates their manly breasts defend,
And crooked sabres at their sides depend.

   Thus sate the monarch, and from high beheld
Th' assembled nations marshal'd on the field;   90
While, as the squadrons pass'd his lofty seat,
They bow'd their arms and ensigns at his feet.

   First march'd the forces drawn from Egypt's lands,
Four were their chiefs, and each a troop commands.
Two came from upper, two from lower Nile,   95
Where ocean's waters once o'erspread the soil:
Now lie far distant from the briny flood
Those fields which once the coasting sailor view'd.

   First of the squadrons mov'd the ready train
That dwell in Alexandria's wealthy plain;   100
Along the land that westward far declines,
Whose wide extent with Afric's border joins.
Araspes was their chief, who more excell'd
In close device than action in the field.
The troops succeed, on Asia's coast who lie,   105
Against the beams that gild the morning sky:
These leads Aronteus, not by virtue fir'd,
But with the pride of titles vain inspir'd:
No massy helm, ere this, had press'd his brows,
Nor early trump disturb'd his soft repose: 110

But now from ease to scenes of toil he came,
By false ambition lur'd with hopes of fame.
The next that march'd, appear'd no common band,
But a huge host that cover'd all the land:
It seem'd that Egypt's fields of waving grain   115
Could scarce suffice their numbers to sustain:
Yet these within one ample city dwell'd;
These mighty Cairo in her circuit held.
From crowded streets she sends her sons to war;
And these Campsones brings beneath his care.   120
Then, under Gazel, march'd the troop who till'd
The neighbouring glebe with generous plenty fill'd;
And far above, where loud the river roars,
And from on high its second cataract pours.
No arms but swords and bows th' Egyptians bear,
Nor weighty mail, nor shining helmets wear: 126
Their habits rich, not fram'd to daunt the foe,
But rouze to plunder with the pompous show.

 Next Barca's tawny sons, a barbarous throng,
Beneath their chief, Alarcon, march'd along: 130
Half arm'd they came; these, long to plunder train'd,
A hungry life on barren sands sustain'd.
Zumara's king a fairer squadron leads;
To him the king of Tripoly succeeds:
           Both

Both weak in steady fight, but skill'd to dare 135
In sudden onset, and a flying war.
Then those whose culture each Arabia claim'd,
The stony that, and this the happy nam'd.
The last ne'er doom'd (if fame the truth declare)
The fierce extremes of heat and cold to bear. 140
Here odoriferous gums their sweets diffuse;
Th' immortal phœnix here his youth renews;
Here, on a pile of many a rich perfume,
Prepares at once his cradle and his tomb!
Less costly these their vests and armour wore; 145
But weapons, like the troops of Egypt bore.
To these succeed the wandering Arab train,
Who shift their canvas towns from plain to plain:
Their accents female, and their stature low;
A sable hue their gloomy features show, 150
And down their backs the jetty ringlets flow.
Long Indian canes they arm with pointed steel,
And round the plain their steeds impetuous wheel:
Thou wouldst have thought the winds impell'd their course,
If speed of winds could match the rapid horse. 155
Arabia's foremost squadron Syphax leads;
Before the second bold Aldine proceeds.

The

The third have Albiazar at their head;
A chief in rapine, not in knighthood, bred.
Then from the various Islands march'd a train,   160
Whose rocks are 'compass'd by th' Arabian main:
There were they wont, in arts of fishing skill'd,
To draw rich pearls from ocean's watery field.
And join'd with those, the neighbouring lands that lie
Beside the Red-sea shore, their aids supply.   165
Those Agricaltes, these Mulasses guides,
Who every faith and every law derides.
Next march'd the swarthy troops from Meroe's soil,
That dwell 'twixt Astaborn and fruitful Nile;
Where Ethiopia spreads her sultry plains,   170
Whose vast extent three different states contains:
Two Assimirus and Canarius sway'd;
These Macon's laws and Egypt's rule obey'd,
And 'gainst the Christian host their forces led.
The third, whose sons the pure religion knew,   175
Mix'd not its warriors with the Pagan crew.

Two tributary kings their squadrons show,
That bear in fight the quiver and the bow.
Soldan of Ormus one, a barren land,
Where the vast gulph of Persia laves the strand.   180
One in Boëcan held his regal place,
Whose kingdom oft the rising tides embrace;

But

But when the ebbing waves forsake the shore,
With feet unbath'd the pilgrim passes o'er.

 Not thee, O Altamorus! from the plain   185
Thy faithful spouse could in her arms detain:
She wept, she beat her breast, she tore her hair,
And begg'd thee oft thy purpose to forbear.
Dost thou to me prefer, unkind! (she cry'd)
The dreadful aspect of the stormy tide?   190
Are weapons gentler burthens to thy arms,
Than thy dear son, who smiles in infant charms?

 Samarcand's realms this powerful king obey;
No subject crown, no tributary sway:
In fields he shone, conspicuous in the fight,   195
And stood supreme in courage as in might.
The cuirass on their breast his warriors brace;
Their side the sword, their saddle bears the mace.

 Next from the seats of morn, beyond the shores
Of Ganges' stream, Adrastus brings his pow'rs: 200
Around his limbs a serpent's skin he drew,
Diversify'd with spots of sable hue;
While for his steed he press'd (tremendous sight!)
A mighty elephant of towering height.

 Then came the regal band, the Caliph's boast,   205
The flower of war and vigour of the host:

             All

All arm'd in proof, well furnish'd for the field,
On foaming steeds their rapid course they held.
Rich purple vestments gleam upon the day,
And steel and gold reflect a mingled ray! 210
Alarcus here and Hidraótes came;
Here Odemarus rode, a mighty name!
Here midst the valiant Rimedon appear'd,
Whose daring soul nor toil nor danger fear'd.
Tigranes here and Ormond fierce was found; 215
Ripoldo, once for piracy renown'd:
And Marlabustus bold, th' Arabian nam'd,
Since late his might the rebel Arabs tam'd.
Here Pirgas, Arimon, Orindus shone;
Brimartes, fam'd for many a conquer'd town: 220
Syphantes, skill'd the bounding steed to rein:
And thou, Aridamantes! form'd to gain
The prize of wrestling on the dusty plain!
Here Tifaphernes, with a dauntless air,
Tower'd o'er the rest, the thunderbolt of war! 225
Whose force in battle every force excell'd,
To lift the javelin or the falchion wield.

O'er these the sway a brave Armenian bears,
Who left the Christian faith in early years
For Pagan lore; his former name estrang'd, 230
To Emirenes then was Clement chang'd:

Yet

Yet was he well esteem'd for faith sincere,
And far o'er all his sovereign held him dear.

No more remain'd; when now, to sudden view,
The fair Armida with her squadron drew. 235
High on a stately car, the royal dame
In martial pomp (a female archer!) came:
A slender belt her flowing robe restrain'd;
Her side the shafts, her hand the bow sustain'd.
Ev'n sweet in wrath, her charms the gazer move, 240
And while she threats her threatening kindles love!
Her radiant car, like that which bears the sun,
Bright with a jacynth and pyropus shone.
Beneath the golden yoke, in pairs constrain'd,
Four unicorns the skilful driver rein'd. 245
A hundred maids, a hundred pages, round
Attend; the quivers on their shoulders sound:
Each in the field bestrides a milk-white steed,
Practis'd to turn, and like the wind in speed.
Her troop succeeds, which Aradine commands, 250
And Hidraótes rais'd in Syria's lands.

As when, again reviv'd, the phœnix soars
To visit Ethiopia's much-lov'd shores,
And spreads his vary'd wings with plumage bright,
(Sky-tinctur'd plumes that gleam with golden light!)

On

On either hand the feather'd nations fly, 256
And wondering trace his progress through the sky:
So pass'd the fair, while gazing hosts admire
Her graceful looks, her gesture and attire.
If thus her face, in awful anger arm'd, 260
Such various throngs with power resistless charm'd;
Well might her softer arts each bosom move,
With winning glances and the smiles of love.

 Armida past; the king of kings commands
Brave Emirenes, from the martial bands, 265
T' attend his will; to him he gives the post,
O'er all the chiefs, to guide the numerous host.
He came, his looks with grace majestic shin'd,
And spoke him worthy of the rank design'd.
At once the guard divides; a path is shown; 270
He treads the steps ascending to the throne:
There, on his humble knee, the ground he press'd,
And bow'd his head low-bending o'er his breast.
To him the king—This sceptre, chief, receive,
To thee the rule of yonder host I give. 275
Thou, Emirenes! now my place supply;
Deliver Sion's king, our old ally:
Swift on the Franks my dread resentment pour;
Go—see—and conquer—in th' avenging hour

No Christian 'scape; their name no more be known,
And bring the living, bound, before my throne. 281

   The Monarch spoke; the warrior from his hand
Receiv'd the sovereign ensign of command.

   This sceptre from unconquer'd hands (he cry'd)
I take, O King! thy fortune is my guide.   285
Arm'd in thy cause I go, thy captain sworn,
T'avenge the wrongs which Asia's realms have borne:
Nor will I e'er return, but crown'd with fame;
Death, if I fail, shall hide a warrior's shame!
Should unexpected ills, ye powers! impend,   290
On me alone let all the storm descend:
Preserve the host, while, victors, from the plain
They bring their chief in glorious triumph slain.

   He ceas'd; the troops with loud applause reply,
And barbarous clangors echo to the sky.   295

   And now departs, amid the mingled sound,
The king of kings, with peers encompass'd round:
These, summon'd to the lofty tent of state,
In equal honours with the Monarch sate;
Himself benignant ev'ry chief addrefs'd,   300
And gave to each a portion of the feast.
There, for her arts, fit time Armida found,
While pleasure reign'd, and festive sport went round.

The banquet o'er, the dame, who well defcries
That all beheld her charms with wondering eyes;
Slow from her feat arofe, with regal look,   306
And thus refpectful to the Caliph fpoke.

O mighty King! behold with thefe I ftand
To guard our faith, and combat for the land.
A damfel, yet I boaft a royal name;   310
Nor fcorns a queen to mix in fields of fame.
Who fecks to reign, in arts of ruling fkill'd,
By turns the fceptre and the fword muft wield.
This hand in battle can the javelin ufe,
And, where it ftrikes, the wound the ftrokes purfues.
Haft thou not heard how once I prifoners made   316
The braveft knights whofe arms the Crofs difplay'd?
Thefe overcome, in rugged chains confin'd,
To thee a glorious prefent I defign'd:
So had thy powers (their braveft champions loft) 320
With fure fuccefs o'erthrown the Chriftian hoft.
But fierce Rinaldo, who my warriors flew,
Releas'd, in evil hour, the captive crew.
'Tis he! the wretch of whom I wrong'd complain,
And unreveng'd thefe wrongs I yet fuftain.   325
A juft refentment hence my bofom warms,
And fires with added zeal my foul to arms.—

But

But what my wrongs hereafter times shall speak;
Let this suffice—a great revenge I seek!
Revenge be mine!—and sure, not sent in vain, 330
Some pointed shaft may fix him to the plain.
Heaven oft from righteous hands directs the dart,
And guides the weapon to the guilty heart.
But should some knight, by thirst of glory led,
Bring me, from yonder field, the Christian's head, 335
These eyes with joy the welcome gift shall view;
The victor-chief shall find a victor's due:
My hand in marriage shall the hero gain,
With ample dowry and a large domain.
Say—is there one who will the prize regard, 340
And dare the peril meet for such reward?

 While thus the damsel spoke, with longing eyes
Adrastus views her, and at length replies.

 Forbid it, Heaven! that e'er Rinaldo's heart
Should feel the vengeance of Armida's dart: 345
Shall such a wretch to thee resign his breath,
And sweetly perish by an envy'd death?
In me thy minister of wrath survey,
His forfeit head before thy feet I'll lay;
This hand shall rend his breast, and scatter far 350
His mangled body to the fowls of air.

While thus the Indian proud Adraſtus ſpoke,
Theſe haughty words from Tiſaphernes broke.

 And what art thou, whoſe empty pride can dare
Before our Monarch thus thy vaunts declare? 355
Know many a chief (tho' ſilent here) exceeds
Thy boaſted valour with his martial deeds.

 To him his rival with indignant ſcorn:
Lo! one for action, not for vaunting, born:
And elſewhere hadſt thou dar'd our wrath provoke,
Thy laſt of words, infenſate! hadſt thou ſpoke. 361

 Thus furious they; but with his awful hand,
Their common lord the growing ſtrife reſtrain'd;
Then to Armida thus—Thy manly mind
Seems far exalted o'er thy ſofter kind: 365
With thee remains the power, tranſcendent dame!
To calm theſe warriors, and their rage reclaim;
'Tis thine, at will, to bid their fury glow
With nobler vengeance on the public foe:
Then ſhall each champion's valour ſtand confeſs'd,
While emulation breathes from breaſt to breaſt. 371

 This ſaid, the Monarch ceas'd; and either knight
Vow'd in her cauſe to wield the ſword in fight.
Nor theſe alone; but all, whom glory warms,
Now vaunt their courage and their force in arms:

All

All to the damsel proffer certain aid, 376
And vow deep vengeance on Rinaldo's head.

While thus against the hero, once belov'd,
Such various powers, such mighty foes she mov'd,
He, whom her hate pursu'd, the land forsook, 380
And through the main his prosperous voyage took.
The wind, that late impell'd the pilot's sails,
Now favour'd her return with western gales.
The youth the pole and either bear survey'd,
And all the stars that gild night's sable shade: 385
He view'd the foamy flood, the mountains steep,
Whose shaggy fronts o'ershade the silent deep:
Now of the camp he asks, and now enquires
Of different nations, and their rites admires.
Thus through surrounding waves the warriors fly, 390
Till the fourth morning paints the eastern sky;
And when the setting sun to sight was lost,
The rapid vessel gain'd the destin'd coast.
Then thus the virgin—Here our voyage ends,
Here Palestine her welcome shore extends. 395

The heroes land, and from their wondering eyes
The mystic pilot in a moment flies.
Now o'er the prospect eve her mantle threw,
And every object from the sight withdrew.

O 2 Uncertain

Uncertain midſt the ſandy wilds they ſtray, 400
No friendly beam to guide them on their way.
At length the pale-orb'd queen of ſilent night,
Slow riſing, ſtreak'd the parting clouds with light:
Sudden the chiefs a diſtant blaze behold,
With rays of ſilver, and with gleams of gold. 405
Approaching then, they radiant arms ſurvey'd,
On which the moon with full reflection play'd.
Thick ſet as ſtars, with many a coſtly ſtone,
The golden helm and poliſh'd cuiraſs ſhone.
An aged tree the maſſy burden held: 410
Againſt the trunk was hung the mighty ſhield;
Myſterious forms emblaz'd its ſpacious field.
Beneath the branches from his ruſtic ſeat
A courteous hermit roſe, the knights to meet.

  When now the Dane and Ubald nearer drew, 415
In him their friend their ancient hoſt they knew:
At once they greet the ſage with glad ſurpriſe,
The ſage with mild benevolence replies;
Then tow'rds Rinaldo, who with wonder view'd
His reverend form, he turn'd, and thus purſu'd. 420

  For thy arrival, chief! and thine alone,
I here have ſtay'd in deſert ſhades unknown.
In me thy friend behold—let theſe relate
How far my care has watch'd thy former ſtate.

Theſe,

These, taught by me, th' enchantress' power defy'd,
And freed thy soul, in magic fetters ty'd.   426
Attend my words, nor harsh their tenour deem,
Though far unlike the Syren's wanton theme:
Deep in thy heart repose each sacred truth,
Till holier lips instruct thy listening youth.   430
Think not our good is plac'd in flowery fields,
In transient joys which fading beauty yields:
Above the steep, the rocky path it lies,
On virtue's hill, whose summit cleaves the skies.
Who gains th' ascent must many toils engage,   435
And spurn the pleasures of a thoughtless age.
Wilt thou, dismay'd, the arduous height forego,
And lurk ignobly in the vale below?
To thee a face erect has Nature given
And the pure spirit of congenial heaven,   440
That far from earth thy generous thoughts might rise,
To gain, by virtuous deeds, th' immortal prize.
She gave thee courage, not with impious rage
T' oppress thy friends, and civil combats wage;
But that thy soul with noble warmth might glow,   445
In fields of fight against the common foe.
Wisdom to proper objects points our ire,
Now gently cools, now fans the rising fire.

He spoke: with downcast eyes the hero stood,
While thus the words of truth resistless flow'd.   450
Full well his secret thoughts the hermit view'd;
Now lift thy eyes, O son! (he thus pursu'd)
See in that shield thy great forefathers shown,
Whose mighty deeds to distant times are known:
Wilt thou the honours of thy line disgrace,   455
And lag behind in glory's sacred race?
Rise! gallant youth! and while thy sires I name,
From their example catch the generous flame.

He said; with eager gaze the knight beheld
The sculptur'd stories to his sight reveal'd.   460

There, in a narrow space, the master's mind,
With wondrous art, a thousand forms design'd:
There shone great Estè's race, whose noble blood
From Roman source in streams unsully'd flow'd.
With laurel crown'd the godlike chiefs appear'd; 465
The sage their honours and their wars declar'd.
Caius he show'd, who (when th'imperial sway
Declining fell to alien hands a prey)

A willing

Ver. 464. *From Roman source* —] The house of Estè was said to be descended from Actius, related by the mother's side to Augustus.

Ver. 467. *Caius he show'd* —] At the time of the emperors Arcadius and Honorius, anno 403, Stilico, incited by
ambition

A willing people taught to own his power,
And first of Estè's line the sceptre bore. 470
When now the Goth (a rude destructive name!)
Call'd by Honorius, big with ruin, came;
When Rome, oppress'd and captive to the foe,
Fear'd one dire hour would all her state o'erthrow;
He show'd how brave Aurelius from the bands 475
Of foreign foes preserv'd his subject lands.
Forestus then he nam'd, whose noble pride
The Huns, the tyrants of the north, defy'd:

Fierce ambition to weaken Honorius, who ruled in the west, invited into Italy Alaric and Radagasso, kings of the Goths and Vandals; at which time this Caius Actius governed in Estè in the name of the emperor, where the Barbarians committing every kind of outrage, and the emperor taking no measures against them, Actius was by general consent elected absolute sovereign, in order to defend the country from these invaders.

Ver. 471. *When now the Goth*—] When Honorius, exasperated with the Romans, transferred the imperial seat to Ravenna, and invited Alaric again into Italy, who had been before invited by Stilico, Aurelius conducted himself so artfully, that the Goths, in their march towards Rome, with design to destroy that city, passed through his territories without committing the least depredations.

Ver. 477. *Forestus then he nam'd*—] Attila king of the Huns, in the year 450, through an irreconcileable hatred to

Fierce Attila their lord, of savage mien,
By him subdu'd in single fight was seen.   480
See next the patriot chief, with ceaseless care,
For Aquileia's strong defence prepare;
Th' Italian Hector in the task of war!
But ah! too soon he ends his mortal state,
And with his own includes his country's fate.   485
Then Acarinus to his father's fame
Succeeds, the champion of the Roman name,
Not to the Huns, but Fate, Altinus yields,
And, far retir'd, a surer kingdom builds:

Deep

'the Christians, prepared to march to the attack of Aquileia, as the key to Italy; and was several times defeated by Forestus, the son of Aurelius, with the assistance of the forces of Gilio, king of Padua, his relation. Forestus is said to have fought with Attila hand to hand.

Ver. 486. *Then Acarinus —*] Acarinus succeeded his father Forestus in the government of Estè and Monselice, and gained many victories over Attila.

Ver. 488. *Not to the Huns, but Fate, Altinus yields.*] The forces of Altinus met with such continued ill success with Attila, that their misfortunes seemed to have been the immediate dispensation of Providence; and hence the poet says, that Altinus gave way to Fate, and not to the Huns.

Ver. 489. *And, far retir'd, a surer kingdom builds.*] It was under the conduct of Acarinus that Aventino, Anzio,

Trento,

Deep in the vale of Po his city rose, 490
(A thousand scatter'd cots his town compose)
Which distant ages shall with pride proclaim
The seat of empire of th' Estensian name.
Th' Alani quell'd, Acarius, in debate
With Odoacer, meets the stroke of fate: 495
For Italy he bravely yields his breath,
And shares paternal honour in his death.
With him the gallant Alphorisius dies:
To exile Actius, with his brother, flies;
But soon return'd (th' Erulean king o'erthrown) 500
Again in council and in arms they shone.

Next, Trento, and other neighbouring villages, were reduced into the form of a city, and defended by a mole against the floods of the Po; and this was the foundation of the future town of Ferrara.

Ver. 494. *Th' Alani quell'd* —] At this time Acarinus was captain of horse, anno 463.

Ver. 495. *With Odoacer, meets the stroke of fate.*] Acarius, and Alphorisius his brother, opposed king Odoacer, one of the chiefs in the army of Attila, who had made a descent into Italy, with many others, the remains of the forces of that barbarian.

Ver. 499. *To exile Actius* —] Actius and Constantius, sons of Acarinus, being invaded by Odoacer, were despoiled of all their possessions, and obliged to abandon Italy.

Ver. 500. *Th' Erulean king.*] Odoacer, who was three times defeated by Theodoric Amalo, king of the Ostrogoths,

Next, as his eye receiv'd the barbed steel,
A second brave Epaminondas fell:
See! where with smiles he seems his life to yield,
Since Totila is fled, and safe his shield.   505
His son Valerian emulates his name,
And treads the footsteps of paternal fame:
Scarce yet a man, of manly force possess'd,
His daring hand th' encroaching Goth repress'd.

goths, and two years besieged in Ravenna, and at last killed, after Actius and Constantius had recovered their possessions.

Ver. 502. —— *as his eye receiv'd the barbed steel.*] By the title of second Epaminondas is meant Bonifacius. This event happened in the year 556, when Narsetes, sent by the emperor Justinian, overcame Totila, king of the Goths; in which battle Bonifacius being present, was shot in the right eye by an arrow, which passed through the nape of his neck; he was carried on his shield into his tent, where he soon expired. The poet compares him to Epaminondas, the Theban general, of whom it is related, that at the battle of Mantanea, being carried mortally wounded into his tent, he demanded if his shield was safe, and being told it was, he ordered it to be brought to him, and having kissed it with great apparent satisfaction, immediately died.

Ver. 508. *Scarce yet a man* —] At the death of his father this youth was only fourteen years of age, and at that time was with Narsetes at the overthrow of the Goths.

Near him with warlike mien Erneſtus roſe, 510
Who routs in field the rough Sclavonian foes.
With theſe intrepid Aldoard is ſhown,
Who 'gainſt the Lombard king defends Monſcelce's town,
Henry and Berengarius then appear'd,
Who ſerv'd where Charles his glorious banners rear'd. 515
Then Lewis follow'd, who the war maintain'd
Againſt his nephew that in Latium reign'd.

Next

Ver. 510. —— *Erneſtus roſe.*] Erneſtus, ſon of Eribert of Eſtè, performed many great actions in Dalmatia; which, from the name of Schiavi, took the name of Sclavonia: he defeated the Sclavonians ſo effectually in 711, that they were never again able to make head.

Ver. 512. *With theſe intrepid Aldoard* —] Agilulpho, by his marriage with Theodolinda, became king of the Lombards, and, making peace with France, invaded Italy, and took Padua, at firſt defended by the princes of the houſe of Eſtè; and he endeavoured to do the ſame by Monſcelce.

Ver. 514. *Henry and Berengarius* —] Henry, ſon of Erneſtus: Berengarius, ſon of Henry.

Ver. 515. *Who ſerv'd where Charles* —] Charles the Great, ſerved with great valour by Henry and Berengarius.

Ver. 516. *Then Lewis follow'd* —] After the death of Charles, Berengarius entered into the ſervice of his ſon Lewis,

Next Otho with his sons, a friendly band;
Five blooming youths around their father stand.
There Almeric, Ferrara's Marquis, came, 520
(Ferrara, plac'd by Po's majestic stream)
See! where he lifts to heaven his pious eyes;
Beneath his care what hallow'd fanes arise!
The second Actius fill'd a different side,
Who bloody strife with Berengarius try'd; 525

wis, who was created emperor, and carried on a war against Bernardo the son of Pepin, the other son of Charles, who had been by his father made king of Italy: he was defeated by Berengarius, taken prisoner, and afterwards stript of his kingdom and deprived of his sight, anno 819.

Ver. 518. *Next Otho with his sons* —] Otho, brother to Berengarius: his five sons were Marino, Sigifredo, Uberto, Hugo, and Amizono.

Ver. 520. *There Almeric* —] Almeric was son of Amizono: through the favour of Hugo king of Italy, by whom he was greatly esteemed, Almeric was called to the government of Ferrara, where he ruled with sovereign authority, and obtained the title of Marquis: he gave a considerable part of his revenues to the maintenance of churches and abbeys, and employed his private fortune in building others, amongst which was the church of Saint George, afterwards the principal one of Ferrara.

Ver. 524. *The second Actius* —] He carried on a war with Berengarius II. king of Italy, anno 950.

But,

But, after many various turns of fate,
Subdu'd his foe, and rul'd th' Italian ſtate:
Albertus now appear'd, his valiant ſon,
Who from Germania mighty trophies won;
Who foil'd the Danes; and to his nuptial bed,   530
With ample dowry, Otho's daughter led.
Next Hugo, who the haughty Romans quell'd,
And o'er the Tuſcan lands dominion held.
Tedaldo then; and now the ſculpture ſhow'd,
With Beatrice where Bonifacius ſtood.   535

No

Ver. 530. *Who foil'd the Danes; and to his nuptial bed,*
With ample dowry —] He obtained from the emperor Otho his daughter Adelaide to wife, with the dowry of Friburg, in Germany, and ſeveral places in Italy, anno 973.

Ver. 532. *Next Hugo, who the haughty Romans quell'd.*] This Hugo perform'd many exploits againſt the Romans, in behalf of pope Gregory, and the emperor Otho, about the year 995.

Ver. 534. *Tedaldo then* —] Son of Actius II, duke of Ferrara, and marquis of Eſtè, count of Canoſſa, lord of Lucca, Placentia, Parma, and Rheggio, anno 970.

Ver. 535. *With Beatrice where Bonifacius ſtood.*] There were two of the name of Bonifacius, one ſon of the before-named Albertus, and the other ſon of Tedaldo, duke of Ferrara; this laſt ſucceeded to the poſſeſſions of his father,

and

No male succeeding to the large domain,
No son the father's honours to maintain,
Matilda follow'd, who, with virtues try'd,
Full well the want of manly sex supply'd:
In arts of sway the wife and valiant dame   540
O'er crowns and sceptres rais'd the female fame:
The Norman there she chac'd! here quell'd in field
Guiscard the brave, before untaught to yield:

and obtained besides Mantua and Modena, and was imperial vicar anno 1007. He married Beatrice daughter of the Emperor Conrade II. and received Verona with her in dowry in 1034.

Ver. 536. *No male succeeded*—] Bonifacius left only one male child, which died under the care of its mother Beatrice.

Ver. 538. *Matilda follow'd*—] Daughter of Bonifacius and Beatrice, according to the poet, and so likewise delivered by Pigna; but other authors differ in the account of the parentage of this celebrated woman.

Ver. 542. *The Norman there she chac'd!*—] The Normans had then, and some years before, under Roberto Guiscardo, taken possession of Puglia and Calabria, and endeavoured to lower the power of Matilda, but she defeated them several times; and Roberto, having afterwards concluded a peace with this Matilda, joined with her in assisting the pope against Henry IV.

Henry she crush'd (the fourth that bore the name)
And with his standards to the temple came;   545
Then in the Vatican, with honours grac'd,
In Peter's chair the sovereign Pontiff plac'd.
See the fifth Actius near her person move,
With looks of reverence and of duteous love.
Actius the fourth a happier race has known;   550
Thence Guelpho issues, Kunigunda's son;

Retiring,

Ver. 544. *Henry she crush'd*—]. The emperor Henry IV. a bitter enemy to the church: he endeavoured to deprive her of the right of creating bishops, and prosecuted the legitimate popes, and twice created antipopes.

Ver. 545. *And with his standards*—] This happened in Canossa, 1081, at the time Gregory IX. was besieged there by Henry. This religious and magnanimous woman replaced two pontiffs in the papal chair; the one was Alexander II. who had been driven out by Giberto of Parma, sent by the emperor Henry IV. into Italy, which Henry favoured Candalo, who probably by his means was made antipope; the other was Gregory IX. persecuted by the same Henry.

Ver. 548. *See the fifth Actius*—] This, according to Pigna, was second husband to Matilda, after the death of her first husband Gottifredo Gibboso: but it being afterwards discovered that they were related, the marriage was annulled, and they were divorced by command of the pope.

Ver. 550. *Actius the fourth*—] This Actius was more fortunate in point of children than Bonifacius, who left
only

Retiring, to Germania's call he yields,
By fate transplanted to Bavarian fields:
There on the Guelphian tree, with age decay'd,
Great Estè's branch its foliage fair display'd: 555
Then might you soon the Guelphian race behold
Renew their sceptres and their crowns of gold.
From hence Bertoldo rose, of matchless fame;
Hence the sixth Actius, bright in virtue, came.

 Such were the chiefs whose forms the shield ex-
  press'd; 560
And emulation fir'd Rinaldo's breast:
In fancy rapt, each future toil he view'd,
Proud cities storm'd, and mighty hosts subdu'd.
Swift o'er his limbs the burnish'd mail he throws,
Already hopes the day, and triumphs o'er the foes.

 And now the Dane, who told how Sweno fell 566
In fatal fight beneath the Pagan steel,

---

only Matilda to succeed him; but this Actius had for his son Guelpho, by Kunigonda, daughter of Guelpho IV. duke of Bavaria.

 Ver. 558. *From hence Bertoldo rose.*—] Bertoldo son of Actius V. by Judith, born of Conrado II; and of her was born Actius VI. This Bertoldo was father of Rinaldo; so that this shield contained all his progeny from the first original.

To brave Rinaldo gave the deſtin'd blade;
In happy hour receive this ſword (he ſaid)
Avenge its former lord, whoſe worth demands, 570
Whoſe love deſerves, this vengeance at thy hands.

Then thus the hero—Grant, O gracious Heaven!
The hand to which this fated ſword is given,
With this may emulate its maſter's fame,
And pay the tribute due to Sweno's name. 575

So they. But now the ſage without delay
Impell'd the warriors on their purpos'd way:
Haſte, let us ſeek the Chriſtian camp (he cry'd)
Myſelf will thro' the waſte your journey guide.

He ſaid; and ſtrait his ready car aſcends; 580
(Each knight obſequious at his word attends:)
He gives the ſteeds the rein, the laſh applies:
Swift to the eaſt the rolling chariot flies.
Again the hoary hermit ſilence broke,
And ſudden, turning to Rinaldo, ſpoke. 585

To thee 'twas given the ancient root to trace,
Whence ſprang the branches of th' Eſtenſian race:
Still ſhall that ſtock ſucceeding years ſupply,
Nor, damp'd with age, the pregnant virtue die.
O! could I now, as late the paſt I told, 590
The future ages to thy view unfold,

Succeeding

Succeeding heroes should thy wonder raise,
Great as the first in number as in praise:
But truths like these are hidden from my sight,
Or seen through dusky clouds with doubtful light.
Yet hear, and trust to what my words disclose; 596
Since from a purer source this knowledge flows;
(From him*, to whose far-piercing mind 'tis given
To view, unveil'd, the deep decrees of Heaven)
Thy sons, the heroes of the times to come, 600
Shall match the chiefs of Carthage, Greece, or Rome!
But o'er the rest shall rise Alphonso's fame,
Alphonso, second of the glorious name!
Born when an age corrupt, to vice declin'd,
Shall boast but few examples to mankind: 605
He, while a youth, in mimic scenes of war,
Shall certain signs of early worth declare;
In forest wilds shall chace the savage train,
And the first honours of the list obtain;
In riper years in war unconquer'd prove, 610
And hold his subjects in the bands of love!
'Tis his to guard his realms from all alarms,
Midst mighty powers and jarring states in arms:
To cherish arts, bid early genius grow,
And splendid games and festivals bestow; 615

* PETER.

In

In equal scales the good and bad to weigh;
And guard with care for every future day.
O! should he rise against that impious race,
Whose deeds shall then the earth and seas deface;
Who, in those times, shall hold mankind in awe, 620
And give to more enlighten'd minds the law;
Then shall his righteous vengeance wide be known;
For shrines profan'd, and altars overthrown:
In that great hour, what judgment shall he bring
On the false sect, and on their tyrant king! 625
The Turk and Moor, with thousands in their train,
Shall seek to stop his conquering arms in vain:
Beyond the climate where Euphrates flows;
Beyond Mount Taurus, white with endless snows,
Beyond the realms of summer, shall he bear 630
The Cross, the Eagle, and the Lily fair;
The secret source of ancient Nile shall trace,
And in the faith baptize the sable race.

He spoke: and transport fill'd the warrior's breast,
To hear the glories of his line exprest. 635
Now had the light proclaim'd the dawning day,
And the east redden'd with a warmer ray;
When high above the tents they saw from far
The streaming banners trembling in the air.

Then thus the reverend fire began anew: 640
Before our eyes the fun afcending view!
Whofe friendly rays difcover wide around
The plains, the city, and the tented ground.
Hence may you pafs without a further guide:
A nearer profpect is to me deny'd. 645

He faid; and inftant bade the chiefs adieu;
And thefe, on foot, their ready way purfue.
Meanwhile the news of their arrival came
To all the camp, divulg'd by flying fame;
And Godfrey, rifing from his awful feat, 650
With fpeed advanc'd, the welcome knights to meet.

THE END OF THE SEVENTEENTH BOOK.

THE EIGHTEENTH BOOK OF JERUSALEM DELIVERED.

THE ARGUMENT.

RINALDO returns to the camp, and is gracioufly received by Godfrey. After offering his devotions on Mount Olivet, he enters upon the adventure of the enchanted wood. He withftands all the illufions of the Demons, and diffolves the enchantment. The Chriftians then build new machines: In the mean time Godfrey has intelligence of the approach of the Egyptian army to raife the fiege. Vafrino is fent as a fpy to the Egyptian camp. Godfrey attacks the city with great refolution: The Pagans make an obftinate defence. Rinaldo particularly fignalizes himfelf, and firft fcales the walls. Ifmeno is killed. The archangel Michael appears to the Chriftian general, and fhews him the celeftial army, and the fouls of the warriors, that were flain in battle, engaged in his caufe. Victory now declares for the Chriftians: Godfrey firft plants his ftandard on the wall, and the city is entered on all fides.

THE EIGHTEENTH BOOK OF JERUSALEM DELIVERED.

AND now they met: Rinaldo first began,
And thus sincere address'd the godlike man,
O prince! the care t'efface my honour's stain
Impell'd my vengeance on the warrior slain:
But, late convinc'd, the rash offence I own;   5
And deep contrition since my soul has known.
By thee recall'd, I seek the camp again;
And may my future deeds thy grace obtain!

Him lowly bending, with complacent look
Godfrey beheld, embrac'd, and thus bespoke.   10

No more remembrance irksome truths shall tell;
The past shall ever in oblivion dwell:
Lo! all th' amends I claim—thy weapons wield,
And shine the wonted terror of the field.

'Tis thine t' affift thy friends, amaze thy foes, 15
And the dire fiends in yonder wood oppofe.
Yon wood, from whence our warlike piles we made,
Conceals deep magic in its dreadful fhade;
Horrid it ftands! of all our numerous hoft,
No hands to fell th' enchanted timbers boaft. 20
Then go!—'tis thine the mighty tafk to try;
There prove thy valour, where the valiant fly,

 Thus he. In brief again the warrior fpoke,
And dauntlefs on himfelf th' adventure took.
Then to the reft he ftretch'd his friendly hand, 25
And gladly greeted all the focial band.
Brave Tancred now and noble Guelpho came,
With each bold leader of the Chriftian name.
The vulgar next he view'd with gracious eye,
And affable receiv'd the general joy. 30
Nor round him lefs the fhouting foldiers prefs'd,
Than if the hero, from the conquer'd eaft,
Or mid-day realms, enrich'd with fpoils of war,
Had rode triumphant on his glittering car.
Thence to his tent he pafs'd; there plac'd in ftate, 35
Encircled by his friends, the champion fate.
There much he anfwer'd; much to know defir'd;
Oft of the war and wondrous wood enquir'd.
            At

At length, the rest withdrawn, the hermit broke
His silence first, and thus the youth bespoke. 40

O chief! what wonders have thy eyes survey'd!
How far remote thy erring feet have stray'd!
Think what thou ow'st to him who rules on high:
He gave thee from th' enchanted seats to fly:
Thee, from his flock a wandering sheep, he sought,
And, now recover'd, to his fold has brought: 46
By Godfrey's voice he calls thee to fulfil
The mighty purpose of his sacred will.
But think not yet, impure with many a stain,
In his high cause to lift thy hand profane: 50
Nor Nile, nor Ganges, nor the boundless sea,
With cleansing tides, can wash thy crimes away.
Sincere, to GOD thy secret sins declare,
And sorrowing seek his grace with fervent prayer.

He said; and first the prince, in humble strain, 55
Bewail'd his senseless love and rage as vain:
Then low before the sage's feet he kneel'd,
And all the errors of his youth reveal'd.
The pious hermit then absolv'd the knight,
And thus pursu'd—With early dawn of light, 60

Ver. 56. *Bewail'd his senseless love and rage as vain.*] His love for Armida, and his rage exercised against Gernando.

On yonder mount thy pure devotion pay,
That rears its front againſt the morning ray.
Thence ſeek the wood whoſe monſters thou muſt
    quell;
Let no vain frauds thy daring ſteps repel:
Ah! let no tuneful voice, nor plaints beguile,　　65
Nor beauty win thee with enticing ſmile:
Sternly reſolv'd, avoid each dangerous ſnare,
And ſcorn the treacherous look and well-diſſembled
    prayer.
So counſel'd he. The youth obſequious heard,
And eager for th' important deed prepar'd:　　70
In thought he paſs'd the day, in thought the night;
And, ere the clouds were ſtreak'd with growing light,
Encloſ'd his limbs in arms, and o'er him threw
A flowing mantle of unwonted hue.
Alone, on foot, his ſilent way he took,　　75
And left his comrades, and the tents forſook.
Now night with day divided empire held,
Nor this was fully riſ'n, nor that expell'd:
The chearful eaſt the dawning rays diſplay'd,
And ſtars yet glimmer'd through the weſtern ſhade.
To Olivet the penſive hero paſs'd,　　81
And, muſing deep, around his looks he caſt,

　　　　5　　　　　　　　　Alternate

Alternate viewing here the spangled skies,
And there the spreading light of morning rise.

 Then to himself he said—What beams divine 85
In heaven's eternal sacred temple shine!
The day can boast the chariot of the sun,
The night the golden stars and silver moon!
But ah! how few will raise their minds so high!
While the frail beauties of a mortal eye,   90
The transient lightenings of a glance, a smile
From female charms, our earthly sense beguile!

 While thus he mus'd, he gain'd the hill's ascent,
There low on earth with humble knee he bent:
Then on the east devoutly fix'd his eyes,   95
And rais'd his pious thoughts above the skies.

 Almighty Father, hear!—my prayers approve!
Far from my sins thy awful sight remove:
O let thy grace each thought impure control,
And purge from earthly dross my erring soul! 100

 Thus while he pray'd, Aurora, rising bright,
To radiant gold has chang'd her rosy light:
O'er all his arms th' increasing splendor plays,
The hallow'd mount and grove reflect the rays.
Full in his face the morn her breeze renews, 105
And scatters on his head ambrosial dews:

            His

His robe, with lucid pearls befprinkled o'er,
Receives a fnowy hue unknown before.
So with the dawn the drooping floweret blooms;
The ferpent thus a fecond youth affumes.   110

   Surpris'd his alter'd veft the warrior view'd,
Then turn'd his fteps to reach the fatal wood.
And now he came where late the bands retir'd,
Struck with the dread the diftant gloom infpir'd:
Yet him nor fecret doubts nor terrors move,   115
But fair in profpect rofe the magic grove.
While, like the reft, the knight expects to hear
Loud peals of thunder breaking on his ear,
A dulcet fymphony his fenfe invades,
Of Nymphs or Dryads warbling through the fhades,
Soft fighs the breeze, foft purls the filver rill,   121
The feather'd choir the woods with mufic fill:
The tuneful fwan in dying notes complains;
The mourning nightingale repeats her ftrains:
Timbrels and harps and human voices join;   125
And in one concert all the founds combine!

   In wonder wrapt awhile Rinaldo ftood,
And thence his way with wary fteps purfu'd:
When lo! a cryftal flood his courfe oppos'd,
Whofe winding train the foreft round enclos'd.   130

On

On either hand, with flowers of various dyes,
The smiling banks perfum'd the ambient skies.
From this a smaller limpid current flow'd,
And pierc'd the bosom of the lofty wood:
This to the trees a welcome moisture gave,   135
Whose boughs, o'erhanging, trembled in its wave.

Now here, now there, the ford the warrior try'd,
When sudden rais'd a wondrous bridge he 'spy'd;
That, built of gold, on stately arches stood,
And show'd an ample passage o'er the flood: 140
He trod the path, the further margin gain'd;
And now the magic pile no more remain'd:
The stream so calm, arose with hideous roar,
And down its foamy surge the shining fabric bore.

The hero, turning, saw the tide o'erflow,   145
Like sudden torrents swell'd with melting snow.
Then new desires incite his feet to rove
Thro' all the deep recesses of the grove.
As, searching round, from shade to shade he strays,
New scenes at once invite him and amaze.   150
Where'er he treads, the earth her tribute pours
In gushing springs, or voluntary flowers:
Here blooms the lily; there the fragrant rose:
Here spouts a fountain; there a riv'let flows:

From every spray the liquid manna trills; 155
And honey from the softening bark distills.
Again the strange, the pleasing sound he hears
Of plaints and music mingling in his ears:
Yet nought appears that mortal voice can frame,
Nor harp nor timbrel whence the music came. 160

As fix'd he silent stands in deep surprise,
And reason to the sense her faith denies;
He sees a myrtle near, and thither bends,
Where in a plain the path far-winding ends:
Her ample boughs the stately plant display'd 165
Above the lofty palm or cypress' shade;
High o'er the subject trees sublime she stood,
And seem'd the verdant empress of the wood.

While round the champion cast a doubtful view,
A greater wonder his attention drew: 170
A labouring oak a sudden cleft disclos'd;
And from its bark a living birth expos'd;
Whence (passing all belief!) in strange array,
A lovely damsel issu'd to the day.
A hundred different trees the knight beheld, 175
Whose fertile wombs a hundred nymphs reveal'd:
As oft in pictur'd scenes we see display'd
Each graceful goddess of the sylvan shade;

With

With arms expos'd, with vesture girt around,
With purple buskins, and with hair unbound: 180
Alike to view, before the hero stood
These shadowy daughters of the wondrous wood;
Save that their hands nor bows nor quivers wield;
But this a harp, and that a timbrel held.
Now, in a circle form'd, the sportive train 185
With song and dance their mystic rites began;
Around the myrtle and the knight they sung:
And in his ear these tuneful accents rung,

All hail! and welcome to this pleasing grove,
Armida's hope, the treasure of her love! 190
Com'st thou! (O long expected!) to relieve
The painful wounds the darts of absence give?
This wood, that frown'd so late with horrid shade,
Where pale despair her mournful dwelling made,
Behold at thy approach reviv'd appears, 195
At thy approach a gentler aspect wears!

Thus they—Low thunders from the myrtle rose,
And strait the bark a cleft wide-opening shows;
In wonder wrapt have ancient times survey'd
A rude Silenus issuing from the shade; 200
A fairer form the teeming tree display'd.
A damsel thence appear'd, whose lovely frame
Might equal beauties of celestial name;

On

On her Rinaldo fix'd his heedful eyes,
And saw Armida's features with surprise: 205
On him a sad, yet pleasing look she bends;
And in the glance a thousand passions blends.

Then thus—And art thou now return'd from flight,
Again to bless forlorn Armida's sight?
Com'st thou the balm of comfort to bestow, 210
To ease my widow'd nights, my days of woe?
Or art thou here to work me further harms,
That thus thy limbs are sheath'd in hostile arms?
Com'st thou a lover or a foe prepar'd;
Not for a foe the stately bridge I rear'd: 215
Not for a foe unlock'd th' impervious bowers,
And deck'd the shade with fountains, rills, and flowers.
Art thou a friend?—That envious helm remove;
Disclose thy face, return the looks of love:
Press lips to lips, to bosom bosom join; 220
Or reach at least thy friendly hand to mine!

Thus as she spoke, she roll'd her mournful eyes,
And bade soft blushes o'er her features rise:
Unwary pity here, with sudden charm,
Might melt the wisest, and the coldest warm: 225
While, well advis'd, the knight no longer stay'd,
But from the scabbard bar'd the shining blade;

Then,

Then, swift advancing, near the myrtle drew:
With eager haste to guard the plant she flew;
The much-lov'd bark with eager arms enclos'd, 230
And, with loud cries, the threatening stroke oppos'd.

 Ah! dare not thus with savage rage invade
My darling tree, the pride of all the shade!
O cruel!—lay thy dire design aside,
Or thro' Armida's heart the weapon guide! 235
To reach the trunk, this bosom shall afford
(And this alone) a passage to thy sword!

 But, deaf to prayers, aloft the steel he rear'd;
When lo! new forms, new prodigies appear'd!
Thus, oft in sleep we view, with wild affright, 240
Dire monstrous shapes, the visions of the night!
Her limbs enlarge; her features lose their grace;
The rose and lily vanish from her face:
Now, towering high, a giant huge she stands,
An arm'd Briareus with a hundred hands. 245
With dreadful action fifty swords she wields,
And shakes aloft as many clashing shields;
Each nymph, transform'd, a horrid Cyclop stood;
Unmov'd the hero still his task pursu'd;
Against the tree redoubled strokes he bent; 250
Deep groans, at every stroke, the myrtle sent:

Infernal glooms the face of day deform;
And winds, loud roaring, raife a hideous ftorm:
With thunders hoarfe the diftant fields refound,
And lightenings flafh, and earthquakes rock the
 ground. 255
But not thefe horrors can his force reftrain,
And not a blow his weapon aims in vain:
Now, finking low, the nodding myrtle bends:
It falls—the phantoms fly—th' enchantment ends.

The winds are hufh'd, the troubled ether clears,
The foreft in its wonted ftate appears: 261
No more the dark retreat of magic made,
Though awful ftill, and black with native fhade.
Again the victor try'd if aught withftood
The lifted fteel to lop the fpreading wood: 265
Then fmiling thus he faid—O phantoms vain!
Shall thefe illufions e'er the brave reftrain?

Now to the camp with hafty fteps he prefs'd;
Meanwhile the hermit thus the bands addrefs'd:
Already freed I fee th' enchanted ground! 270
Behold the chief returns with conqueft crown'd!
He faid: when from afar, confefs'd to fight,
In dazzling arms appear'd the victor knight:
High on his creft the filver eagle fhone,
And blaz'd with brighter beams againft the fun. 275

The

The troops falute him with triumphant cries;
From man to man the fpreading clamors rife.
Then to his valour pious Godfrey pays
The willing tribute of unenvy'd praife:
When to the leader thus Rinaldo faid : 280
At thy command I fought yon dreadful fhade;
The deep receffes of the grove I view'd,
The wonders faw, and every fpell fubdu'd:
Now may thy train the region fafe explore,
No magic charms fhall vex their labours more. 285

Thus he; and ftrait the band the foreft fought,
Whence mighty timbers to the camp they brought.
O'er all their work an able chief prefides;
William, Liguria's lord, the labour guides.
But late the empire of the feas he held, 290
Till forc'd before the Pagan fleets to yield;
With all their naval arms the failor train
He brings, t' increafe the forces on the plain.
To him fuperior knowledge Heaven imparts:
A fearching genius in mechanic arts! 295
A hundred workmen his commands obey,
Their tafks performing as he points the way.
Vaft battering rams againft the city rife,
And miffive engines of enormous fize.

Ver. 298. *Vaft battering rams*——] The account of thefe military engines and towers is according to the hiftory.

Of timbers huge he built a spacious tower; 300
A hundred wheels the mighty fabric bore:
With junctures strong he fix'd the solid sides,
And 'gainst the fire secur'd with moisten'd hides.
Suspended from below, with horned head,
The ram resistless on the bulwarks play'd; 305
While from the midst a bridge was form'd to fall,
That join'd th' approaching engine to the wall:
And from the top was seen at will to rise
A lesser tower, high-pointing to the skies.
The gazing throngs admire in every part 310
The strange invention and the workman's art:
Soon, like the first, two other piles they frame,
The same their figure and their height the same.

  Thus they: While from the walls the Pagan spies
Observ'd the Christian camp with heedful eyes; 315
They saw the pines and elms in many a load
Drawn to the army from the friendly wood:
They saw them rise in warlike structures high,
But scarce could thence their distant forms descry.
They too machines compose with equal care, 320
Their ramparts strengthen, and their walls repair.
Ismeno midst the rest his engines brought,
From Sodom's lake, with fatal sulphur fraught,

                                                  From

From hell's black flood, whose waters foul and flow
Nine times enfold the realms of endless woe! 325
Horrid with these, a fiery pest he stood,
Resolv'd t' avenge his violated wood.

While thus the city and the camp prepar'd,
This to assault, and that the works to guard,
High o'er the tents in all the army's view, 330
An airy dove with rapid pinions flew;
Now, from the lofty clouds declining down,
With nearer flight approach'd the sacred town:
When lo! a falcon chac'd her from above,
And threatening to the high pavilion drove: 335
Just as his claws the trembling bird oppress'd,
She shelter sought in pious Godfrey's breast:
The pitying chief the dove from fate repriev'd,
Then round her neck a slender band perceiv'd:
Beneath her wing a tablet hung conceal'd, 340
Which, open'd, to his sight these words reveal'd.

To thee th' Egyptian chief his zeal commends,
And health to great Judæa's Sovereign sends.
Fear not, O Monarch! still thy towers defend,
Till the fifth morn her welcome light extend: 345
Then shall our arms relieve your threaten'd wall,
Sion shall conquer, and the Christians fall.

Such was the secret in the tablet seal'd,
In barbarous phrase and characters reveal'd.
These winged heralds thus the mandates bear   350
Of eastern nations through the fields of air.

The prince now set the captive dove at large,
But she (a guiltless traitress to her charge)
As conscious of th' event, no more return'd,
But distant from her lord in secret mourn'd.   355

The leader then conven'd the princely train,
The tidings strait disclos'd, and thus began.

Behold, O friends! how heaven's high Monarch
    shows
Th' important secrets of our wily foes,
No more delay—this present time demands   360
Our boldest hearts and most experienc'd hands,
Be every toil, be every peril try'd,
The way to conquer on the southern side.
There, well by nature fenc'd on every part,
The forts are less secur'd by works of art;   365
There, Raymond, let thy strength resistless fall,
There, with thy engines, shake the doubtful wall,
While I, upon a different side, prepare,
Against the northern gate, the storm of war,
So may the foes their forces thither bend,   370
And there, deceiv'd, our chief assault attend.

From

From thence convey'd, shall then my lofty tower
On other parts unlook'd-for vengeance pour.
Near me, Camillus, thou the toils shalt share,
And the third pile be trusted to thy care.   375

   He ceas'd: when Raymond, pondering in his breast
The public welfare, Godfrey thus address'd.

   So well for all, O chief! thy cares provide,
Nor aught can be retrench'd, nor aught supply'd.
Yet let me wish some artful spy were sent   380
To Egypt's camp, to sound their deep intent;
Who to our host might all their motions tell,
And certain tidings of their force reveal.

   Then Tancred spoke! a faithful squire is mine,
Who seems well form'd to further your design; 385
He every wile, with ready wit, prepares;
He dares all perils, yet with caution dares.
Swift in the race he lightly skims the field;
His pliant tongue in every speech is skill'd:
He shifts his mien, his action and his tone,   390
And makes the modes of various climes his own.

   The 'squire, now call'd, before th' assembly stands,
And cheerful hears the task his lord demands;
Then smiling thus: To me consign the care,
This instant see me for th' attempt prepare: 395

Q 4   Swift

Swift will I reach (an unexpected spy)
The distant land where Egypt's forces lie;
There pierce the swarming vale at noon of day,
And every man and every steed survey.
I promise soon (nor vain esteem my boast)   400
To bring the state and numbers of their host;
To penetrate their leader's secret thought,
And view each purpose in his bosom wrought.
Thus bold Vafrino spoke; nor more delay'd,
But swift in vesture long his limbs array'd: 405
He bar'd his neck, and round his forehead roll'd
A turban huge in many a winding fold:
His back the Syrian bow and quiver bore,
And all his looks a foreign semblance wore.
The wondering crowds admir'd his ready tongue,
On which each nation's different accent hung;   411
That Egypt well might claim him for her own,
Or Tyre receive him as her rightful son.
Now from the camp he issu'd on a steed
That scarcely bent the grass beneath his speed. 415
Ere yet they view'd the third succeeding day,
The Franks, industrious, gain'd the rugged way.
In vain the rolling hours to rest invite,
They join to day the labours of the night:

            Till

Till all is for the great assault prepar'd, 420
And nought remains that can their schemes retard.

  The Christian chief, on pious thoughts intent,
In humble prayer the day preceding spent,
And bade the faithful host their sins confess,
And take, from sacred hands, the bread of peace.
He then began his vast machines to show 426
On divers parts, t' amuse the thoughtless foe.
The foe, deceiv'd, with joyful looks descry'd
His force directed on their strongest side.

  But, soon as evening stretch'd her welcome shade,
He thence with ease his warlike pile convey'd: 431
This tow'rds the ramparts' weaker parts he brought,
Where less expos'd his hardy soldiers fought.
Experienc'd Raymond with his lofty tower
Against the southern hill his forces bore: 435
And, with the third, the brave Camillus press'd
Against the side declining to the west.

  When now the chearful harbinger of day
Had ting'd the mountains with a golden ray;
The foes the mighty tower with terror view'd 440
Far distant from the place where late it stood;
And all around, till then unseen, beheld
Enormous engines thickening o'er the field.

With

With every art the wary Pagans form
Their beſt defence againſt th' approaching ſtorm.
No leſs intent, the prudent chief, who knew   446
That nearer now th' Egyptian army drew,
Each paſs ſecures; and, calling from the bands
Guelpho and either Robert, thus commands.

You watchful on your ſteeds in arms remain, 450
While I attempt yon hoſtile wall to gain,
Where leaſt defence appears: be yours the care
To guard our rear from unexpected war.

He ceas'd: and, breathing courage man to man,
Three fierce aſſaults the Chriſtian powers began. 455
Then hoary Aladine, with cares decay'd,
In arms, long ſince difus'd, his limbs array'd;
Trembling with feeble feet and tottering frame,
The aged king oppos'd to Raymond came.
Stern Solyman for Godfrey ſtood prepar'd;   460
And fierce Argantes good Camillus dar'd.
Here Tancred, led by fate, approach'd the wall,
Where by his arms his daring foe might fall.

The ready archers now their bows apply;
In deadly poiſon drench'd their arrows fly;   465
The face of heaven is all in darkneſs loſt,
Such clouds of weapons iſſue from the hoſt.

With

With greater force the mural engines pour
Their sudden vengeance in a mingled shower.
Hence, sheath'd with iron, javelins huge are thrown;
Hence rocky fragments thunder on the town.   471
Not in the wound the javelins lose their force,
But furious hold their unremitted course;
Resistless here their bloody entrance find,
And issuing there, leave cruel death behind!   475
Where'er the stones alight, with dreadful sway
Through men and arms they force their horrid way;
Sweep life before 'em, crush the human frame,
And hide at once the figure and the name!

 Still unappall'd the Pagan troops remain,   480
And boldly still the bold assault sustain:
Already had they spread with heedful care
Their woolly fences 'gainst the threatening war;
And where expos'd the thickest ranks they 'spy,
With missile weapons send a fierce reply: 485
Yet undismay'd the brave assailants press,
Nor from the threefold charge, intrepid, cease.
Some under vast machines securely move,
While storms of arrows hiss in vain above.
Some wheel th' enormous engines near the foes: 490
The Syrians, from the walls, th' attempt oppose.

            Each

Each ready tower to launch its bridge essays;
Its iron head each ram incessant plays.

 Meanwhile in generous doubt Rinaldo stands,
No vulgar deeds his glorious arm demands: 495
He rolls his ardent eyes; his thoughts aspire
To tempt the pass from which the rest retire.
Then to the warriors, late by Dudon led,
Th' intrepid hero turn'd, and thus he said.

 O shame to fight! while here our squadrons press,
Behold yon fortress still remains in peace,   501
No perils e'er can brave designs control,
All deeds are open to the dauntless soul.
Haste, let us thither march, and 'gainst the foes
A sure defence, with lifted shields, oppose.   505

 He spoke: The warriors with one soul obey'd,
And o'er their heads extend an ample shade,
The bucklers join'd secur'd the moving train,
While from on high the ruins roll in vain.
Now to the walls they came; with eager haste   510
A scaling-ladder bold Rinaldo plac'd;
A hundred steps it bore, the hero's hand
Aloft with ease th' enormous weight sustain'd.
Spears, beams, and rafters from the ramparts pour;
Dauntless he mounts amid the ponderous shower: 515

Nor toils nor death the daring youth could dread,
Though pendent rocks had nodded o'er his head.
His ample shield receiv'd a feather'd wood;
His back sustain'd a falling mountain's load:
This arm the bulwarks shook; and that before 520
His towering front the fencing buckler bore.
His great example every warrior fir'd;
Each gallant chief to scale the works aspir'd.
But various fates they prove: Some headlong fall;
And some are slaughter'd ere they mount the wall; 525
While he, ascending still, securely goes,
His friends encourages, and threats his foes.
The thronging numbers, with collected might,
Attempt in vain to hurl him from his height:
Still in th' unequal combat firm he stands, 530
And bears alone th' united furious bands.
And now his sword the spacious rampart clears,
And frees the passage for his brave compeers.
To one the hero gave a wish'd relief,
(Eustatius, brother to the pious chief) 535
With ready hand he stopp'd his fatal fall,
And friendly guarded while he gain'd the wall.
The Christian leader, on a different side,
With various perils various fortune try'd:

Nor

Nor men with men alone the combat fought, 540
There pile with pile, with engine engine, fought.
Above the walls a trunk the Syrians raife;
(A veffel's towering maft in ancient days)
To this athwart a maffy beam fufpend;
Thick iron plates the folid head defend: 545
This with ftrong cables back the Pagans drew,
Then, fwift recoiling, on the tower it flew.
The yielding timbers with the fury fhook,
The joint gave way before the frequent ftroke:
But foon the tower its needful arms fupplies: 550
Two fcythes prepar'd are rais'd of mighty fize,
That, clofing, with their fharpen'd edge divide
The twifted cords to which the beam is ty'd.
As, loos'd by time, or by rude tempefts torn,
A rock's huge fragment from a mountain borne, 555
Impetuous whirling down the craggy fteeps,
Woods, cots, and herds before its fury fweeps:
So drew the dreadful engine, in its fall,
Arms, men, and ruins, from the fhatter'd wall.
The tower's vaft fummit nodded from on high! 560
The bulwarks tremble, and the hills reply.

 Victorious Godfrey now, advancing on,
Already deem'd the hoftile ramparts won:

When

When from the foes, with roaring thunders, broke
Whirlwinds of flame and deluges of fmoke! 565
Not Ætna from her raging womb expires
Such pois'nous ftreams and fuffocating fires;
Not fuch dire fumes the clime of India yields,
When noxious vapours taint her fultry fields.
Thick fulphur pours and burning javelins fly; 570
Dark clouds arife, and intercept the fky.
The tower's ftrong planks the fcorching mifchief meet;
The moiften'd hides now fhrivel in the heat:
Around afcends a black and fanguine flame,
And the laft ruin threats the mighty frame. 575
 Before the reft the glorious leader ftood,
With looks unchang'd the growing danger view'd,
And on the pile commands his troops to pour
The cooling waters in a copious fhower.
Now deep diftrefs the troubled hoft affails; 580
The fire increafes, and the water fails;
When from the north a fudden wind arofe,
And turn'd the raging flames againft the foes:
The blazing fury on the Pagans falls,
Where numerous works were rais'd to guard the walls.
The light materials catch! the fparks afpire; 586
And all their fences crackle in the fire.
       O favour'd

O favour'd chief! th' Almighty's care approv'd:
By him defended, and by him belov'd:
Heaven in thy caufe auxiliar arms fupplies,   590
And at thy trumpet's call the winds obedient rife!

But dire Ifmeno, who the flames beheld
By Boreas' breath againft himfelf repell'd,
Refolv'd once more to prove his impious fkill,
And force the laws of nature to his will.   595
With two magicians, that his arts purfue,
The dreadful forcerer towers in open view:
Black, fqualid, foul! he rifes o'er the bands:
So 'twixt two furies Dis or Charon ftands.
And now the murmuring of the words was heard   600
By Phlegethon and deep Cocytus fear'd:
Already now the air difturb'd was feen,
The fun with clouds obfcur'd his face ferene:
When from an engine flew, with hideous fhock,
A ponderous ftone, the fragment of a rock,   605
Through all the three its horrid paffage tore,
Crafh'd every bone, and drench'd their limbs in gore:

Ver. 606. *Through all the three*—] Though the particular character of Ifmeno is entirely the invention of the poet, yet hiftory relates the death of certain magicians, that had placed themfelves on the walls of Jerufalem, in order to oppofe the machines of the Chriftians.

With

With groans the sinful spirits take their flight
From the pure air and seats of upper light,
And seek th' infernal shades of endless pain: 610
O mortals! hence from impious deeds refrain.

At length the tower, preserv'd from threaten'd flame
By friendly winds, more near the ramparts came;
Now, from the midst, the bridge was seen to fall,
And now was fix'd upon the lofty wall: 615
But thither Solyman intrepid flies,
And there to cut the bridge his falchion tries:
Nor had he try'd in vain, but, sudden rear'd,
Another tower upon the first appear'd:
Above the loftiest spires was seen on high 620
The wondrous fabric rising to the sky.
Struck with the sight th' astonish'd Pagans stood,
While far beneath the pile the town they view'd.
But still the fearless Turk his post maintain'd,
Though on his head a rocky tempest rain'd; 625
Nor yet despairs to part the bridge, and loud,
With threats and cries, incites the timorous crowd.

To Godfrey then, unseen by vulgar eyes,
Appear'd th' Archangel Michael from the skies,

In

Ver. 628. *To Godfrey then—*] This fiction seems to be taken from miracles recorded in the history of the crusade. The arch-

In glorious panoply, divinely bright, 630
More dazzling than the sun's unclouded light.

 Lo! Godfrey (he began) the hour at hand
To free from bondage Sion's sacred land:
Decline not then to earth thy looks dismay'd:
Behold where Heaven assists with heavenly aid! 635
I now remove the film, and teach thy sight
To bear the presence of the sons of light.
The souls of those, now heavenly beings, view,
That champions once for CHRIST their weapons drew:
With thee they fight, with thee they come to share 640
The glorious triumph of the sacred war.
There, where thou seest the dust and smoak on high
In mingled waves, where heaps of ruin lie,
There, wrapt in darkness, Hugo holds his place,
And heaves the bulwark from its lowest base. 645

archbishop of Tiro relates, that the Christians being engaged with the Infidels, and nearly defeated, a soldier was seen to descend from Mount Olivet, bearing a shield of wonderful lustre, who encouraged the Christians to renew the battle with double vigour, and immediately disappeared. It was likewise said, that at the siege of Antioch, Pyrrhus, a Turk, saw an infinite army of soldiers on white horses, with white arms and vestments, who fought on the side of the Christians. These afterwards disappeared, and were supposed to be angels and the souls of the blessed, sent from God to succour the Christians.

See! Dudon, arm'd againſt the northern towers,
With fire and ſword celeſtial vengeance pours.
Yon ſacred form that on the mount appears,
Who ſolemn robes with wreaths of prieſthood wears,
Is Ademar, a ſaint confeſs'd he ſtands; 650
See! ſtill he follows, bleſſes ſtill the bands.
But higher raiſe thy looks, behold in air
Where all the powers of heaven combin'd appear.

The hero rais'd his eyes, and ſaw above
A countleſs army of celeſtials move. 655
Three ſquadrons rang'd the wondrous force diſplay'd,
Three fulgent circles every ſquadron made,

Orb

Ver. 650. *Is Ademar*—] The Archbiſhop of Tiro gives the following extraordinary account. "That day Ademar, biſhop of Poggio, a man of exemplary virtue and piety, who loſt his life near Antioch, was ſeen by numbers in the holy city: and numbers, whoſe teſtimony is worthy of credit, affirmed that they ſaw him among the firſt to ſcale the walls, and inciting others to enter the town." All theſe traditions were authority ſufficient for the beautiful machine with which Taſſo has adorned his poem: the whole paſſage of which is taken from the ſublime fiction of Virgil, in the 2d Æneid, where Æneas ſees the gods of Greece engaged in the deſtruction of his native city.

Ver. 656. *Three ſquadrons rang'd*—] The Italian commentator explains theſe to mean the three celeſtial hierarchies, each divided into three orders: the firſt, ſeraphim, cherubim,

Orb within orb; by juſt degrees they roſe,
And nine bright ranks the heavenly hoſt compoſe.

and thrones: the ſecond, dominations, principalities, and powers: the third, virtues, angels, and archangels—this opinion is according to St. Gregory and St. Bernard, from which other authors have differed.

Ver. 658. *Orb within orb; by juſt degrees they roſe,*
And nine bright ranks the heavenly hoſt compoſe.] Some theologiſts have ſaid that theſe circles diminiſhed till they came to an indiviſible point, wherein was centered the eſſence of Divinity. This abſtruſe and whimſical doctrine is mentioned by Dante, which paſſage may not be unpleaſing to the curious reader; where he ſpeaks of theſe nine choirs or orders in the following manner.

> Un punto vidi, che raggiava lume
>   Acuto sì, che'l viſo ch'egli affoca,
>   Chiuder convienſi per lo forta acume:
> Diſtante intorno al punto un cerchio d'igne
>   Si girava ſi ratto, ch' avria vinto
>   Quel moto che piu toſto il mondo cigne,
> E queſto era d'un altro circoncinto
>   E quel del terzo e'l terzo poi dal quarto
>   Dal quinto il quarto, e poi dal ſeſto il quinto
> Sovra ſeguia il ſettimo ſi ſparto
>   Già di larghezza che'l mezzo di Giuno
>   Intero a contenerlo farebbe arto.
> Coſi l'ottavo, e'l nono: e ciaſcheduno
>   Più tardo ſi movea, ſecondo ch'era,
>   In numero diſtante, più da l'uno.
>   PARADISO, Canto xxviii.

His sense no more sustain'd the blaze of light, 660
And all the vision vanish'd from his sight.
Then round the plain his martial bands he 'spy'd,
And saw how conquest smil'd on every side.
With brave Rinaldo numbers scale the wall;
Before his arms in heaps the Syrians fall; 665
No longer Godfrey then his zeal restrain'd,
But snatch'd the standard from Alfiero's hand;
And, rushing o'er the bridge, the passage try'd:
The furious Turk all passage there deny'd:
A little space is now the glorious field 670
Where valour's deeds a great example yield!
Here let me nobly fall! (the Pagan cries)
Be glory mine, let life the vulgar prize.
O burst the bridge! and me alone expose;
I shall not meanly sink beneath the foes. 675
But now he sees th' affrighted numbers fly,
And now beholds the dread Rinaldo nigh:
What should I do? (the wavering Soldan said)
If here I fall, in vain my blood is shed.
Then, other schemes revolving in his mind, 680
He slowly to the chief the pass resign'd,
Who threatening follow'd, with impetuous haste,
And on the wall the holy standard plac'd.

The conquering banner, to the breeze unroll'd,
Redundant streams in many a waving fold : 685
The winds with awe confess the heavenly sign,
With purer beams the day appears to shine :
The swords seem bid to turn their points away,
And darts around it innocently play :
The sacred mount the purple cross adores, 690
And Sion owns it from her topmost towers.

Then all the squadrons rais'd a shouting cry,
The loud acclaim of joyful victory !
From man to man the clamor pours around:
The distant hills re-echo to the sound. 695
And now, incens'd, impatient of delay,
Against Argantes Tancred forc'd his way;
At once he launch'd his bridge, the passage made,
And straight his standard on the walls display'd.

But tow'rds the south where aged Raymond fought,
And 'gainst the Pagan king his forces brought; 701
There deeper toil engag'd the Christian power,
There rocky paths delay'd the cumbrous tower.
At length th' assailants and defenders hear
The echoing shouts of conquests from afar. 705
To Aladine and Raymond soon 'tis known,
That tow'rds the plain are Sion's ramparts won :

The

Then thus the earl aloud—O hear, my friends!
Before the Chriſtian arms the city bends!
And does ſhe, when ſubdu'd, our courage dare? 710
Shall we alone no glorious triumph ſhare?

But ſoon the Syrian king withdrew his force,
Nor longer ſtrove t' oppoſe the victor's courſe;
Retreating thence a lofty fort he gain'd,
From which he hop'd their fury to withſtand. 715

Now all the conquering bands, oppos'd no more,
Swarm o'er the walls and through the portals pour,
The thirſty ſword now rages far and wide,
Death ſtalks with grief and terror at his ſide:
Blood runs in rivers, or in pools o'erflows, 720
And dead and dying, heap'd, a horrid ſcene compoſe!

THE END OF THE EIGHTEENTH BOOK.

THE

NINETEENTH BOOK

OF

JERUSALEM DELIVERED.

THE ARGUMENT.

Tancred and Argantes retire together from the walls, and engage in single combat: After an obstinate defence, the latter is slain; and Tancred himself, weakened by the loss of blood, falls into a swoon. In the mean time Rinaldo pursues the Infidels, and compels many of them to take refuge in Solomon's temple. Rinaldo at length bursting open the gate, the Christian troops enter, and make a terrible slaughter. Solyman and Aladine fortify themselves in David's tower. Solyman defends the pass with great intrepidity, but at last retires within the fort at the appearance of Godfrey and Rinaldo: Night puts an end to the operations on both sides. Vafrino enters the Egyptian camp, where he meets with Erminia. In their way to the Christian tents, they find Tancred in appearance dead: Erminia's lamentation; she recovers Tancred from his swoon, and, at his desire, he is conveyed with the body of Argantes to the city. Vafrino gives an account to Godfrey of the discoveries he has made; upon which the general determines to hold his army in readiness to encounter the Egyptian forces.

THE
NINETEENTH BOOK
OF
JERUSALEM DELIVERED.

NOW wide-destroying death, or pale affright,
Remov'd the Pagans from their ramparts' height:
Alone, still fix'd to triumph or to fall,
Argantes turns not from th' abandon'd wall;
Secure he stands, his front undaunted shows,   5
And singly combats midst a host of foes:
Far more than death he dreads a sully'd name,
And, if he dies, would close his days with fame.
  Before the rest intrepid Tancred flies,
And lifts his falchion, and the chief defies: 10
Well, by his mien and arms confess'd to view,
His plighted foe the fierce Argantes knew.
Thus dost thou, Tancred! keep thy faith? (he cry'd)
Late art thou come our battle to decide:

We

We meet not here as heroes heroes dare; 15
Thou com'ft a bafe artificer of war!
Thofe engines are thy guard, thofe troops thy fhield;
Thou bring'ft ftrange weapons to difgrace the field!
Yet hope not from this hand, in dreadful ftrife,
(Thou woman's murderer!) now t'efcape with life!

   He faid; and Tancred, fmiling with difdain, 21
In words indignant thus reply'd again.
Late am I come?—Supprefs thy fenfelefs fcorn;
Soon fhalt thou find too fpeedy my return;
When thou fhalt wifh, to eafe thy doubtful foul, 25
That 'twixt us Alps might rife, or oceans roll;
And know, by fatal proof too well difplay'd,
Nor fear detain'd my arms, nor floth delay'd.
Come, glorious chief! thou terror of the plain,
By whom are heroes quell'd and giants flain! 30
With me retire, and prove thy boafted might,
The woman's murderer dares thee to the fight!

   Then to his troops—With-hold your wrathful hands,
This warrior now my fword alone demands;
No common foe; by challenge, him I claim; 35
By former promife mine, and mine by fame.

   Defcend (again the proud Circaffian cry'd)
Or fingly, or with aid, the caufe decide:

The

The place frequented or the desart try;
With every odds thy prowess I defy! 40
 The stern convention made, at once they move,
With mutual ire, the dreadful fight to prove.
Already Tancred hopes the glorious strife,
And burns with zeal to take the Pagan's life:
He claims him wholly, all his blood demands, 45
And envies even a drop to vulgar hands.
He spreads his shield, forbids the threatening blow,
And guards from darts and spears his mighty foe.
They leave the walls, impatient of delay,
And through a winding path pursue their way. 50
At length, amid surrounding hills, they view'd
A narrow valley black with shady wood;
That seem'd a sylvan theatre, design'd
For chace or combat with the savage-kind.
Here both the warriors stopp'd; when, pensive grown,
Argantes turn'd to view the suffering town. 56
Tancred, who saw his foe no buckler wield,
Straight cast his own at distance on the field;
Then thus began—What means this sudden gloom?
Think'st thou, at last, thy destin'd hour is come? 60
If such foreboding thoughts a doubt create,
Too late thy prescience, and thy fears too late.
           Yon

Yon city fills my mind (the chief reply'd)
The queen of nations, and Judæa's pride,
That vanquish'd now must fall, while I in vain   65
Attempt her sinking ruins to sustain:
How poor a vengeance can thy life afford,
Thy life by Heaven devoted to my sword!

  He ceas'd; then wary each to combat drew:
For each his adverse champion's valour knew.   70
Tancred was light, his joints were firmly knit,
Swift were his hands, and ready were his feet.
Argantes tower'd superior by the head,
With larger limbs, with shoulders broader spread.
Now Tancred wheels, now bends t' elude the foe,   75
Now, with his sword, averts th' impending blow.
But high, erect, the bold Argantes stood,
And equal art, with different action, show'd:
Now here, now there, impetuous from above,
Against the prince the brandish'd steel he drove.   80
That, on his art and courage most relies;
This, on his mighty strength and giant size.

  Two vessels thus their naval strife maintain,
When no rude wind disturbs the watery plain:
Their bulk though different, equal is the fight,   85
In swiftness one, and one excels in height.

                                        But

But while the Christian seeks to reach the foe,
And shuns the sword that seems to threat the blow,
Full at his face the point Argantes shook;
Then swift, as Tancred turn'd to ward the stroke, 90
He pierc'd his flank, and, loud exulting, said:
Behold the crafty now by craft betray'd!

With rage and shame indignant Tancred burn'd,
And all his thoughts to glorious vengeance turn'd;
Then with his falchion to the boast replies, 95
Where to his aim the vizor open lies.
Argantes breaks the blow: with shorten'd sword
On him intrepid rush'd the Christian lord:
The Pagan's better hand he seiz'd, and dy'd
With many a ghastly wound his bleeding side. 100
Receive this answer (loud the hero cries)
The vanquish'd to his victor thus replies!

The fierce Circassian foams with rage and pain,
But strives to free his captive arm in vain:
At length, dependent from the chain, he leaves 105
The trusty falchion, and his hand reprieves.
Each other now in rude embrace they press'd,
Arms lock'd in arms, and breast oppos'd to breast.

Ver. 105. —— *from the chain* ——] In Ariosto it is frequently mentioned, that the sword was fastened to the wrist by a chain, though this is the only passage where such a custom is alluded to by Tasso.

Not

Not with more vigor, on the sandy field,
Great Hercules the mighty giant held. 110
Such is their conflict, so the warriors strain,
Till both together, sidelong, press the plain.
Argantes, as he fell, by chance or skill,
Bore high his better arm releas'd at will:
But Tancred's hand, that should the weapon wield, 115
Was held beneath him prisoner on the field.
Full well the Frank th' unequal peril view'd,
And, soon recovering, on his feet he stood.
   More slow the Saracen the ground forsook,
And, ere he rose, receiv'd a sudden stroke. 120
But as the pine, whose leafy summit bends
To Eurus' blast, at once again ascends:
So from his fall arose the Pagan knight
With equal wrath and unabated might.
Again, with flashing swords, the war they wag'd: 125
Now less of art and more of horror rag'd.
From Tancred's wounds appear'd the trickling blood;
But from Argantes pour'd a crimson flood:
Tancred full soon his feeble arm beheld
Slow and more slow the weighty falchion wield: 130
All hatred then his generous breast forsook,
And, back retreating, mildly thus he spoke.
Yield, dauntless chief! enough thy worth is shown;
Or me, or fortune, for thy victor own:

                    I ask

I afk no fpoils, no triumph from the fight,   135
Nor to myfelf referve a conqueror's right.
  At this with rage renew'd the Pagan burn'd:
Ufe what thy fortune gives—(he fierce return'd)
And dar'ft thou then from me the conqueft claim?
Shall bafe conceffions ftain Argantes' fame?   140
Alike thy mercy and thy threats I prize;
This arm fhall yet thy fenfelefs pride chaftife.
As, near extinct, the torch new light acquires,
Revives its flame, and in a blaze expires:
So he, when fcarce the blood maintain'd its courfe,
With kindled ire recruits his dying force;   146
Refolv'd his laft of days with fame to fpend,
And crown his actions with a glorious end.
Grafp'd in each hand, his vengeful fteel he took:
In vain the Chriftian's fword oppos'd the ftroke: 150
Full on his fhoulder fell the deadly blade,
Nor, deaden'd there, its eager fury ftay'd,
But, glancing downward, deeply pierc'd his fide,
And ftain'd his armour with a purple tide.
Yet Tancred's looks nor doubt nor fear confefs'd;
For Nature's felf had fteel'd his dauntlefs breaft. 156
A fecond ftroke the haughty Pagan try'd;
The wary Chriftian now his purpofe 'fpy'd,
And flipt, elufive, from the fteel afide.

Then,

Then, spent in empty air thy strength in vain, 160.
Thou fall'st, Argantes! headlong on the plain:
Thou fall'st! yet (unsubdu'd alike in all)
None but thyself can boast Argantes' fall!

 Fresh stream'd the blood from every gaping wound,
And the red torrent delug'd all the ground: 165
Yet on his arm and knee the furious knight
His bulk supported, and provok'd the fight.
Again his hand the courteous victor stay'd:
Submit, O chief! preserve thy life (he said:)
But, while he paus'd, the fierce insidious foe 170
Full at his heel directs a treacherous blow,
And threats aloud: Then flash from Tancred's eyes
The sparks of wrath, while thus the hero cries:
And dost thou, wretch! such base return afford
For life so long preserv'd from Tancred's sword? 175

 He said; and as he spoke, no more delay'd,
But through his vizor plung'd th' avenging blade.
Thus fell Argantes; as he liv'd he dy'd;
Untam'd his soul, unconquer'd was his pride:
Nor droop'd his spirit at th' approach of death, 180
But threats and rage employ'd his latest breath.

 Then Tancred in the sheath his sword bestow'd,
And paid to GOD the thanks his conquest ow'd:

But

But dear his triumph has the victor cost:
His senses fail, his wonted strength is lost. 185
Again he strives to pass the valley o'er,
And tread the steps his feet had trod before.
Not far his tottering knees their load sustain,
His utmost strength he tries, but tries in vain.
Now, laid on earth, his arm supports his head, 190
(His arm, that trembles like a feeble reed)
Each object swims before his giddy sight;
The cheerful day seems chang'd to dusky night;
He faints;—he swoons! and scarce to mortal eyes
The victor differing from the vanquish'd lies. 195

While these, inflam'd with private hate, engag'd,
The wrathful Christians through the city rag'd.
What tongue can tell the woes that then were known,
And speak the horrors of a conquer'd town!
Each part is fill'd with death, with blood defil'd; 200
The ghastly slain appear in mountains pil'd.
There on th' unbury'd corse the wounded spread;
The living here interr'd beneath the dead.
With flowing hair pale mothers fly distress'd,
And clasp their harmless infants to the breast: 205
The spoiler here, impell'd by thirst of prey,
Bears on his laden back the spoils away:

The foldier there, by luft ungovern'd fway'd,
Drags by her graceful locks th' affrighted maid.

But tow'rds the mountain where the temple ftood,
The bold Rinaldo drove the trembling crowd: 211
Nor helm nor buckler could his force withftand;
Th' unarm'd alone efcap'd his vengeful hand.
He fought the brave, but fcorn'd with great difdain
To wreak his fury on a helplefs train. 215
Then might you wondrous deeds of valour view,
How thefe he threatening chac'd, and thofe he flew;
How with unequal rifk, but equal fear,
The arm'd and naked fugitives appear.

Already, mingled with th' ignobler band, 220
A troop of warriors had the temple gain'd,
That, oft o'erthrown, and oft confum'd by flame,
Still bears its antient founder's glorious name.
Great Solomon the ftately fabric rear'd,
Where marble, gold, and cedar once appear'd: 225
Lefs coftly now; but 'gainft the hoftile powers
Secur'd with iron gates, and guarded towers.

Rinaldo rais'd his threatening looks on high,
And view'd the fortrefs with an angry eye:
Now here, now there, he feeks fome pafs to meet,
And twice furrounds it with his rapid feet. 231

So

So when a wolf, beneath the friendly shades,
With hopes of prey the peaceful fold invades;
He traverses the ground with fruitless pain,
Licks his dry chaps, and thirsts for blood in vain. 235
The chief now paus'd before the lofty gate,
The Pagans, from above, th' encounter wait.
While thus the hero stood, by chance he 'spies
A beam beside him of enormous size;
(Whate'er the use design'd) so high, so vast,   240
The largest ship might claim it for a mast:
This in his nervous arms aloft he shook,
And with repeated blows the portal struck:
Not the strong ram with greater fury falls,
Nor bombs more fiercely shake the tottering walls.
Nor steel nor marble could the force oppose;   246
The fence gives way before the driving blows:
The bars are burst, the sounding hinges torn,
And hurl'd to earth the batter'd gates are borne.
Swift through the pass, the victor to sustain,   250
Fierce as a torrent rush th' exulting train.

    Then, dire to see! the dome devote to GOD,
With carnage swell'd, and pour'd a purple flood.
O! sacred justice of th' Almighty, shed,
Tho' late, yet certain, on the guilty head!   255

Thy awful providence now stands confess'd,
And kindles wrath in every pious breast.
The Pagan with his blood must cleanse from stain
Those sacred shrines which once he durst profane.

   But Solyman, meanwhile, to David's tower   260
Retreated with the remnant of his power;
His troops with sudden works the fort enclose,
And stop each entrance from th' invading foes.
And Aladine the tyrant thither flies;
To whom aloud th' intrepid Soldan cries;   265

   Come, mighty monarch! haste! the fortress gain,
Whose strength shall yet preserve thy threaten'd reign;
Here may'st thou still defend thy life, secur'd
From the dire fury of the wasting sword.
Ah me! relentless fate (the king reply'd)   270
O'erturns the city, levels all her pride!—
My days are run—my empire now is o'er—
I liv'd—I reign'd—but live and reign no more!
'Tis past!—we once have been! behold our doom—
The last, th' irrevocable hour is come!   275

   To whom with generous warmth the Soldan said:
Where, prince! is all thy antient virtue fled?

Ver. 260. —*David's tower*] The citadel of Jerusalem was so called.

Though

Though of his realms by fortune dispossess'd,
A monarch's throne is seated in his breast.
But come, and, here secur'd from hostile rage, 280
Refresh thy limbs decay'd with toils and age.
Thus counsel'd he; and strait, with careful haste,
The hoary king within the bulwarks plac'd.
Himself to guard the dangerous pass appear'd,
With both his hands an iron mace he rear'd: 285
He girt his trusty falchion to his side,
And all the forces of the Franks defy'd.
On every part his thundering weapon flew,
And these he overturn'd, and those he slew.
All fled the guarded fort, with wild affright, 290
Where'er they saw his mace's fury light.
Now, led by fortune, with his dauntless train,
The fearless Raymond rush'd the pass to gain:
Against the Turk in vain he aim'd the blow;
But not in vain return'd his haughty foe: 295
Full in his front the reverend chief he found,
And stretch'd him pale and trembling on the ground.

Again the vanquish'd breathe, the victors fly,
Or in the well-defended entrance die.
The Soldan then, who, midst the vulgar dead, 300
Beheld on earth the Christian leader spread,

Incites his followers, with repeated cries,
To drag within the works their prostrate prize.
　All spring to take him (a determin'd band)
But toils and dangers their attempt withstand.　305
What Christian can his Raymond's care forego?
At once they fly to guard him from the foe.
There rage, here piety, maintains the fight;
No common cause demands each warrior's might:
For Raymond's life or freedom they contend;　310
And those would seize the chief, and these defend.
Yet had the Soldan's force at length prevail'd,
For shields and helms before his weapon fail'd;
But sudden, to relieve the faithful band,
A powerful aid appear'd on either hand;　315
At once the chief of chiefs, resistless, came,
And he *, the foremost of the martial name.
　As when loud winds arise, and thunders roll,
And glancing lightenings gleam from pole to pole,
The shepherd-swain, who sees the darkening air, 320
Withdraws from open fields his fleecy care;
And, thence retreating, to some covert flies
To shun the fury of th' inclement skies;
And with his voice and crook his flock constrains;
Himself, behind them, last forsakes the plains. 325

* RINALDO.

So

So the fierce Pagan, who the storm beheld,
That like a whirlwind swept the dusty field,
Who heard the shouts of legions rend the air,
And saw the flash of armour from afar,
Compell'd his troops within the sheltering tower; 330
Himself, reluctant, from superior power
Retires the last, with unabated heat,
In caution brave, intrepid in defeat.

 Scarce were they enter'd, when, with headlong haste,
Rinaldo o'er the broken fences pass'd;   335
Desire to vanquish one so fam'd in fight,
His plighted vows the hero's soul excite:
For still he keeps his solemn oath in view,
To take the warrior's life who Sweno slew.
Then had his matchless arm the walls assail'd, 340
Then had their strength to shield the Soldan fail'd:
But here the general bade surcease the fight,
For all th' horizon round was lost in night.
There Godfrey strait encamp'd his martial train,
Resolv'd at morn the hostile fort to gain.   345
Then chearful thus his listening host he warms:
Th' Almighty favours now the Christian arms!
At early dawn yon fortress shall be ours;
The last weak refuge of the faithless powers!

Meantime

Meantime your thoughts to pious duties bend, 350
The sick to comfort, and the wounded tend.
Go—pay the rites those gallant friends demand,
Who purchas'd with their blood this fated land;
This temper better suits the Christian name,
Than souls with avarice or revenge on flame. 355
Too much, alas! has slaughter stain'd the day;
Too much has lust of plunder borne the sway.
Then cease from spoil, each cruel deed forbear;
And let the trumpet's sound our will declare.

   He said; and went where, scarce repriev'd from
      death, 360
Still Raymond groan'd with new-recover'd breath.
Nor Solyman less bold, his friends address'd,
While in his thought the chief his doubts suppress'd.
O warriors! scorn the change of fortune's power;
Still cheerful hope maintains her blooming flower;
Safe is your king, and safe his chosen train: 366
These walls the noblest of the realm contain.
Then let the Franks their empty conquest boast;
Swift fate impends o'er all th' exulting host:
While rage and plunder every soul employ, 370
And lust and murder are their savage joy:
Amidst the mingled tumult shall they fall,
And one destructive hour o'erwhelm 'em all;

If Egypt's troops, now haſtening to our aid,
With numerous force their ſcatter'd bands invade. 375
From hence our miſſile weapons can we pour,
To whelm the city with a rocky ſhower;
And with our engines from afar defend
The paths that to the ſepulchre aſcend.

 While deeds like theſe were wrought, Vafrino
  goes;   380
A truſty ſpy, amidſt a hoſt of foes:
The camp he left, his lonely way he took,
What time the ſun the weſtern ſky forſook;
By Aſcalon he paſs'd, ere yet the day
Shed from his orient throne the golden ray: 385
And when his car had reach'd the midmoſt height,
The hoſtile camp appear'd in open ſight.
There, pitch'd around, unnumber'd tents he ſees,
Unnumber'd ſtreamers waving to the breeze.
Diſcordant tongues aſſail his wondering ears; 390
Timbrels and horns and barbarous notes, he hears.
The elephant and camel mix their cries;
The generous ſteed, with ſhriller ſound, replies.
Surpris'd he ſees ſuch numerous forces join'd,
Where Aſia's realms and Afric's ſeem combin'd. 395

 Now here, now there, his watchful looks he throws,
And marks what different works the camp encloſe;
                  Nor

Nor seeks in unfrequented parts to lie;
Nor shuns the observance of the public eye;
But boldly to each high pavilion goes, 400
And fearless communes with th' unconscious foes.
Wise were his questions, well his answers made,
And deepest prudence all his actions sway'd.
The warriors, steeds, and arms, attract his view;
Full soon each leader's rank and name he knew. 405
At length, as wandering through the vale he went,
Chance led his footsteps to the general's tent:
There, while immers'd in deepest thought he stay'd,
His searching eyes a friendly gap survey'd;
From this each voice within distinct was heard, 410
Through this reveal'd th' interior parts appear'd.
There watch'd Vafrino, while he seem'd employ'd
To mend the torn pavilion's opening side.

Bare-headed there he saw the chief confess'd,
With limbs in armour sheath'd, and purple vest: 415
Two pages bore his helmet and his shield;
His better hand a pointed javelin held;
He view'd a warrior, who beside him stood,
Of limbs gigantic, and of semblance proud.
Vafrino stay'd, intent their words to hear, 420
And sudden Godfrey's name assail'd his ear.

Think'ft thou (the leader thus the knight befpoke)
That Godfrey fure fhall fall beneath thy ftroke?
Then he: He furely falls! and here I fwear
Ne'er to return, but victor from the war.   425
This hand my fellows' fwords fhall render vain;
And let my deed this fole reward obtain;
A glorious trophy of his arms to raife
In Cairo's town, and thus infcribe my praife:
" Thefe from the Chriftian chief, whofe force o'er-
  " run   430
" All Afia's lands, in battle Ormond won;
" And fix'd them here, that future times might tell
" How, by his prowefs vanquifh'd, Godfrey fell."
Think not our grateful king (the leader cries)
Will view th' important act with thanklefs eyes: 435
Full gladly will he yield to thy demand,
And crown thy fervice with a bounteous hand.
But now with fpeed the vefts and arms prepare;
The approaching day of combat claims thy care.
All, all is now prepar'd—the knight reply'd: 440
And here the converfe ceas'd on either fide.

Thus they: A ftranger to the hidden fenfe,
The words Vafrino heard in deep fufpenfe;
Oft-times debating, in his anxious mind,
What arms were purpos'd, and what wiles defign'd.

He

He parted thence, and sleepless pass'd the night, 446
And watch'd impatient for the dawning light;
But when the camp, as early morning shin'd,
Unfurl'd the waving banners to the wind,
Mix'd with the rest he went, with these he stay'd; 450
And round from tent to tent uncertain stray'd.

One day he came to where, in regal state,
Amidst her knights and dames Armida sate:
Pensive she seem'd, with various cares oppress'd,
A thousand thoughts revolving in her breast: 455
On her fair hand her lovely cheek she plac'd,
And prone to earth her starry eyes she cast,
All moist with tears: Full opposite he saw
Adrastus motionless with silent awe:
Fix'd on her charms, he gaz'd with fond desire, 460
And with the prospect fed his amorous fire.
But Tisaphernes both by turns beheld,
While different passions in his bosom swell'd:
His changing looks a quick succession prove,
Now fir'd with hatred, now inflam'd with love. 465
From thence Vafrino cast his sight aside,
And midst the damsels Altamorus 'spy'd;
Who curb'd the licence of his roving eyes,
Or snatch'd his wary glances by surprise;

Her

Her hand, her face, with secret rapture view'd, 470
And oft, by stealth, a sweeter search pursu'd,
T' explore the passage where th' uncautious vest
Reveal'd the beauties of her ivory breast.

 At length her downcast looks Armida rears,
While through her grief a transient smile appears. 475
O brave Adrastus! in thy glorious boast,
I feel (she cries) my former anguish lost:
And soon I trust a sweet revenge to find;
For sweet is vengeance to an injur'd mind.

 To whom the Indian—Bid thy sorrows cease, 480
O royal fair! compose thy soul to peace.
Doubt not to view (ere many days are fled)
Cast at thy feet Rinaldo's impious head;
Else shall he come, if so thy will ordains,
To servile dungeons, and eternal chains. 485

 To Tisaphernes smiling then she said:
And wilt not thou, O chief! Armida aid?

 It suits not me (he taunting thus reply'd)
With such a knight to combat side by side.
But I more slow, in fields of battle new, 490
Must far behind thy champion's steps pursue.

 Sternly he said; the word the monarch took,
And strait incens'd with pride ungovern'd spoke:

'Tis

'Tis thine, indeed, a diftant war to wage,
Nor dare like me in nearer fight engage.   495

  Then Tifaphernes fhook his haughty head:
O were I mafter of this arm! (he faid)
Could I at will this faithful falchion wield,
We foon fhould fee who beft could brave the field:
Fierce as thou art, thy threats with fcorn I hear!   500
Not thee, but Heaven and tyrant love, I fear.

  He ceas'd: Adraftus ftern his force defy'd;
But here Armida interpos'd, and cry'd:

  O warriors! wherefore now, your promife vain,
Will you fo foon refume your gift again?   505
My champions are ye both—let this fuffice
To bind your jarring fouls in friendly ties:
At my command, this rafh contention ceafe;
He meets my anger firft who wounds the peace.

  Thus fhe: At once the rage their breaft forfook, 510
And hearts difcordant bow'd beneath her yoke.

  Vafrino, prefent, all their converfe knew,
Then, penfive, from the lofty tent withdrew;
He faw, though deeply yet in clouds enfhrin'd,
Some treafon 'gainft the Chriftian chief defign'd: 515
He queftion'd oft, refolv'd each means to try
To bear the fecret thence, or bravely die.

                              In

In vain his search—till chance at length display'd
The treacherous snares for pious Godfrey laid.
Again he sought the tent, and view'd again   520
The princess seated midst her warrior train:
Then near a damsel with familiar air
He drew, and sportive thus address'd the fair.

 I too would gladly draw th' avenging blade,
Th' elected champion of some lovely maid: 525
Perhaps this arm Rinaldo's self may feel,
Or Godfrey breathless sink beneath my steel.
Ask from this hand (to me that service owe)
The head devoted of some barbarous foe.

 So spoke the squire; and smiling as he spoke,   530
A virgin view'd him with attentive look:
Sudden her eyes his well-known face confess'd,
Beside him soon she stood, and thus address'd.

 From all the train I here thy sword demand,
Nor ask ignoble service at thy hand: 535
I chuse thee for my champion; hence retire,
I now thy converse, as my knight, require.

 She said; and drew him from the throng aside:
I know thee well, Vafrino! (then she cry'd)
Know'st thou not me?—Confus'd the Christian stood,
Till with a smile he thus his speech renew'd.   541

Ne'er have I seen thy charms, exalted fair,
Nor is the name thou speak'st the name I bear:
Born on Biserta's shore, my birth I claim
From Lesbin', and Almanzor is my name.   545
   Long have I known thee (thus the maid reply'd)
Then seek no more in vain thyself to hide:
Dismiss thy fear—thou seest a faithful friend
For thee prepar'd her dearest life to spend.
Behold Erminia! born of royal kind,   550
And once with thee in Tancred's service join'd:
Two happy moons, a blissful captive there,
I liv'd in peace beneath thy gentle care.
   Then on her face he bent his earnest view,
And soon the features of Erminia knew.   555
   Rest on my faith secure (the damsel cries)
I here attest the sun and conscious skies!
Ah! let me now thy pitying aid implore;
Erminia to her former bonds restore!
In irksome freedom since my hours were led,   560
Care fills my days, and slumber flies my bed.
Com'st thou the secrets of the host to spy?
In happy time—on me thou may'st rely:
I shall at full their purpos'd frauds explain,
Which thou, perchance, had'st long explor'd in
    vain.   565
                 Thus

Thus she; while doubtful still Vafrino mus'd
In silent gaze, with various thoughts confus'd:
He call'd Armida's former arts to mind:
Woman's a changeful and loquacious kind:
A thousand schemes their fickle hearts divide,   570
Insensate those that in the sex confide!
At length he spoke: If hence you seek to fly,
Haste, let us go—your trusty guide am I.
Be this resolv'd—but let us yet beware,
And further speech, till fitter time, forbear.   575

Thus having said, they fix'd without delay,
Before the troops decamp'd, to take their way.
Vafrino parted thence; the cautious maid
Awhile in converse with the damsels stay'd,
Amus'd them with her champion lately gain'd,   580
And with a plausive tale each ear detain'd:
Till at th' appointed time the squire she join'd;
Then mounts her steed, and leaves the camp behind.

The Pagan tents were vanish'd from the view;
And near an unfrequented place they drew;   585
When bold Vafrino spoke—Now, courteous fair!
The treason, fram'd for Godfrey's life, declare.

Eight knights (she cry'd) the dire adventure claim,
But Ormond fierce excels the rest in fame:

T 2   These,

These, urg'd by hatred, or inflam'd with ire, 590
In murderous league against your chief conspire:
Then hear their arts—what time on Syria's plain
Th' embattled host contend for Asia's reign;
These on their arms the purple Cross shall bear,
Disguis'd as Franks in white and gold appear, 595
Like Godfrey's guard, amid the mingled war.
But on his helm, shall each a signal show,
Which, in the thickening fight, their friends may know.
These shall the Christian leader's life pursue,
And deadly venom shall their steel imbrue. 600
To me 'twas given each false device to frame;
Compell'd to act what now I loath to name!
Hence from the camp I fly with just disdain,
From the dire mandates of an impious train:
I scorn my thoughts with treason to defile, 605
T' assist the traitor, and partake the guile.
For this—yet not for this alone, I fled—
She ceas'd; and ceasing blush'd with rosy red:
Declin'd to earth she held her modest look,
And half again recall'd what last she spoke. 610
 But what her virgin scruples strove to hide,
He sought to learn, and gently thus reply'd.

Why

Why wilt thou strive thy sorrows to conceal,
Nor to my faithful ear thy cares reveal?
She breath'd a sigh that instant from her breast, 615
Then, with a faltering voice the squire address'd.

    Farewel, ill-tim'd reserve! no more I claim
The modesty that fits a virgin's name.
Such thoughts should long ere this my heart have
    sway'd;
But ah! they suit no more a wandering maid; 620
That fatal night, my country's overthrow,
When Antioch bow'd before the Christian foe;
From that, alas! my following woes I date,
The early source of my disastrous fate!
Light was a kingdom's loss, an empire's boast, 625
For with my regal state myself I lost!
Thou know'st, Vafrino! how I trembling ran,
Midst heaps of plunder and my subjects slain,
To seek thy lord and mine, when, first in view,
All sheath'd in arms he near my palace drew: 630
Low at his feet I breath'd this humble prayer:
Unconquer'd chief! a helpless virgin hear!
Not for my life I now thy mercy claim;
But save my honour, guard my spotless fame!
Ere yet I ceas'd, my hand the hero took, 635
And rais'd me from the earth, and courteous spoke:

                     O lovely

O lovely maid! in vain thou shalt not sue;
In me thy friend, thy kind preserver, view.
He said; a sudden pleasure fill'd my breast,
A sweet sensation every thought possess'd,   640
That, deeply spreading through my soul, became
A wound incurable, a quenchless flame!

  He saw me oft; he gently shar'd my grief;
With words of comfort gave my woes relief.
To thee (he cry'd) thy freedom I resign;   645
Nor aught of all thy treasures shall be mine.
O cruel gift! O bounty vainly shown!
For, giving me myself, myself he won!
And while he thus restor'd th' ignobler part,
Usurp'd the sovereign empire o'er my heart.   650
Alas! in vain I sought to hide my shame—
How oft with thee I dwelt on Tancred's name!
Thou saw'st the tokens of a mind distress'd,
And said'st—Erminia! love disturbs thy breast.
Still I deny'd, but still deny'd in vain: 655
My looks, my sighs, reveal'd my secret pain.
At length, resolv'd my wishes to pursue,
Love all respect of fear and shame o'erthrew.
To seek my lord I went, in luckless hour:
(He gave the wound, and he alone could cure.)   660

                                               But

But lo! new dangers in my way I met,
A band of barbarous foes my steps beset:
From these I scarce with life and freedom fled:
Thence to the distant woods my course I sped;
There chose with shepherd-swains retir'd to dwell,
An humble tenant of the lonely cell.   666
But when my flame, awhile by fear suppress'd,
Once more, returning, kindled in my breast;
Again I sought the paths I sought before;
Again was cross'd by fickle Fortune's power: 670
A troop of spoilers in my way I found;
(Egyptian forces, and to Gaza bound)
Me to their chief they led: with gentle ear
Their chief vouchsaf'd my mournful tale to hear:
So was my virtue safe preserv'd from stain,   675
Till plac'd in safety with Armida's train,
Behold me thus (so changing fate decreed)
Now made a captive, now from bondage freed;
Yet thus enslav'd, and thus releas'd again,
I still am held in fond affection's chain.   680
O thou! for whom such soft distress I prove,
Repulse not with disdain my proffer'd love;
But to a maid a kind reception give,
And to her bonds a wretch forlorn receive.

T 4   Thus

Thus spoke Erminia. All the night and day 685
They journey'd on, and commun'd on their way.
Vafrino shun'd the beaten track, and held
His course through shorter paths, and ways conceal'd.
Now near the town they came at evening light, 689
What time the shade foretold th' approach of night:
When here they saw the ground distain'd with blood,
And, stretch'd on earth, a slaughter'd warrior view'd:
His face was upward turn'd, with dauntless air,
His aspect menac'd, ev'n in death severe.
In him, as near the squire attentive drew, 695
Some Pagan warrior by his arms he knew.
Not far from thence another prone was seen,
His garb was different, different was his mien.
Behold some Christian there (Vafrino said)
Then mark'd his well-known vest with looks dismay'd: 700
He quits his steed, the features views, and cries—
Ah me! here slain unhappy Tancred lies!

Meanwhile th' ill-fated maid behind him stood,
And with attentive gaze the Pagan view'd:
But soon her ear the cruel sounds confess'd, 705
As if a shaft had pierc'd her tender breast.
At Tancred's name she starts in wild despair,
No bounds can now restrain th' unhappy fair:

She

She sees his face with paleness all o'er-spread,
She leaps, she flies impetuous from her steed; 710
Low-bending o'er him, forth her sorrow breaks;
And thus, with interrupted words, she speaks.

 Was I for this, by fortune here convey'd?
O dreadful object to a love-sick maid!
Long have I sought thee with unweary'd pain, 715
Again I see thee:—yet I see in vain!
Tancred no more Erminia present views;
And, finding Tancred, I my Tancred lose!
Ah me!—and did I think thou e'er should'st prove
A sight ungrateful to Erminia's love? 720
Now could I wish to quench the beams of light,
And hide each object in eternal night!
Alas! where now are all thy graces fled!
Where are those eyes that once such lustre shed!
Where are those cheeks, replete with crimson glow!
Where all the beauties of thy manly brow! 726
But senseless thus and pale thou still canst please!
If yet thy gentle soul my sorrow sees,
Yet views, not wholly fled, my fond desires,
Permit th'embolden'd theft which love inspires: 730
Give me (since fate denies a further bliss)
From thy cold lips to snatch a parting kiss:

Those

Those lips from whence such soothing words could
 flow,
To ease a virgin's and a captive's woe!
Let me, at least, this mournful office pay, 735
And rend in part from death his spoils away.
Receive my spirit ready wing'd for flight,
And guide from hence to realms of endless light.

She said; her bosom swell'd with labouring sighs,
And briny torrents trickled from her eyes. 740
At this the knight, who seem'd of sense depriv'd,
Wash'd with her tears, by slow degrees reviv'd;
A sigh he mingled with the virgin's sighs;
He sigh'd, but rais'd not yet his languid eyes.
His breath, returning, soon the dame perceiv'd; 745
A dawn of hope her fainting soul reliev'd.
See, Tancred! feel (exclaim'd the tender maid)
The mournful rites by dear affection paid,
Behold I come, thy fortune to divide—
Thus will I sink, thus perish by thy side! 750
Yet, yet awhile thy fleeting life retain—
O! hear my last request, nor hear in vain!

Then Tancred strove to view the cheerful light,
But soon again withdrew his swimming sight:
Again Erminia vents her tears and sighs; 755
Again she mourns: Forbear! (Vafrino cries)
 Still,

Still, still he breathes, be then our care essay'd
To heal the living ere we weep the dead.

  He strait disarms the chief, she trembling stands,
And to the office lends her friendly hands; 760
Then views the hero's wounds with skilful eyes,
And feels new hopes within her bosom rise:
But midst those desarts nought the fair can find,
Nought but her slender veil, his wounds to bind:
Yet love, inventive, every scheme ran o'er; 765
Love taught her various arts untry'd before.
Her locks she cut, with these she gently dry'd
The clotted blood; the bandage these supply'd.
Though there nor dittany nor crocus grew,
Yet different herbs of lenient power she knew. 770
Already now, his mortal sleep dispell'd,
The languid prince again his eyes unseal'd:
He view'd his squire, he saw th' attending maid
In foreign vesture clad, and faintly said;
From whence, Vafrino! dost thou hither stray? 775
And who art thou, my kind preserver! say?
She doubtful still, 'twixt joy and sorrow, sighs;
Then blushes rosy red, and thus replies:
All shalt thou know; but now from converse cease:
Hear my commands, and calm thy thoughts to peace.

I, your

I, your physician, will your health restore; 781
Be grateful for my care—I ask no more.

 Then in her lap his head she gently laid:
In anxious doubt awhile Vafrino stay'd,
How to the camp his wounded lord to bear, 785
Ere dewy night advanc'd to chill the air:
When sudden near a band of warriors drew,
And soon his eyes the troops of Tancred knew;
Who hither came, by happy fortune brought,
As fill'd with fear their absent chief they sought. 790
These rais'd th' enfeebled hero from the field,
And gently in their faithful arms upheld.
Then Tancred thus:—Shall brave Argantes slain
Be left, a prey to vultures, on the plain?
Ah no!—forbid it, Heaven! nor let him lose 795
A soldier's honours, or sepulchral dues.
I wage no battle with the silent dead;
In fight the glorious debt he boldly paid:
Then on his worth the rightful praise bestow;
'Tis all the living to the lifeless owe. 800

 So he. Obsequious to their lord's command,
His breathless foe they rear'd from off the land.
Behind they bore him, while with guardian care
Vafrino rode beside the royal fair.

Then spoke the prince, as thus they journey'd on: 805
Seek not my tents, but seek th' imperial town:
What chance soe'er this mortal frame shall meet,
There let me find it, in that holy seat:
From thence, where CHRIST a prey to death was given,
My soul may wing her readier flight to heaven: 810
So shall I then my pilgrimage have made,
And the last vows of my devotion paid.

He said: to Sion's walls the train address'd
Their ready course: There soon the warrior press'd
The welcome couch, and sunk to gentle rest. 815
And now Vafrino for the virgin-fair
A secret place provides with silent care:
That done, to Godfrey's sight with speed he goes;
And enters boldly, (none his steps oppose)
Where sate the leader, bending o'er the bed 820
On which the wounded Raymond's limbs were spread;
And round their prince (a great assembly!) stand
The best, the wisest, of the Christian band.
All gaz'd in silence, with attentive look,
While thus Vafrino to the general spoke. 825

O sacred chief! thy high commands obey'd,
I sought the faithless crew, their camp survey'd:

But

But here my skill, to tell their number, fails;
I saw them hide the mountains, fields, and vales:
Their thirst the copious streams and fountains dries;
And Syria's harvest scarce their food supplies.   831
But many a troop of horse and foot, in vain,
Unskill'd in battle, load th' encumber'd plain!
Nor order these obey, nor signals hear,
Nor draw the sword, but wage a distant war: 835
Yet some are forces prov'd, not new to fame,
Who once beneath the Persian standards came:
But chief o'er all those mighty warriors stand,
Th' Immortal Squadron call'd, the Monarch's chosen
    band.
The ranks unthinn'd no slaughter can deface;   840
Still, as one falls, another fills his place.
Brave Emirenes leads the numerous host;
And few can equal skill or courage boast;
And him, in every art of battle skill'd,
The Caliph trusts to draw thee to the field.   845
Ere twice returning morn the day renew,
Expect to find th' Egyptian camp in view.
But thou, Rinaldo! most thy life defend;
For which, ere long, such warriors shall contend:
For this the noblest champions wield their arms;   850
With rival hate each breast Armida warms:

                                    For

For with her beauty shall his deed be paid,
Who from the battle brings thy forfeit head.
Midst these, the noble chief from Persia's lands,
Samarcand's monarch, Altamorus stands. 855
Adrastus there is seen, of giant size,
Whose kingdom near Aurora's confines lies:
No common courser in the field he reins;
His bulk a towering elephant sustains.
There Tisaphernes boasts his glorious name, 860
Who bears in hardy deeds the foremost fame.

Thus he: Rinaldo, fill'd with generous ire,
Darts from his ardent eyes the sparkling fire:
He burns with noble zeal to meet the foes,
And all his soul with martial ardor glows. 865

Then to the chief the squire his speech renew'd:
Yet more remains to speak (he thus pursu'd);
For thee the Pagans deeper wiles prepare;
For thee has treason spread its blackest snare!
He said; and to the listening peers explain'd 870
The fatal purpose of th' insidious band;
Fierce Ormond's boast and proud demand disclos'd,
And all the murderous fraud at full expos'd.

Much was he ask'd; and much again reply'd:
Short silence then ensu'd on every side. 875

At

At length the leader, loft in various thought,
From hoary Raymond's wifdom counfel fought.

 Then he: Attend my words—at morning hour,
With forces deep enclofe yon hoftile tower;
And let the troops awhile recruit their might,   880
And rouze their vigour for a greater fight.
Thou, as fhall beft befeem, O chief! prepare,
For open action, or for covert war.
Yet this I moft o'er every care commend,
In every chance thy valu'd life defend: 885
Thou giv'ft fuccefs to crown our favour'd hoft;
And who fhall guide our arms, if thou art loft?
That all the Pagan fraud may ftand confefs'd,
Command thy guard to change their wonted veft:
So fhall the traitors through the field be known,   890
And on their heads their impious treafon thrown.

 O ftill the fame! (the leader thus replies)
Thou fpeak'ft the friend, and all thy words are wife!
Now hear the purpofe in our thoughts decreed:
Againft the foe our battle will we lead;   895
In walls or trenches ne'er fhall bafely reft
A camp triumphant o'er the fpacious eaft!
'Tis ours to meet yon barbarous troops in fight,
And prove our former worth in open light.

          Before

Before our swords shall fly the trembling train: 900
Thus shall we firmly fix our future reign:
The tower shall soon our stronger force obey,
And, unsupported, yield an easy prey.

　　He ceas'd; and to his tent his steps address'd;
For now the sinking stars invite to rest. 905

THE END OF THE NINETEENTH BOOK.

THE

TWENTIETH BOOK

OF

JERUSALEM DELIVERED.

THE ARGUMENT.

The Egyptian army arrives; the generals, on both sides, prepare for the battle. The speeches of Godfrey and Emirenes. The Christians make the onset: Gildippe signalizes herself and engages Altamorus, who had made great havock of the Christians. Ormond is killed by Godfrey, and his associates are all cut to pieces. Rinaldo attacks the Moors and Arabs, and defeats them with great slaughter: He passes by Armida's chariot; her behaviour on that occasion. Solyman, from the tower, takes a prospect of the battle, and, fired with emulation, leaves his fortress: Aladine, and the rest of the Pagans, accompany him. Raymond is felled to the ground by Solyman; but Tancred, hearing the tumult, issues from the place where he lay ill of his wounds, and defends him from the enemy. Aladine is slain by Raymond. The Soldan, having forced his way through the Syrians and Gascons that surrounded the tower, enters the field of battle. The deaths of Edward and Gildippe. Adrastus is killed by Rinaldo, and Solyman falls by the same hand. Emirenes endeavours, in vain, to rally his troops. Tisaphernes performs great actions, till he is slain by Rinaldo. Armida flies from the field; Rinaldo pursues her: The interview between them. Godfrey kills Emirenes, and takes Altamorus prisoner. The Pagans fly on all sides; and Godfrey enters the temple victorious, and pays his devotions at the tomb.

THE TWENTIETH BOOK OF JERUSALEM DELIVERED.

THE sun had rouz'd mankind with early ray,
And up the steep of heaven advanc'd the day:
When from the lofty tower the Pagans 'spy
A dusty whirlwind, that obscur'd the sky,
Like evening's shade: At length, reveal'd to sight, 5
Th' Egyptian host appear'd in open light:
The numerous ranks the spacious champaign fill'd,
Spread o'er the mountains, and the plains conceal'd.
Then sudden, from the troop besieg'd ascends
A general shout, that all the region rends.   10
With such a sound the cranes embody'd fly
From Thracian shores, to seek a warmer sky;
With noise they cut the clouds, and leave behind
The wintry tempest, and the freezing wind.

Now hope, rekindling, fires the Pagan band; 15
Swells every threat, and urges every hand.
This soon the Franks perceiv'd, and instant knew
From whence their foes' recover'd fury grew.
They look'd; and midst the rolling smoke, beheld
The moving legions that o'erspread the field. 20
At once a generous rage each bosom warms;
At once each valiant hero pants for arms:
Around their chief with eager looks they stand,
And loud the signal for the war demand.

But, well advis'd, the prudent chief denies 25
To wage the battle till the morn arise:
He rules their ardor, he controls their might,
And points a fitter season for the fight.
They hear, observant, and his voice obey,
But burn impatient for the dawning ray. 30

At length, high seated on her eastern throne,
The breezy morn with welcome lustre shone;
Wide o'er the skies she shed her ruddy streams,
And glow'd with all the sun's enlivening beams;
While heaven, serene and cloudless, would survey 35
The glorious deeds of that auspicious day.

Ver. 35. *While heaven, serene and cloudless,* —] The history relates, that the morning on which the armies engaged was uncommonly fine.

Soon as the dawn appears, with early care,
His army Godfrey leads in form of war;
But leaves, t' enclose the foes' beleaguer'd tower,
Experienc'd Raymond with the Syrian power, 40
That from the neighbouring lands auxiliar came,
And hail'd with joy their great deliverer's name;
A numerous throng!—nor these alone remain,
To these he adds the hardy Gascon train.

Now tow'rd the leader, with exalted mien, 45
While certain conquest in his eyes was seen,
With more than wonted state he seem'd to tread;
A sudden youth was o'er his features spread:
Celestial favour beam'd in every look,
And every act a more than mortal spoke. 50

Now near advanc'd, the pious hero view'd
Where, deeply throng'd, th' Egyptian squadrons
  stood;
And strait to seize a favouring hill he sends,
Whose height his army's left and rear defends.
His troops he rang'd; the midst the foot contain'd;
In either wing the lighter horse remain'd. 56
The left, that to the friendly hill was join'd,
The chief to either Robert's care consign'd:
The midst his brother held; himself the right,
Where open lay the dangers of the fight: 60

Here mix'd with horse, accuftom'd thus t' engage,
A diftant war on foot the archers wage.
Behind, th' advent'rers to the right he led,
And plac'd the bold Rinaldo at their head.

In thee, intrepid warrior! (Godfrey cries) 65
Our ftrong defence, our hope of conqueft, lies.
Behind the wing awhile remain conceal'd:
But when the foes advance t' invade the field,
Affail their flank, as vainly they contend
To wheel around us, and our rear offend. 70

Then on a rapid fteed, in open view,
From rank to rank, 'twixt horfe and foot, he flew:
From his rais'd helm his piercing looks he caft;
His eyes, his figure, lighten'd as he pafs'd!
The chearful he confirm'd, the doubtful rais'd, 75
And, for their former deeds, the valiant prais'd.
He bade the bold their antient boafts regard;
Some urg'd with honour's, fome with gold's reward.
At length he ftays where thickening round him ftand
The firft, the braveft of the martial band: 80
Then from on high his fpeech each hearer warms,
Swells the big thought, and fires the foul to arms.
As from fteep hills the rufhing torrents flow,
Increas'd with fudden falls of melting fnow:

So

So from his lips, with swift effusion, pours 85
Mellifluous eloquence in copious showers.

O you, the scourge of Jesus' foes profess'd,
O glorious heroes! conquerors of the east!
Behold the day arriv'd, so long desir'd,
The wish'd-for day to which your hopes aspir'd! 90
Some great event th' Almighty sure designs,
Who all his rebels in one force combines:
See! in one field he brings your various foes,
That one great battle all your wars may close.
Despise yon Pagans, an ungovern'd host, 95
Lost in confusion, in their numbers lost!
Our mighty force can troops like these sustain?
A rout undisciplin'd, a straggling train!
From sloth or servile labours brought from far,
Compell'd, reluctant, to the task of war! 100
Their swords now tremble, trembles every shield;
Their fearful standards tremble on the field.
I hear their doubtful sounds, their motions view,
And see death hovering o'er the fated crew.
Yon leader fierce and glorious to behold, 105
In flaming purple and refulgent gold,
Might quell the Moorish and Arabian train,
But here his valour, here his worth is vain;

Wise though he be, what methods shall he prove
To rule his army, or their fears remove?   110
Scarce is he known, and scarce his troops can name,
Nor calls them partners of his former fame:
We every toil and every triumph share,
Fellows in arms, and brothers of the war!
Is there a warrior but your chief can tell   115
His native country, and his birth reveal?
What sword to me unknown? What shaft that flies
With missile death along the liquid skies?
I ask but what I oft have gain'd before:
Be still yourselves, and Godfrey seeks no more. 120
Preserve your zeal! your fame and mine attend:
But, far o'er all, the faith of CHRIST defend!
Go—crush those impious on the fatal plain:
With their defeat your sacred rights maintain.
What should I more?—I see your ardent eyes! 125
Conquest awaits you!—seize the glorious prize,

  He ceas'd; and instant, like a flashing light,
When stars or meteors stream through dusky night,
A sudden splendor on his brow was shed,
And lambent glories play'd around his head: 130
All wondering gaze! and some the sign explain,
The certain omen of his future reign.

Perchance

Perchance (if mortal thoughts so high may soar,
Or dare the secrets of the skies explore)
From heavenly seats his guardian angel flew,   135
And o'er the chief his golden pinions threw.

  While Godfrey thus the Christian host prepares;
Th' Egyptian leader, press'd with equal cares,
Extends his numerous force to meet the foes:
The midst the foot, the wings the horse compose: 140
Himself the right; the midst Mulasses guides:
There, in the central war, Armida rides,
In pomp barbaric near the leader stand
India's stern king, and all the regal band:
There Tisaphernes lifts his haughty head;   145
But where the squadrons to the left were spread,
(A wider space) there Altamorus brings
His Afric Monarchs, and his Persian Kings:
From thence their slings, their arrows they prepare,
And all the missile thunder of the war.   150

  Now Emirenes every rank inspires,
The fearful raises, and the valiant fires:
To those he cry'd—What mean your looks depress'd?
What fear unmanly harbours in your breast?
Our near approach shall daunt yon hostile train,   155
Our shouts alone shall drive them from the plain.

To these—No more delay, ye generous bands!
Redeem the pillage from the spoilers' hands.
In some he 'waken'd every tender thought,
Each lov'd idea to remembrance brought: 160
O! think by me your country begs (he cries)
And thus, adjuring, on your aid relies!
Preserve my laws, preserve each sacred fane,
Nor let my children's blood my temples stain:
Preserve from ruffian force th' affrighted maid; 165
Preserve the tombs and ashes of the dead!
To you! opprefs'd with bending age and woe,
Their silver locks your hoary fathers show:
To you, your wives, your lisping infants sue;
All ask their safety, and their lives from you. 170

He said, and ceas'd; for nearer now was seen
Th' advancing powers, and small the space between.
Now front to front in dreadful pause they stand,
Burn for the fight, and only wait command.
The streaming banners to the wind are spread, 175
The plumage nods on every crested head;
Arms, vests, devices, catch the sunny rays,
And steel and gold with mingled splendor blaze!
Each spacious host on either side appears
A steely wood, a grove of waving spears. 180

They

They bend their bows, in rest their lances take,
They whirl their slings, their ready javelins shake;
Each generous steed to meet the fight aspires,
And seconds, with his own, his master's fires;
He neighs, he foams, he paws the ground beneath, 185
And smoke and flame his swelling nostrils breathe.

Even horror pleas'd in such a glorious sight,
Each beating bosom felt severe delight:
While the shrill trumpets, echoing from afar,
With dreadful transports animate the war. 190
But still the faithful bands superior stood,
More clear their notes, more fair their battle show'd:
Their louder trumpets rouz'd a nobler flame,
And from their arms a brighter lustre came!

The Christians sound the charge; the foes reply;
And the mix'd clangors rattle in the sky: 196
Strait on their knees the Franks the soil adore,
And kiss the hallow'd earth, and Heaven implore.
And now between the troops the space is lost;
With equal ardor joins each adverse host. 200

What hero first, amidst the Christian name,
Gain'd from the faithless bands a wreath of fame?
'Twas thou, Gildippe! whose resistless hand
O'erthrew Hircanes, who in Ormus reign'd:

(Such

(Such glory Heaven on female arms display'd) 205
Deep in his breast the spear a passage made;
Headlong he falls; and, falling, hears the foe
With joyful shouts applaud the forceful blow.
Her javelin broke, her trusty sword she drew,
And pierc'd the Persians, and Zopyrus slew; 210
Cleft where the circling belt his armour bound,
He falls, divided, on the purple ground.
Through fierce Alarcus' throat her weapon hew'd
The double passage of the voice and food;
Then Artaxerxes in the dust she laid, 215
And through Argeus thrust her furious blade.
At Ishmael's arm her rapid steel she guides,
And the close juncture of the hand divides:
The sever'd hand at once the rein forsook;
Above the startled courser hiss'd the stroke; 220
He rear'd aloft, and, seiz'd with sudden fright,
Broke through the ranks, and discompos'd the fight.
All these, and numbers more, her fury feel,
Whose names in silence ages past conceal:
But 'gainst her now the thronging Persians came, 225
And Edward ran t' assist the matchless dame.
With force united then, the faithful pair
Undaunted bore the rushing storm of war.
       Neglectful

Neglectful of themselves amidst the strife,
Each guards, with pious care, the other's life.   230
Her ready shield the warlike damsel spread,
And turn'd the weapons aim'd at Edward's head.
He, o'er his spouse, his fencing buckler throws:
Each seeks for each the vengeance on the foes.
By him the daring Artaban was slain,   235
Who in Boëcan's island held his reign:
By him his instant fate Alvantes found,
Who durst at fair Gildippe aim the wound.
Then Arimontes' brow she cleft in two,
Who, with drawn sword, against her consort flew.   240
While these resistless midst the Persians rag'd;
More dire Samarcand's king the Franks engag'd.
Where-e'er he turn'd his steed, or drove his steel,
The horse and foot before his fury fell:
And those that 'scape the falchion's milder death,   245
Beneath the courser's feet groan out their struggling
 breath!

Ver. 230. *Each guards, with pious care, the other's life.*] The circumstance of a male and female warrior, so tenderly connected with each other, makes a beautiful and affecting picture, and adds variety to the poem: it seems to have been first introduced by Tasso, and has already been observed to have its foundation in history. See note to Book i. ver. 424.

By

By Altamorus on the dreadful plain,
Brunello strong, Ardonio huge, was slain;
Of that the helm and head the sword divides;
The gory visage hangs on equal sides.   250
This pierc'd where laughter first derives its birth,
And the glad heart dilates to pleasing mirth,
(Wondrous and horrid to the gazer's eyes!)
Now laughs constrain'd, and as he laughs he dies!
With these Gentonio, Guasco, Guido dy'd: 255
And good Rosmondo swell'd the crimson tide.
What tongue can tell the throng depriv'd of breath,
The wounds describe, or dwell on every death?

None yet appear'd, of all the warring band,
Who durst sustain his valour hand to hand.   260
Alone Gildippe 'gainst the monarch came;
No fear could damp her generous thirst of fame.
Less bold on fair Thermodoön's winding shore,
Each warlike Amazon her buckler bore,
Or rear'd her axe; than now, with glorious heat, 265
Gildippe rush'd the Persian's rage to meet.
She rais'd her sword, and struck the regal crown
That round his helm with pomp barbaric shone.
The glittering honours from his brows she rent;
Beneath the force the mighty warrior bent.   270

The

The king with shame the powerful arm confess'd,
And swift t' avenge the blow his steel address'd:
Full on her front so fierce the dame he struck,
That sense her mind, and strength her limbs forsook.
Then had she fall'n, but near with ready hand   275
Her faithful lord her sinking weight sustain'd.
No more the lofty foe his stroke pursu'd,
But with disdain an easy conquest view'd:
So the bold lion, with a scornful eye,
Scowls on the prostrate prey, and passes by.   280

 Meantime fierce Ormond, who, with murderous care,
Had spread for Godfrey's life the fatal snare,
Disguis'd, was mingled with the Christian band,
And near their chief his dire associates stand.
So prowling wolves an entrance seek to gain,   285
Like faithful dogs, amongst the woolly train;
They watch the folds when welcome shades arise,
And hide their quivering tails between their thighs.
Th' insidious band advanc'd, and now in view
Near pious Godfrey's side the Pagan drew.   290
Soon as the prince the white and gold survey'd,
(The certain token which their wile betray'd)
Behold the traitor there confess'd (he cries)
Who veils his treason with a Frank's disguise!

At me his followers aim the deadly blow— 295
He said, and rush'd against the treacherous foe:
On Ormond swift th' avenging blade he rais'd;
Th' astonish'd wretch, without resistance, gaz'd:
And, while a sudden terror froze his blood,
With stiffening limbs, a senseless statue stood. 300
Each sword was turn'd against the fraudful crew,
At these the shafts from every quiver flew:
In pieces hewn their bodies strew the plains;
And not a single corse entire remains!

Now, stain'd with slaughter, Godfrey bent his course
To where the valiant Altamorus' force 306
His squadrons pierc'd, that fled with timorous haste,
Like Afric sands before the southern blast.
Loud to his troops th' indignant hero cry'd,
Stay'd those that fled, and him that chac'd defy'd. 310

Between those mighty chiefs a fight ensu'd,
More dire than Ida or Scamander view'd.
Meanwhile betwixt the foot the battle bled;
Those Baldwin rul'd, and these Mulasses led.
Nor less, in other parts, the conflict rag'd, 315
Where next the mountain, horse with horse engag'd.
There Emirenes dealing fate was found;
There fought the two * in fields of death renown'd.

* ADRASTUS and TISAPHERNES.

Two Roberts there the Pagan force defy'd:
With Emirenes one the combat try'd, 320
While conquest yet declar'd on neither side:
But one, with armour pierc'd and helmet hew'd,
In harder conflict with Adrastus stood.
Still Tisaphernes finds no equal foe
To mate his strength, and measure blow for blow;
But rushes where he sees the thickest train, 326
And with a mingled carnage heaps the plain.

  Thus far'd the war; while neither part prevails,
And hope and fear are pois'd in equal scales.
O'erspread with shatter'd arms the ground appears,
With broken bucklers, and with shiver'd spears. 331
Here swords are stuck in hapless warriors kill'd,
And useless there are scatter'd o'er the field.
Here, on their face, the breathless bodies lie;
There turn their ghastly features to the sky! 335
Beside his lord the courser press'd the plain;
Beside his slaughter'd friend the friend is slain;
Foe near to foe; and on the vanquish'd spread
The victor lies; the living on the dead!
An undistinguish'd din is heard around, 340
Mix'd is the murmur, and confus'd the sound:
The threats of anger, and the soldiers' cry,
The groans of those that fall, and those that die.

The splendid arms that shone so gay before,
Now, sudden chang'd, delight the eyes no more. 345
The steel has lost its gleam, the gold its blaze:
No more the vary'd colours blend their rays:
Torn from the crest the sully'd plumes are lost,
And dust and blood deform the pomp of either host!

Now, on the left, with Ethiopia's train, 350
The Moors and Arabs wheel around the plain.
The slingers next, and archers from afar,
Pour'd on the Franks a thick and missile war:
When lo! Rinaldo with his squadron came,
Dire as an earthquake, swift as lightening's flame!
From Meroë, first of Ethiopia's bands, 356
Full in his passage Assimirus stands:
Rinaldo reach'd him, where the sable head
Join'd to the neck, and mix'd him with the dead.
Soon as his sword the taste of blood confess'd, 360
New ardor kindled in the hero's breast.
Through all the throng the dreadful victor storm'd,
And deeds, transcending human faith, perform'd.
As, when th' envenom'd serpent shoots along,
Furious he seems to dart a triple tongue: 365
At once the chief appears three swords to wield,
And hurl a threefold vengeance round the field.

The

The swarthy kings, the Libyan tyrants die;
Drench'd in each other's blood confus'd, they lie.
Fierce with the rest his following friends engage, 30
His great example animates their rage.
Without defence th' astonish'd vulgar fall;
One universal ruin levels all!
'Twas war no more, but carnage thro' the field;
Those lift the sword, and these their bosoms yield.
No longer now the Pagans sink, oppress'd 376
With wounds before, all honest on the breast;
Lost are their ranks, they fly with headlong fear,
And pale confusion trembles in their rear:
Behind, Rinaldo pours along the plain, 380
And breaks and scatters wide the timorous train.
At length his generous arm from slaughter ceas'd,
And 'gainst a flying foe his wrath decreas'd.
So when high hills or tufted woods oppose,
With double force the wind indignant blows; 385
No more oppos'd, no more its rage prevails,
But o'er the lawn it breathes in gentle gales.
So midst the rocks the sea resounding raves,
But, unconfin'd, more calmly rolls its waves.
Next on the foot the warrior bent his force, 390
Where late the Afric and Arabian horse

The squadrons flank'd; but now dispers'd around,
They take their flight, or gasp upon the ground.
Swift on th' unguarded files Rinaldo flew;
As swift behind his brave compeers pursue: 395
Spears, darts, and swords, in vain his might withstand,
Whole legions fall beneath his dreadful hand!
Not with such rage a bursting tempest borne,
Sweeps o'er the field, and mows the golden corn.
The streaming blood in purple torrents swell'd, 400
And arms and mangled limbs the earth conceal'd:
There, uncontrol'd, the foaming coursers tread,
Bound o'er the plain, and trample on the dead!

Now came Rinaldo where, with martial air,
Appear'd Armida in her glittering car.   405
A train of lovers near her person wait,
A glorious guard, the nobles of the state!
She sees! she knows!—conflicting passions rise,
Desire and anger tremble in her eyes.
A transient blush the hero's visage burns;   410
But heat and cold possess her heart by turns.
The knight, declining from the car, withdrew,
Not unregarded by the rival-crew;
Those lift the sword, and these the lance protend;
Ev'n she prepares her threatening bow to bend, 415

She

She fits the shaft, disdain her thoughts impell'd,
But love awhile the purpos'd stroke with-held;
Thrice in her hand the missile reed she tries;
And thrice her faltering hand its strength denies.
At length her wrath prevails, she twangs the string,
And sends the whizzing arrow on the wing: 421
Swift flies the shaft—as swiftly flies her prayer,
That all its fury may be spent in air!
She hopes, she fears, she follows with her eye,
And marks the weapon as it cuts the sky.   425
The weapon, not unfaithful to her aim,
Against the warrior's stubborn corslet came;
Harmless it fell; aside the hero turn'd:
She deem'd her power despis'd, her anger scorn'd:
Again she bent her bow, but fail'd to wound,   430
While love with surer darts her bosom found.

 And is he then impervious to the steel,
And fears he not (she cry'd) the stroke to feel?
Does tenfold adamant his limbs invest,
That adamant which guards his ruthless breast? 435
So well secur'd, that safely he defies
The sword of battle, or the fair one's eyes?
What further arts for wretched me remain?—
Attempt no more—for every art is vain!

X 4

Arm'd

Arm'd or difarm'd an equal fate I know,   440
Alike contemn'd, a lover or a foe!
Where now, alas! is every former boaſt?—
Behold my warriors faint!—my hopes are loſt!
Againſt his valour every ſtrength muſt fail;
Nor courage can withſtand, nor arms avail!   445
  While thus ſhe thought, her champions round ſhe view'd
O'erthrown, or ta'en, or weltering in their blood.
What ſhould ſhe do?—alone, unhelp'd remain?
Already now ſhe dreads the victor's chain:
Nor dares (the bow and javelin at her ſide)   450
In Pallas' or Diana's arms confide.
As when the fearful cygnet ſees on high
The ſtrong-pounc'd eagle ſtooping from the ſky,
Trembling ſhe cowers beneath th' impending fate;
So ſeem'd Armida, ſuch her dangerous ſtate.   455
  But Altamorus, who from ſhameful flight
Still held the Perſians, and maintain'd the fight,
Her peril view'd, and, careleſs of his fame,
His troops forſook, and to her reſcue came.
With rapid ſword he breaks amid the war,   460
And wheels around her, and defends the car;
While dire deſtruction rages through his bands,
O'erthrown by Godfrey and Rinaldo's hands.

This

This sees th' unhappy prince, but sees in vain:
Armida succour'd, now he turns again,   465
But flew too late t' assist his routed train!
There all was lost; a general panic spread;
Dispers'd, around the broken Persians fled.
In other parts the fainting Christians yield;
Two Roberts there in vain direct the field;   470
One scarce escap'd with life; his wounded breast
And bleeding front the hostile steel confess'd;
While fierce Adrastus one his prisoner made:
Thus equal chance the dubious battle sway'd.

But Godfrey now his hardy warriors warm'd, 475
Again to fight his ready bands he form'd;
Then bravely on the victor-forces flew;
They join, they thicken, and the war renew.
Each side appears distain'd with adverse gore;
Each side the glorious signs of triumph bore.   480
Conquest and fame on either part are seen,
And Mars and Fortune doubtful stand between.

While thus the combat rages on the plain
Betwixt the Christian and the Pagan train;
High on the tower the haughty Soldan stood,   485
From whence, intent, the distant strife he view'd;
Struck with the sight, his breast with envy swell'd,
He burn'd to mingle in the fatal field.

All

All arm'd besides, he snatch'd with eager haste,
And on his head his radiant helmet plac'd: 490
Rise! rise! (he said) no longer slothful lie—
Behold the time to conquer or to die!
Then, whether Heaven's high providence inspir'd
His daring purpose, and his fury fir'd,
That thus at once the Pagan reign might end, 495
And all its glories on that day descend:
Or whether, conscious of his death to come,
He felt an impulse now to meet his doom:
Sudden he bade the sounding gates unbar,
And issu'd forth with unexpected war; 500
Nor waits his following band, but singly goes;
Himself alone defies a thousand foes.
But soon the rest his martial rage partook,
Ev'n aged Aladine the fort forsook:
The base, the cautious, catch at once the fires; 505
Nor hope excites them, but despair inspires.
  The first the Turk before his passage found,
His valour tumbled breathless to the ground.
So swift he thunder'd on the faithful train,
That, ere they view th' assault, their friends are slain.
First of the Christians, struck with panic fear, 511
The trembling Syrians for their flight prepare.

But still unrouted stood the Gascon band,
Though nearer these the Soldan's rage sustain'd,
And fell in heaps beneath his slaughtering hand. 515
Not with such wrath the savage beast indu'd,
Leaps o'er the fold, and dies the ground with blood:
Not with such fury, through th' ethereal space,
Voracious vultures rend the feather'd race.
Through plated steel his strength resistless drives, 520
While his keen falchion drinks the warriors' lives!
With Aladine the Pagans quit the tower,
And furious on their late besiegers pour.

But Raymond now advanc'd with fearless haste,
And saw where Solyman his squadron press'd; 525
Nor yet the hoary chief his steps forbore,
Nor shunn'd that arm whose force he felt before.
Again to combat he defies the foe,
Again his front receives a dreadful blow:
Again he falls; in vain declining age, 530
With strength unequal, would such power engage.
Behold a hundred swords and shields display'd;
And these defend the knight, and those invade.
But thence with speed th' impetuous Soldan flies;
(He deems him slain, or deems an easy prize) 535
Descending, o'er the ruin'd works he goes
To distant plains, where fiercer battle glows:

Far

Far other scenes his barbarous rage demands,
Far other deaths must glut his cruel hands!

Meanwhile around the late beleaguer'd tower, 540
New vigour had infpir'd the Pagan power;
The warmth their leader breath'd they ftill retain;
And with the Chriftians ftill their fears remain.
Thofe feek to finifh what their chief began;
And thefe, retreating, feem to quit the plain: 545
In due array the hardy Gafcons yield;
The Syrians wide are fcatter'd o'er the field.
The tumult thickens near where Tancred lies,
He hears the din of arms, the foldiers' cries:
Strait from the couch his wounded limbs he rears, 550
And lo! at once the mingled fcene appears:
He fees on earth th' ill-fated Raymond laid,
Some flowly yield, and fome in flight furvey'd.
That courage true to every noble breaft,
Nor loft by weaknefs, nor by pain fupprefs'd, 555
Now fwell'd the hero's foul; he grafp'd his fhield,
Nor feem'd too faint the ponderous orb to wield;

Ver. 550. —— *from the couch his wounded limbs he rears.*] Taffo feems to have caught this circumftance from an incident in Boyardo, where Sacripant, in like manner, iffues forth, armed only with his fword and fhield, againft Agrican, who had gained an entrance into Albracca.

His right hand held unsheath'd his glittering blade,
Nor other arms he sought, nor more delay'd;
But issuing thus—O! whither would you fly,   560
And leave your lord neglected here to die?
Shall then these Pagans rend his arms away,
And in their fanes suspend the glorious prey?
Go—seek your country—to his son reveal
That, where you fled, his noble father fell!   565

He said; and durst against a thousand foes
His breast, still feeble with his wounds, oppose;
While with his ample shield (a fencing shade,
With seven tough hides and plates of steel o'erlaid)
He kept the hoary Raymond safe from harms,   570
From swords, and darts, and all the missile arms:
He whirls his falchion with resistless sway:
The foes repuls'd forego their wish'd-for prey.
But soon the venerable hero rose,
His face with shame, his heart with anger, glows;   575
In vain he seeks the chief by whom he fell,
Then 'gainst the vulgar turns his vengeful steel.
The Gascons, rally'd, soon the fight renew,
And strait their gallant leader's steps pursue:
Now fears the troop that danger late disdain'd,   580
And courage now succeeds where terror reign'd.

They

They chace that yielded, those that chac'd give way:
So chang'd at once the fortune of the day!
While Raymond rag'd with unresisted hand,
And fought the noblest of the hostile band: 585
The realm's usurper, Aladine, he view'd,
Who midst the thickest press the fight pursu'd;
He saw, and 'gainst him rais'd his fatal steel,
Cleft through the head the dying monarch fell;
Prone on his kingdom's soil resign'd his breath, 590
And groaning bit the bloody dust in death.
Now various passions move the Pagan foes:
Some 'gainst the spear their desperate breasts oppose;
While some, with terror seiz'd, the fight forsake,
And in the fort their second refuge take: 595
But entering, mix'd with these, the victor-train
At once the conquest of the fortress gain.
Now all is won—in vain the Pagans fly;
Within they fall, or at the portal die.
Sage Raymond then ascends the lofty tower, 600
The mighty standard in his hand he bore,
There full in view, to either host display'd,
The Cross triumphant to the winds he spread;
Unseen of Solyman, who thence afar,
Impatient flew to mingle in the war: 605

And

And now he reach'd the fatal fanguine field,
Where more and more the purple torrent fwell'd.
There death appear'd to hold his horrid reign,
There raife his trophies on the dreadful plain.
The Soldan feiz'd a fteed, the combat fought, 610
And fudden to the fainting Pagans brought
A fhort but glorious aid—So lightening flies,
And unexpected falls, and inftant dies;
But leaves in rifted rocks, with furious force,
The tokens of its momentary courfe. 615
A hundred warriors, great in arms, he flew;
Yet from oblivion fame has fnatch'd but two.
O Edward and Gildippe! faithful pair!
Your haplefs fate, your matchlefs deeds in war,
(If equal praife my Tufcan mufe can give) 620
Confign'd to diftant times fhall ever live!
Some pitying lover, when the tale he hears,
Shall grace your fortune and my verfe with tears.

Th' intrepid heroine fpurr'd her fteed, and flew
To where the raging Turk the troops o'erthrew: 625
Two mighty ftrokes her valiant arm impeil'd,
One reach'd his fide, one pierc'd his plated fhield:
The furious chief her well-known veft defcry'd:
Behold the ftrumpet with her mate (he cry'd)

Hence

Hence to thy female tasks! the distaff wield, 630
Nor dare with spear and sword to brave the field.

 He said, and dreadful as the words he spoke,
His thundering weapon through her corslet broke:
Deep in her breast the ruthless falchion drove,
Her gentle breast, the seat of truth and love! 635
Her languid hand foregoes the useless rein;
Approaching death creeps cold in every vein.
To save his wife, unhappy Edward flies!
Too late he comes—his lov'd Gildippe dies!
What should he do?—distracting thoughts prevail,
Pity and wrath at once his heart assail: 641
That, bids his arm a kind support bestow,
This, prompts his vengeance on the barbarous foe.
While with his left he seeks to hold the fair,
His better hand provokes th' unequal war: 645
But vain his effort to support his bride,
Or reach the murderous chief by whom she dy'd.
The sword the Pagan through his arm impell'd,
That with a fruitless grasp his consort held.
As when an axe the stately elm invades, 650
Or storms uproot it from its native shades,
It falls—and with it falls the mantling vine,
Whose curling folds its ample waist entwine:

            So

So Edward funk beneath the Pagan steel;
So, with her Edward, fair Gildippe fell.   655
They strive to speak, their words are lost in sighs,
And on their lips th' imperfect accent dies.
Each other still with mournful looks they view,
And, close embracing, take the last adieu:
Till, losing both the cheerful beams of light,   660
Their gentle souls together take their flight!

    Soon spreading fame the dire event declares,
And soon the tidings to Rinaldo bears:
Compassion, grief, and wrath at once conspire,
And all his generous thoughts to vengeance fire: 665
But first Adrastus, in the Soldan's sight,
His passage cross'd, and dar'd him to the fight.

    Then thus the king—By every sign display'd,
Thou sure art he for whom my search is made.
Each buckler have I long explor'd in vain,   670
And oft have call'd thee through th' embattled plain.
Now shall my former vows be fully paid,
And justice sated with thy forfeit head:
Come!—let us here our mutual valour show,
Armida's champion I, and thou her foe!   675

    Boastful he spoke; then whirl'd his flashing steel;
Swift on the Christian's head the tempest fell:

In vain—the temper'd cafque the force withftood;
But oft the warrior in the faddle bow'd:
Rinaldo's falchion then Adraftus found, 680
And in his fide imprefs'd a mortal wound:
Prone falls the giant-king, no more a name!
One fatal blow concludes his life and fame!

With horror feiz'd, the gazing Pagans ftood,
While fear and wonder froze their curdling blood.
Ev'n Solyman furpris'd the ftroke beheld, 686
His alter'd looks his troubled thoughts reveal'd:
He fees his doom, and (wondrous to relate!)
Sufpended ftands to meet approaching fate.
But Heaven's high will, for ever uncontrol'd, 690
Unnerves the mighty, and confounds the bold!
As oft the fick in dreams attempt to fly,
What time the fainting limbs their fpeed deny;
In vain their lips a vocal found effay,
Nor cries nor voice can find their wonted way. 695
So ftrove the Soldan now th' affault to dare,
He rouz'd his foul to meet the threaten'd war;
In vain—no more the thirft of fame prevail'd;
His fpirits droop'd, his wonted vigour fail'd;
He fcorn'd to yield or fly: yet, unrefolv'd, 700
A thoufand thoughts his wavering mind revolv'd.

While

While thus he paus'd, the conquering chief drew
    nigh,
Furious he rush'd, tremendous to the eye!
He seem'd to move with more than mortal course,
And look'd a match for more than mortal force. 705
The Pagan scarce resists, yet even in death
Preserves his fame, and nobly yields his breath;
Nor shuns the sword, but, midst his ruin great,
Without a groan receives the stroke of fate!
Thus he, who, when subdu'd by stronger foes, 710
From every fall like old Antæus rose
With force renew'd, now reach'd his destin'd hour,
And press'd at length the earth, to rise no more.

Then fame from man to man the tidings bears;
A doubtful face no longer fortune wears; 715
No longer then the war's event suspends,
But joins the Christians, and their arms befriends.
Soon from the fight recede the regal band,
The pride, the strength, of all the eastern land;
Once call'd Immortal; now the name is lost, 720
And ruin triumphs o'er an empty boast!
Th' astonish'd bearer with the standard fled,
Him Emirenes stopp'd, and sternly said.

Art thou not he, selected from the train,
Our monarch's glorious banner to sustain? 725

Was it for this (O! scandal to the brave!)
That to thy hand th' important charge I gave?
And canst thou, Rimedon, thy chief survey,
Yet basely leave him, and desert the day?
What dost thou seek?—thy safety?—here it lies— 730
With me return—death waits for him who flies.
Here let him bravely fight who hopes to live;
Here honour's deeds alone can safety give.

He heard, and instant to the field return'd;
Disdain and shame his conscious bosom burn'd. 735
No less the rest th' intrepid chief retain'd,
These urg'd by threats, and those by force constrain'd.
Who dares to fly from yonder swords, (he cries)
Who dares to tremble, by this weapon dies!
Thus rang'd again his routed files he view'd, 740
The war rekindled, and his hopes renew'd:
While Tisaphernes with resistless might
Maintain'd the combat, and forbade the flight.
Brave deeds that day renown'd the warrior's hand;
His single force dispers'd the Norman band: 745
By him were chac'd the Flemings from the plain,
And Gernier, Gerrard, and Rogero slain.
When acts like these had grac'd his last of days,
And crown'd his short but glorious life with praise;

As

As carelefs what fucceeding fate might yield, 750
He fought the greateft perils of the field;
He faw Rinaldo, well the youth he knew,
Though all his arms were dy'd to fanguine hue.
Lo! there the terror of the plain (he cries)
May Heaven affift my daring enterprize! 755
So fhall Armida her revenge obtain:
O! Macon! let my fword this conqueft gain,
And his proud arms fhall hang devoted in thy fane.

Thus pray'd the knight; his words are loft in air,
No Macon hears his unavailing prayer. 760
As the bold lion, eager to engage,
With lafhing tail provokes his native rage:
So fares the furious warrior; love infpires,
Swells all his foul, and roufes all his fires.
He bears aloft his fhield; he fpurs his fteed; 765
The Latian hero rufh'd with equal fpeed.
At once they meet; at once, on either hand,
In deep fufpenfe the gazing armies ftand.
Such fkill, fuch courage, either champion fhows,
So fwift their weapons, and fo fierce their blows; 770
Each fide awhile forget their wonted rage,
And drop their arms, to fee the chiefs engage.
In vain the Pagan ftrikes; fecur'd from harms,
The Chriftian combats in ethereal arms;

From him more fatal every stroke descends; 775
The foe from wounds no temper'd steel defends;
His shield is rent away, his helm is hew'd,
And the plain blushes with a stream of blood.
  The fair enchantress, who the fight survey'd,
Beheld how fast her champion's strength decay'd. 780
She saw the rest, a pale and heartless train,
That scarce from flight their trembling feet restrain;
Till she, who late such guards around her view'd,
Alone, forsaken, in her chariot stood:
She loaths the light, and servitude she fears, 785
Of conquest or revenge alike despairs.
Then, leaping from her car in pale affright,
She mounts a steed, and takes her speedy flight.
But, like two hounds that snuff the tainted dew,
Anger and love her parting steps pursue. 790
When Cleopatra, by her fears betray'd,
Of old from Actium's fatal conflict fled;
And left, to Cæsar's happier arms expos'd,
Her * Roman lord with perils round enclos'd;
He soon, forgetful of his former fame, 795
Spread every sail to join the flying dame:
So Tisaphernes (but his foe withstood)
Had from the field Armida's flight pursu'd:

        * MARK ANTHONY.

His fair-one vanish'd from his longing eyes,
The sun seem'd blotted from the cheerful skies: 800
Fierce at Rinaldo then, in wild despair,
He rais'd aloft his vengeful blade in air.
Not with such weight, to frame the forky brand,
The ponderous hammer falls from Brontes' hand.
Full on his front the thundering stroke he sent: 805
Beneath the force the staggering warrior bent;
But soon recovering, whirl'd his beaming sword:
The thirsty point the Pagan's bosom gor'd;
A furious passage through his cuirass made,
Till at his back appear'd the reeking blade: 810
The steel, drawn forth, a double vent supply'd;
The soul came floating in a purple tide.

Rinaldo, pausing, cast around his view,
To mark what friends to aid, what foes pursue.
Wide o'er the field he sees the Pagans fly; 815
On earth their broken arms and ensigns lie.
And now his thoughts recall th' unhappy fair,
Who furious fled abandon'd to despair;
Her woeful state might well his pity claim,
Her love neglected, and her ruin'd fame! 820
For still in mind his tender faith he bore,
Her champion plighted when he left her shore.

Then, where her rapid courser's track he view'd,
Th' impatient knight the flying dame pursu'd.
   Meanwhile Armida chanc'd a vale to find   825
That seem'd for dire despair and death design'd:
Well-pleas'd herself she saw by fate convey'd
To end her woes in such a grateful shade.
There, 'lighting from her steed, she laid aside
Her bow, her quiver, all her martial pride.   830
Unfaithful arms! (she cries) essay'd in vain,
Return'd unbath'd from such a sanguine plain;
Here bury'd lie, and prove the field no more,
Since you so ill aveng'd the wrongs I bore.
If vainly thus at other hearts you fly,   835
Dare you a female's wretched bosom try?
Here—enter mine, that naked meets the blow;
Here raise your trophies, here your triumph show!
Love knows how well this breast admits the dart,
Love, that so deep has pierc'd my tender heart! 840
Unblest Armida! what is now thy fate,
When this alone can cure thy wretched state?
The weapon's point must heal the wound of Love,
And friendly Death my heart's physician prove.
Fond Love, farewel!—but come, thou fell Disdain!
For ever partner with my ghost remain;   846
                             Together

Together let us rife from realms below,
To haunt th' ungrateful author of my woe;
To bring dire vifions to his fearful fight,
And fill with horror every fleeplefs night!   850
  She ceas'd; and, fix'd her mournful life to clofe,
The fharpeft arrow from her quiver chofe;
When lo! Rinaldo came and faw the fair
So near the dreadful period of defpair:
Already now her frantic hand fhe rear'd,   855
And death already in her looks appear'd:
He rufh'd behind her, and reftrain'd the dart;
The fatal point juft bent againft her heart.

  Armida turn'd, and ftrait the knight beheld,
(Unheard he came, and fudden ftood reveal'd)   860
Surpris'd fhe fees, and, fhrieking with affright,
From his lov'd face averts her angry fight;
She faints! fhe finks!—as falls a tender flower,
Whofe feeble ftem fupports the head no more:
His arms he threw around her lovely waift,   865
Her weight fupported, and her zone unbrac'd;
While, gently bending o'er the fair diftrefs'd,
His forrows bath'd her face and lovely breaft.
As, wet with pearly drops of morning dews,
The drooping rofe her wonted grace renews: 870
                                             So

So she, recovering soon, her visage rears,
All moist and trickling with her lover's tears.
And thrice she rais'd her eyes the youth to view,
Thrice from his face her sight averse withdrew.
Oft from the strict embrace in vain she strove,   875
With languid hand, his stronger arm to move;
The pitying warrior still his grasp retain'd,
And closer to his breast the damsel strain'd.
At length, as thus in dear restraint she lay,
Her words with gushing torrents found their way:
Yet still on earth she bent her steadfast look,   881
Nor dar'd to meet his glance, while thus she spoke.
O cruel! when thou left'st me first to mourn!
And O! as cruel now in thy return!
Why wouldst thou then thy fruitless cares employ
To save a life thy perjuries destroy?   886
Say, to what future wrongs, what future shame,
What woes unknown is doom'd Armida's name?
Full well thy wily purpose I descry—
But she can little dare, who dares not die.   890
One triumph still to grace thy pomp remains;
A hapless princess bound in captive chains;
At first betray'd, then made by force thy prize;
From acts like these thy mighty glories rise!

Once

Once life and happiness 'twas thine to give; 895
Now death alone my sufferings can relieve!
But not from thee this blessing I demand;
All gifts are hateful from Rinaldo's hand!
Yet, cruel as thou art, myself can find
Some friendly way t' elude the ills design'd: 900
If to a helpless wretch in bondage ty'd,
Are poisonous drugs and piercing steel deny'd;
Yet (thanks to Heaven!) a path remains to death;
Thou shalt not long detain this hated breath:
Cease then thy soothing arts, thy feints give o'er, 905
And move my soul with flattering hopes no more.

 Thus mournful she; while love and anger drew
Fast from her beauteous eyes the briny dew.
He, touch'd with pity, melts with equal woe,
And, mix'd with hers, his kindly sorrows flow. 910
At length with tender words he thus reply'd;
Armida! lay thy doubts, thy fears, aside:
Live—not to suffer shame, to empire live;
In me thy champion, not thy foe, receive.
Behold these eyes, if still thou doubt'st my zeal, 915
Let these, the truth of what I speak, reveal.
I swear to place thee on thy regal throne,
The seat of splendor where thy fathers shone.
         O! would

O! would to Heaven! the rays of truth as well
Might from thy mind the Pagan mist dispel,   920
As I shall raise thee to so high a state,
No eastern dame shall match thy glorious fate.

He spoke; and, speaking, sought her breast to move
With sighs and tears, the eloquence of love!
Till, like the melting flakes of mountain snow,   925
Where shines the sun, or tepid breezes blow;
Her anger, late so fierce, dissolves away,
And gentle passions bear a milder sway.

Ah me! I yield! (the soften'd fair replies)
Still on thy faith my easy heart relies!   930
'Tis thine at will to guide my future way,
And, what thou bid'st, Armida must obey!

Thus they. Meanwhile th' Egyptian chief beheld
His regal standard cast upon the field;
And Rimedon all breathless press the plain,   935
By one fierce stroke from mighty Godfrey slain.
Or kill'd, or routed, all his troops appear,
Yet, to the last, he scorns ignoble fear;
And seeks, what now his hopes alone demand,
A death illustrious from a noble hand.   940

He spurs his steed, and swift on Godfrey flies;
No greater foe amid the plain he spies:

Fierce

Fierce as he thunders through the ranks of war,
He shows the last brave tokens of despair:
Then to the chief he rais'd his voice on high: 945
I come by thee in glorious strife to die!
'Tis death I seek—but, ere I yield to fate,
I trust to crush thee with my sinking weight!

  Thus he. At once they rush to meet the fight:
At once, on either side, their swords alight. 950
The Pagan's steel the Christian's buckler cleaves;
His hand, disarm'd, the sudden wound receives.
From Godfrey next descends a mightier blow
Full on the cheek of his unwary foe:
Half back he fell: and, while to rise he strove, 955
Deep in his groin the Frank his falchion drove.

  Now, Emirenes dead, but few remain
Of all the numbers of th' Egyptian train:
While Godfrey these from place to place pursu'd,
Brave Altamorus on the field he view'd, 960
Who midst his foes th' unequal fight maintain'd,
Alone, on foot, with hostile blood distain'd;
With broken sword and shield the king appears,
And close surrounded with a hundred spears.

  Then to his warriors pious Godfrey cry'd: 965
Forbear, my friends! and lay your arms aside:

And thou, O chief! no more conteſt the field;
Forego thy weapons, and to Godfrey yield.

 He ſaid; and he, who till that fatal hour
Ne'er bow'd his lofty ſoul to human power,   970
Soon as the great, the glorious name he heard,
(A ſound from Libya to the pole rever'd)
At once reſign'd his ſword to Godfrey's hands:
I yield! (he cry'd) nor leſs thy worth demands.
Thy triumph gain'd o'er Altamorus' name,   975
Is crown'd no leſs with riches than with fame.
My kingdom with its gold, my pious wife
With jewels, ſhall redeem my forfeit life.

 Heaven has not given me (thus the chief replies)
A mind to covet gold, or jewels prize: 980
Still keep whate'er is thine from India's ſhore,
And ſtill in peace enjoy thy Perſian ſtore:
No price for life, no ranſom I demand;
I war, but traffick not, in Aſia's land.   984

 He ceas'd; and with his guards the monarch plac'd,
Then from the field the ſcatter'd remnants chac'd;
Theſe to the trench in vain their flight purſue;
Inſatiate death o'ertakes the trembling crew;
Gigantic ſlaughter ſtalks on every ſide,
And ſwells from tent to tent the dreadful tide: 990

         Helms,

Helms, crests, and radiant shields are purpled o'er,
And costly trappings drop with human gore!

   Thus conquer'd Godfrey; and as yet the day
Gave from the western waves the parting ray,
Swift to the walls the glorious victor rode,   995
The domes where CHRIST had made his blest abode:
In sanguine vest, with all his princely train,
The chief of chiefs then sought the sacred fane;
There o'er the hallow'd tomb his arms display'd,
And there to Heaven his vow'd devotions paid. 1000

THE END OF THE TWENTIETH AND LAST BOOK.

INDEX.

The Letters denote the Book, the Figures the Verse.

A

ABYLA xv. 164
Achilles, in the review i. 416
—— killed by *Clorinda* ix. 538
Ademar, in the review i. 297
—— in the procession xi. 38
—— killed by *Clorinda* ib. 306
—— is seen by *Godfrey* at the storming of *Jerusalem* xviii. 648
Adrastus, King of *India*, in the review xvii. 199
—— his contention with *Tisaphernes* concerning *Armida* xvii. 342
—— his station in the *Egyptian* army xx. 143
—— takes one of the *Roberts* prisoner ib. 470
—— challenges *Rinaldo* ib. 666
—— is killed by him ib. 680
Adrastus (a *Christian*) endeavours to scale the walls of *Jerusalem* xi. 237
—— is knocked down by a stone from *Argantes* ib. 243
Egyptian Empire, its rise and extent (see *Caliph*) xvii. 23

Egyptian fleet and army xv. 75
—— army passes in review before the Caliph xvii. 89
—— the different nations and leaders characterised xvii. 93—233
—— the army appears in sight of *Jerusalem* xx. 1
—— their order of battle ib. 137
—— the *Egyptian* army totally defeated 350—403, 462, 714, & seq.
Agricalies and *Malosses* killed by *Argillan* ix. 610
Aladine, King of *Jerusalem*, his character i. 621
—— fortifies the city at the approach of the *Christians* ib. 675
—— removes the image of the Virgin *Mary* from the *Christian* temple to the Mosque ii. 47
—— resolves upon a general massacre of the *Christians* in *Jerusalem* ib. 77
—— condemns *Olindo* and *Sophronia* to be burned ib. 235

Z *Aladine*

INDEX.

Aladine welcomes *Clorinda* to the city, and at her intercession pardons them *ib.* 357
—— takes a view of the armies from the walls, and hears the characters of the *Christian* commanders from *Erminia*
   iii. 129, 284, 443
—— endeavours to dissuade *Argantes* from a single combat with the *Christians*
   vi. 65
—— gives consent to his sending a challenge to the *Christians*   *ib.* 105
—— receives intelligence of *Solyman's* design to attack the *Christian* camp
   ix. 105
—— issues from the city with troops to assist the main army   *ib.* 725
—— commands a retreat to be sounded   *ib.* 730
—— in debate with his counsellors   x. 237
—— his speech to them *ib.* 245
—— welcomes the Soldan, and pays him great honour
   ib. 376
—— his vigilance in defence of the city   xi. 178, 199
—— hears the offer of *Argantes* and *Clorinda* of their nocturnal expedition
   xii 65
—— his speech on the occasion
   ib. 75
—— dissuades the Soldan from accompanying them
   ib. 99
—— stands at the gate ready to receive them at their return   *ib.* 66
—— hears from *Ismeno* the account of his placing the Demons to guard the wood, and of the drought that threatened the *Christians*   xiii. 85
Aladine, letter to him from the *Egyptian* commander intercepted by *Godfrey*
   xviii. 328
—— arms himself, and takes his post against *Raymond* at the attack of the city
   ib. 456
—— retires from the walls
   ib. 712
—— fortifies himself with *Solyman* in *David's* tower
   xix. 260
—— issues from thence and attacks the *Christians* that besieged it   xx. 503
—— is killed by *Raymond*
   ib. 584
Alarcon, in the review xvii. 130
Alarcus, in the review xvii. 211
—— killed by *Clorinda* xx. 213
Albazar kills *Ernestus* ix. 318
Albiazar, in the review xvii. 158
Albine killed by *Clorinda* ix. 529
Alcander wounded by *Clorinda*
   iii. 208
—— sees *Erminia*, in *Clorinda's* armour, by night, approaching the *Christian* camp   vi. 762
—— sends a message to *Godfrey*
   ib. 794
Alcastus, in the review   i. 473
—— his character   xiii. 172
—— attempts the enchanted wood   xiii. 179
—— put to flight by the Demons   *ib.* 203
Aldiazelles killed by *Argillan*
   ix. 611
Aldine, in the review xvii. 157
Alecto,

INDEX.

Alecto, a Fury, in a vision, excites *Argillan* to raise a mutiny in the camp viii. 430
—— assumes the shape of *Araspes*, and encourages *Solyman* to assault the *Christian* camp by night ix. 1, 17
—— gives *Aladine* notice of the Soldan's design ix. 105
Aletbes, embassador from *Egypt*, his character ii. 142
—— his artful speech to *Godfrey*, to persuade him to give over his design against *Jerusalem* ib. 472, 599
—— receives a present from *Godfrey*, and is dismissed with a refusal ib. 699
Alexandria xv. 113
Algazelles killed by *Argillan* ix. 601
Algazor killed by *Dudon* iii. 335
Algiers xv. 151
Aliprando finds *Rinaldo's* armour, and brings it to the camp viii. 333
—— relates the circumstances to *Godfrey* ib. 370—409
Almanzor killed by *Dudon* iii. 332
Altamorus, King of *Samarcand*, in the review xvii. 185
—— his character ib. 193
—— in *Armida's* tent, enamoured of her xix. 466
—— his station in the *Egyptian* army xx. 146
—— makes great slaughter of the *Franks* ib. 241
—— kills *Brunello*, *Ardonio*, *Gentonio*, *Guasco*, *Guido*, and *Rosmondo* ib. 247
—— strikes down *Gildippe* ib. 271

Altamorus defends *Armida* ib. 456
—— sees his troops routed ib. 462
—— fights on foot surrounded by the enemy ib. 960
—— surrenders himself to *Godfrey* ib. 969
Alvantes killed by *Edward* ib. 237
Alzerbè xv. 131
Amurath killed by *Dudon* iii. 330
ANGELS, the figure and descent of one described i. 99
—— guardian Angel sent to protect *Raymond* in his combat with *Argantes* vii. 578
—— guardian Angel seen by *Godfrey's* side, during the insurrection in the camp vii. 624
—— Angels invoked by the *Christians* to their assistance xi. 51
—— an Angel heals *Godfrey's* wound ib. 494
—— Angels are seen by *Godfrey* to fight on his side, in the storming of *Jerusalem* xviii. 654
(See *Gabriel*, *Michael*, *Demons*, &c.)
Antioch i. 41
—— governed by *Bœmond* ib. 69
APPARITIONS.
Apparition raised by *Alecto*, before *Argillan* viii. 432
—— seen in the night when *Solyman* attacks the *Christian* camp x. 118
—— commands *Arsetes* to baptize *Clorinda* xii. 272
—— foretells *Clorinda's* death ib. 296

Z 2 Apparition

INDEX.

Apparition of *Clorinda* to *Tancred* in a dream.
   ib. 677
Apparitions guard the enchanted wood   xiii. 195
Apparition of *Hugo* to *Godfrey* in a dream   xiv. 31
(See *Enchanted Wood, Angels,* and *Demons.*)
Aquiline, Raymond's horse, engendered by the wind
   vii. 555
Arabians attack *Sweno's* camp by night   viii. 112
—— attack *Godfrey's* camp
   ix. 161
Aradine, in the review, commands *Armida's* troops
   xvii. 250
Aramantes (one of *Latinus's* sons) with his father and brothers, attacks *Solyman*
   ix. 233
—— is killed by him *ib.* 249
Araspes, in the review xvii. 103
Ardelius, killed by *Clorinda*
   iii. 264
Ardonio, killed by *Altamorus*
   xx. 247
—— his remarkable death
   ib. 251
Argantes comes embassador from *Egypt* with *Alethes*
   ii. 436
—— his character *ib.* 450
—— his speech to *Godfrey*
   ib 665
—— declares war in the name of the King of *Egypt*
   ib. 681
—— receives a present from *Godfrey* *ib.* 701
—— parts from *Alethes,* and repairs to *Jerusalem*
   ib. 711
—— sallies from the town, and engages the *Christians*
   iii. 254
Argantes is thrown from his horse by *Rinaldo* *ib.* 318
—— with *Clorinda,* supports the *Pagans* in their retreat   *ib.* 326
—— kills *Dudon* *ib.* 344
—— his insulting speech over him   *ib.* 357
—— is obliged to retreat with the *Pagans* into the town
   ib. 368
—— his speech to *Aladine,* to induce him to decide the war by a single combat
   vi. 17
—— his reply to *Aladine* vi. 93
—— sends a boasting challenge to the *Christians* vi. 109
—— issues from the walls *ib.* 168
—— fights with *Otho* *ib.* 235
—— overcomes him *ib.* 262
—— fights with *Tancred ib.* 289
—— they are parted by the heralds   *ib.* 364
—— the combat deferred to the sixth day following
   ib. 393
—— his impatience for the battle   vii. 363
—— arms himself on the appointed day, and sends a fresh challenge to the *Christians* *ib.* 371
—— defies the whole *Christian* army   *ib.* 537
—— meets and fights with *Raymond* in *Tancred's* stead
   ib. 612
—— is saved by the interposition of *Beelzebub ib.* 719
—— the armies being engaged afresh, he wounds *Guido,* kills *Ormano,* and fells *Rogero*   *ib.* 780

Argantes

INDEX.

Argantes forced to give way to the *Christians* vii. 808
—— a storm being raised by Demons, in favour of the *Pagans*, he falls again upon the *Christians*, and compels them to quit the field *ib.* 858
—— kills *Ridolphus* *ib.* 866
—— issues from the town with *Clorinda*, to assist the Arab ix. 335
—— kills numbers *ib.* 415, 517
—— leaves the field with reluctance at *Aladine's* entreaty ix. 731
—— his speech to *Aladine* in council x. 257
—— defends the city xi. 188
—— knocks down *Adrastus* *ib.* 240
—— keeps off the *Christian* tower from the walls *ib.* 343
—— defends the breach with *Solyman* *ib.* 428
—— sallies on the *Christians* with *Solyman* *ib.* 437
—— at the appearance of *Tancred*, retires again to the breach *ib.* 456
—— is encountered by *Godfrey* *ib.* 534
—— kills *Sigero* *ib.* 550
—— engages with *Clorinda* to burn the *Christian* tower by night xii. 45
—— goes out with *Clorinda*, breaks through the guard, and sets fire to it *ib.* 330
—— returns to the city *ib.* 366
—— vows revenge on *Tancred* for the death of *Clorinda* *ib.* 757
—— takes his post against *Camillus*, at the attack of the town xviii. 461

Argantes is forced to retire before *Tancred* *ib.* 696
—— his intrepid behaviour on the walls xix. 1
—— reproaches *Tancred* with his breach of faith *ib.* 13
—— retires from the walls to fight with him *ib.* 41
—— their combat described *ib.* 69
—— haughtily rejects the offers made by *Tancred* *ib.* 137
—— is killed by him *ib.* 176
—— his behaviour in his last moments *ib.* 178

Argeus killed by *Gildippe* xx. 216

Argillan, his character viii. 418
—— is excited by *Alecto*, in a dream, to raise a mutiny *ib.* 430
—— his speech to the *Italians*, to urge them to revolt *ib.* 461
—— is imprisoned by *Godfrey* *ib.* 606
—— escapes from prison, and signalizes himself in battle against the *Pagans* ix. 569
—— kills *Algazelles*, *Saladine*, *Agricaltes*, *Mulasses*, *Aldiazelles*, and *Ariadenus* *ib.* 601
—— kills *Lesbinus*, the Soldan's page *ib.* 642
—— is killed by *Solyman* *ib.* 677

Ariadenus kills *Gilbert* and *Philip* *ib.* 316
—— is killed by *Argillan* *ib.* 613
—— as he dies, foretels *Argillan's* death *ib.* 616

Z. 3 *Arida-*

INDEX.

Aridamantes, in the review xvii. 222
Arideus and *Pindorus*, heralds, part *Tancred* and *Argantes* vi. 368
Arimon (a *Christian*) killed by *Clorinda* xii, 376
Arimon (a *Pagan*) in the review xvii. 219
Arimontes, killed by *Gildippe* xx. 239
Armida, her character iv. 181
—— is sent by *Hidraotes* to employ her arts among the *Christian* commanders iv. 185
—— arrives at the camp ib. 221
—— description of her beauty ib. 249—258
—— meets with *Eustatius* ib. 265
—— is conducted by him to *Godfrey's* tent ib. 297
—— begs *Godfrey's* assistance to restore her to her throne ib. 305
—— tells him a long story of her pretended misfortunes ib. 335—470
—— her speech upon his refusing her assistance ib. 516
—— appears inconsolable ib. 542
—— the effects of her grief on the leaders ib. 554
—— obtains her suit by the intercession of *Eustatius* ib. 600
—— her artifices in the *Christian* camp, by which she enflames the commanders 628 *to the end* v. 505
—— endeavours in vain to ensnare *Godfrey* and *Tancred* v. 447

Armida demands the succours promised v. 485
—— ten champions are chosen by lot, and she departs with them from the camp ib. 563
—— is followed by many others ib. 569
—— puts a stop to the contentions between *Eustatius* and *Rambaldo* ib. 596
—— her castle vii. 206
—— sees the combat between *Tancred* and *Rambaldo* ib. 270
—— saves *Rambaldo* by a thick darkness ib. 325
—— takes *Tancred* prisoner ib. 333
—— conveys the Knights, who accompanied her, into her castle x. 436
—— prepares a banquet for them ib. 459
—— turns them into fishes ib. 471
—— restores them to their shape ib. 487
—— threatens them with her vengeance, unless they join their arms to the *Pagans* ib. 491
—— keeps the rest prisoners ib. 504
—— sends them to be presented to the King of *Egypt*, and they are released in the way by *Rinaldo* ib. 509
—— her vexation at the news xiv. 379
—— puts *Rinaldo's* armour on a dead body, to make the *Christians* believe he is killed ib. 389
—— entices *Rinaldo* into an island ib. 421

Armida

INDEX.

Armida lulls him to sleep by her
enchantments *ib.* 479
──── is enamoured of him
ib. 485
──── carries him in her chariot
to a remote part of the
world *ib.* 499
──── her island described
xv. 337
──── the wild beasts and monsters that guard the ascent to her palace
ib. 359—392
──── the summit of the mountain described *ib.* 398
──── her palace and gardens
xvi. 1—120
──── her wanton dalliance with
Rinaldo ib. 121—174
──── her cestus *ib.* 175
──── her grief for *Rinaldo's*
flight *ib.* 251
──── pursues and overtakes him
ib. 273
──── her speech to prevail on
him to suffer her to accompany him *ib.* 313
──── her rage at his refusal,
and her furious answer
ib. 399
──── falls into a swoon *ib.* 425
──── on recovering her senses,
finds him gone, and resolves on revenge *ib.* 445
──── destroys her palace *ib.* 486
──── returns to her castle
ib. 508
──── departs from thence to join
the *Egyptian* army
ib. 538
──── arrives at *Gaza* xvii. 61
──── passes in review before
the Caliph *ib.* 234
──── her person, arms, and chariot described *ib.* 236
──── her speech to the Caliph,
in which she offers herself and kingdom to any
that shall revenge her on
Rinaldo ib. 308
Armida with her lovers in the
Egyptian camp xix. 452
──── her discourse with *Adrastus* and *Tisaphernes*
ib. 474
──── composes the quarrel between them *ib.* 502
──── her station in the *Egyptian*
army xx. 142
──── described in her chariot
surrounded by her lovers
ib. 404
──── sees *Rinaldo* pass by her in
the battle xx. 408
──── lets fly an arrow at him
ib. 415
──── her soliloquy on the occasion *ib.* 432
──── is defended by *Altamorus*
ib. 456
──── flies from the field *ib.* 779
──── her despair *ib.* 825
──── attempts to kill herself
ib. 851
──── is prevented by *Rinaldo*
ib. 857
──── her behaviour at the sight
of him *ib.* 859
──── her speech to him *ib.* 883
──── her resentment is softened,
and she submits herself
to his disposal *ib.* 923
Arnaldo urges *Godfrey* to proceed
against *Rinaldo,* for the
death of *Gernando*
v. 238
Aronteus, in the review xvii. 107
Arsetes, Clorinda's eunuch, endeavours to dissuade her
from her design to burn
the *Christian* tower
xii. 139

Z 4 *Arsetes*

INDEX.

Arsetes relates to her the story of her birth *ib.* 159—304
—— his grief for her death *ib.* 750
Artaban, king of *Boecan*, in the review xvii. 181
—— killed by *Edward* xx. 235
Artaxerxes struck down by *Gildippe* *ib.* 215
Artemidorus, earl of *Pembroke*, one of the champions drawn by lot to accompany *Armida* v. 527
(See *Champions*)
Ascalon, xiv. 235. xv. 69
Assimirus, in the review xvii. 172
—— killed by *Rinaldo* xx. 356
Astagoras, a Fury, urges *Alecto* to raise commotions in the *Christian* camp viii. 7

B.

Baldwin, *Godfrey*'s brother, in the review i. 307
—— characterised *ib.* 65
—— his person described iii. 471
—— demands to fight with *Argantes* vii. 487
—— moves his squadron to attack the *Pagans*, and repulses them *ib.* 784
—— stands armed by *Godfrey*'s side, during the insurrection in the camp viii. 558
—— is in *Godfrey*'s tent, when he is wounded xi. 469
—— his station in the *Christian* army xx. 59
—— encounters *Mulasses* *ib.* 313
BATTLE general, between the *Pagans* of *Jerusalem* and *Christians* iii. 117—399 vii. 749 *to the end*

BATTLE general, between the *Arabs* and *Danes* viii. 112—179
—— between the *Pagans* and *Christians* ix. 161 *to the end*
—— between the *Egyptian* and *Christian* armies xx. 195 *to the end*
Beelzebub raises a phantom in *Clorinda*'s likeness vii. 710
—— incites *Oradine* to wound *Raymond* *ib.* 719
(See *Demons*)
Berlinger killed by *Clorinda* ix. 525
Bethel iii. 439
Bethlehem *ib.* 442
BIRD, a wonderful one in *Armida*'s garden xvi. 93
Biserta xv. 147
Bomond, characterised i. 69
BRIDGE, raised by magic xviii. 137
Brimartes, in the review xvii. 220
Brunello, killed by *Altamorus* xx. 247
Bugia xv. 151

C.

CALIPH of *Egypt*, his character xvii. 41
—— his throne and person described *ib.* 63
—— gives the command of the army to *Emirenes* *ib.* 264
—— his speech to him *ib.* 274
—— entertains the leaders in his tent *ib.* 296
—— stops the contest betwixt *Adrastus* and *Tisaphernes* *ib.* 362
—— his speech to *Armida* *ib.* 366
Calpe xv. 164
Camillus,

INDEX.

Camillus, in the review i. 483
—— has the direction of one of the *Christian* towers, at the assault of the walls xviii. 436
Campsones, in the review xvii. 120
Canarius, in the review ib. 172
Carnuti, earl of, in the review i. 311
Carthage, reflections on its ruins xv. 141
CASTLE of *Armida* vii. 206
—— *Tancred* made prisoner in it ib. 333
—— several other *Christian* knights made prisoners in it x. 446
CELESTIAL ARMY assists *Godfrey* in the taking of *Jerusalem* xviii. 628
CESTUS of *Armida* xvi. 175
CHAMPIONS of *Armida*, chosen by lot v. 525
—— depart with *Armida* v. 555
—— return to the camp, and defeat the *Arabs* ix. 709
—— the manner of their being imprisoned by *Armida*, and released by *Rinaldo*, related to *Godfrey* x. 430—530
Charles, the *Dane*, arrives at the *Christian* camp viii. 29
—— relates to *Godfrey* the death of *Sweno* ib. 39—311
—— accompanies *Sweno* in his march ib. 81
—— falls among the slain ib. 178
—— is miraculously healed by a hermit ib. 191
—— finds *Sweno*'s body ib. 229
—— is commanded to carry *Sweno*'s sword to *Rinaldo* ib. 246
—— sees a wonderful tomb enclose *Sweno*'s body ib. 279
Charles is lodged by the hermit in his cell ib. 295
—— offers to go in search of *Rinaldo* xiv. 199
—— is appointed with *Ubald* for that purpose ib. 203
—— meets with a magician, who conducts him and *Ubald* to his subterraneous dwelling ib. 243—265
—— hears from the magician, the manner of *Rinaldo*'s being ensnared by *Armida*, and receives instructions for his deliverance ib. 369 *to the end.*
—— enters with *Ubald* into the miraculous bark xv. 23
—— their voyage described ib. 69—326
—— lands on *Armida*'s island ib. 337
—— ascends the mountain ib. 355
—— enters the palace xvi. 1.
—— sees *Rinaldo* with *Armida* in the garden ib. 123
—— returns with *Rinaldo* and *Ubald* ib. 249, 443. xvii 392
—— gives *Sweno*'s sword to *Rinaldo* ib. 568
—— arrives at the camp ib. 648
(See *Ubald*)
CHRISTIANS elect *Godfrey* their general i. 247
—— their army reviewed by him ib. 283
—— march towards *Jerusalem* ib. 557
Christians

INDEX.

Christians enter *Emmaus* ii. 427
—— arrive in sight of *Jerusalem*
    iii. 19
—— their joy described *ib.* 33
—— attacked by the *Pagans* in a sally from the town
    ib. 95
—— repulse them with slaughter *ib.* 324
—— discouraged at hearing the provisions sent from the fleet were intercepted by the *Arabs* v. 637
—— engage the *Pagans*
    viii. 750
—— opposed by the Demons, who raise a storm in favour of the *Pagans*
    ib. 828
—— obliged to retreat *ib.* 840
—— lament the absence of *Rinaldo* viii. 336
—— believe him slain *ib* 352
—— a mutiny is raised amongst them viii. 632
—— the tumult appeased
    ib. 632
—— attacked in the night by the *Arabs* ix. 153
—— defeat them *ib.* 705
—— march in religious procession xi. 25
—— assault the town xi. 223
—— retire to their camp at the approach of night
    ib. 562
—— afflicted with a terrible drought xiii. 378
—— part of the army revolts
    ib. 490
—— refreshed by a shower from heaven *ib.* 536
—— their joy on that occasion
    ib. 546
—— their joy at *Rinaldo's* return xviii. 29

Christians, their military operations *ib.* 286, 416, 430, &c *seq*
—— assault the town *ib.* 434
—— enter it victorious *ib.* 716
—— their impatience to engage the *Egyptians* xx. 21
—— their order of battle xx. 51
—— gain a compleat victory
    ib. 354, 462, 714, &c *seq.*
Clorinda arrives at *Jerusalem*, her character ii. 286
—— sees *Olindo* and *Sophronia* ready to be burned
    ib. 314
—— intercedes with the king for them *ib.* 374
—— makes a sally on the *Christians* iii. 95
—— kills *Gardo* *ib.* 107
—— fights with *Tancred*
    ib. 159
—— has an interview with him,
    ib. 206
—— is wounded iii. 222
—— kills *Ardelius* *ib.* 264
—— with *Argantes* supports the *Pagans* in their retreat
    ib. 326
—— issues from the town to escort *Argantes* vi. 161
—— her armour is taken away by *Erminia* *ib.* 631
—— encourages her troops to fall upon the *Christians*
    vii. 846
—— kills *Pyrrhus* *ib.* 867
—— issues from the town with *Argantes*, to assist the *Arabs* ix. 335
—— kills *Berlinger*, *Albine*, and *Gallus* *ib.* 525
—— wounds *Gernier* *ib.* 531
—— kills *Achilles* *ib* 537
—— is wounded by *Guelpho*
    ib. 557
Clorinda

INDEX.

Clorinda leaves the field with reluctance at *Aladine's* entreaty *ib.* 731
—— stands on a tower in the city, and shoots at the *Christians* xi. 279
—— wounds *William* the *English* prince *ib.* 287
—— kills *Stephen* earl of *Amboise*, and *Clotbareus* *ib.* 295
—— wounds the *Flemish* chief *ib.* 299
—— kills *Ademar* and *Palamedes* *ib.* 313
—— wounds *Godfrey* *ib.* 370
—— forms a design to burn the *Christians* tower xii. 15
—— acquaints *Argantes* with her intention *ib.* 29
—— goes with *Argantes* to the king, and declares their joint resolution xii. 65
—— is entreated by her eunuch *Arsetes* to relinquish her enterprise *ib.* 139
—— hears the story of her birth from him *ib.* 157
—— is sent away by her mother in her infancy *ib.* 191
—— receives suck from a tigress *ib.* 222
—— is bred up by *Arsetes* *ib.* 242
—— she continues firm in her resolution, and endeavours to comfort *Arsetes* *ib.* 313
—— goes out with *Argantes*, and sets fire to the tower *ib.* 331
—— is pursued by the *Christians* in her retreat *ib.* 360
—— is shut out of the city while she engages and kills *Arimon* *ib.* 372
Clorinda fights with *Tancred* *ib.* 413
—— their combat described *ib.* 423
—— receives her mortal wound *ib.* 485
—— desires baptism *ib.* 501
—— dies *ib.* 511, & *seq.*
—— her body is carried to *Tancred's* tent *ib.* 551
—— her death lamented by *Tancred* *ib.* 569, 613
—— appears in a dream to *Tancred*, and comforts him *ib.* 677
—— her funeral *ib.* 703
Clotbareus, in the review i. 289
—— killed by an arrow from *Clorinda* xi. 299
Columbus, his voyage and discoveries foretold xv. 216
COMBAT, single, between *Tancred* and *Argantes* vi. 289—363
—— between *Tancred* and *Rambaldo* vii. 272—324
—— between *Raymond* and *Argantes* vii. 634—709
—— between *Tancred* and *Clorinda* xii. 413—494
—— between *Tancred* and *Argantes* xix. 69—181
—— between *Rinaldo* and *Adrastus* xx. 676—683
—— between *Rinaldo* and *Tisaphernes* *ib.* 761—812
—— between *Godfrey* and *Emirenes* *ib.* 949
Corbano killed by *Dudon* iii. 336
Corcutes wounded by *Godfrey* ix. 700
Crete xv. 117
CYPRESS, in the enchanted wood xiii. 273

CYPRESS

INDEX

CYPRESS, inscription on its bark *ib.* 282
—— being cut by *Tancred*, bleeds *ib.* 294
—— a voice is heard from the trunk *ib.* 300

D.

DAVID'S TOWER, *Solyman* retreats to it with *Aladine* xix. 260
—— bravely defended by *Solyman* *ib.* 284
—— blocked up by the *Gascons* and *Syrians* xx. 39
—— taken by *Raymond* *ib.* 596
Damascus iv. 155
Damiata xv. 109
DEMONS meet in council iv. 11
—— their persons described *ib.* 25
—— disperse themselves in various parts to annoy the *Christians* *ib.* 139
A Demon makes *Gernando* envious of *Rinaldo* v. 134
—— raise a storm in favour of the *Pagans* vii. 828
—— hearten them in battle ix. 413
—— are driven from the field by *Michael* the Archangel *ib.* 505
—— raised by the incantations of *Ismeno* xiii. 33
—— take possession of the wood *ib.* 83
—— terrify those who come to cut timber *ib.* 125
—— put *Adrastus* to flight *ib.* 193
—— attempt in vain to stop *Tancred* from entering the wood *ib.* 241
—— delude him with a voice like *Clorinda's* *ib.* 302
—— endeavour to amuse *Rinaldo* with various appearances and sounds, at his entering the wood xviii. 117
DEMONS assume the likeness of *Armida* and her nymphs *ib.* 169
—— take the form of *Cyclops*, to deter the knight from cutting down the trees *ib.* 244
—— are put to flight, and the enchantment dissolved *ib.* 258
DESCRIPTIONS, of the figure, and descent of an Angel i. 99
—— of *Tancred*, and his falling in love *ib.* 344
—— of *Rinaldo* in the review *ib.* 435
—— of the troops arming themselves, and of their appearance with the *Cross* at their head *ib.* 533
—— of their march *ib.* 557
—— of fame flying before them *ib.* 607
—— of *Sophronia's* modesty and beauty ii. 99
—— of her courage *ib.* 136, 156, 178
—— of her behaviour when sentenced to be burned *ib.* 192
—— of *Olindo's* despair *ib.* 200
—— of *Clorinda's* person and appearance *ib.* 286
—— of *Argantes'* indignation at *Godfrey's* rejecting the Caliph of *Egypt's* proposals *ib.* 662
—— of his declaring war *ib.* 681
—— of the appearance of the *Christian*

INDEX.

Christian army before *Jerusalem* iii. 1—74
DESCRIPTIONS, of *Clorinda's* fally from the town *ib.* 95—120
—— of the encounter of *Tancred* and *Clorinda* *ib.* 159
—— of *Rinaldo* at the head of the troops *ib.* 282, 378
—— of *Dudon's* exploits and death *ib.* 332
—— of the fituation of *Jerufalem* *ib.* 421
—— of the forrow at *Dudon's* death, and of his funeral *ib.* 507—566
—— of felling the trees in a foreft *ib.* 567
—— of *Pluto* and the Demons in council iv. 17
—— of *Armida's* perfon *ib.* 249
—— of the furprize of the camp at her beauty *ib.* 223, 259
—— of the manner in which *Armida* receives *Godfrey's* refufal *ib.* 512
—— of the arts fhe makes ufe of to enfnare the *Chriftian* commanders *ib.* 632, *to the end*
—— of *Rinaldo's* killing *Gernando*, and the tumult thereupon v. 184
—— of *Godfrey's* behaviour on the occafion *ib.* 230
—— of *Rinaldo*, when he hears *Godfrey's* defign of calling him to account *ib.* 307
—— of *Argantes'* fending a challenge to the *Chriftians* vi. 127
—— of *Argantes'* iffuing from the walls, and ftanding in fight of the *Chriftian* camp *ib.* 166
DESCRIPTIONS, of *Tancred's* going to fight *Argantes* *ib.* 192
—— of *Otho's* engaging with *Tancred*, and being taken prifoner *ib.* 214
—— of the combat betwixt *Tancred* and *Argantes* *ib.* 289—363
—— of *Erminia's* love, and her concern for *Tancred's* danger *ib.* 405
—— of her putting on *Clorinda's* armour, and leaving the city *ib.* 631
—— of her impatience and folicitude *ib.* 673, 723
—— of her being difcovered by moonlight *ib.* 755
—— of her fear and flight *ib.* 776
—— of her arrival on the banks of the river *Jordan* vii. 19
—— of a fhepherd and his fons tending their flock *ib.* 35
—— of *Erminia's* reception by them *ib.* 43, 121
—— of the life fhe led among the fhepherds *ib.* 127
—— of *Tancred's* fearch after her, fuppofing her to be *Clorinda* *ib.* 169
—— of his arrival at *Armida's* caftle *ib.* 206
—— of his combat with *Rambaldo* *ib.* 272
—— of his being made prifoner in the caftle *ib.* 326
—— of *Argantes'* impatience for the battle *ib.* 364
—— of *Raymond's* guardian Angel defcending to his affiftance *ib.* 577

DESCRIPTIONS,

INDEX.

DESCRIPTIONS, of the combat between *Raymond* and *Argantes* ib. 634—709
—— of *Beelzebub's* breaking the truce ib. 710
—— of the wounding of *Raymond* ib. 730
—— of the armies joining in battle ib. 750
—— of *Argantes*' bravery ib. 795
—— of a storm raised by the Demons, in favour of the Pagans ib. 828
—— of the retreat of the *Christians* ib. 858 *to the end*
—— of the intrepidity of *Sweno* viii. 95
—— of a battle by night ib. 112
—— of *Sweno's* death, and the discovery of his body by the light of the moon, &c. viii. 156—225
—— of an insurrection in the camp ib. 526—615
—— of *Solyman's* march, and his attacking the *Christian* camp by night ix. 97—168
—— of his fury and dreadful appearance ib. 169—204
—— of the deaths of *Latinus* and his five sons ib. 209, 309
—— of *Godfrey's* valour ib. 371, 699
—— of a general battle ib. 399
—— of the blessed in heaven ib. 431—452 xiv. 29
—— of the descent of *Michael* the Archangel ix. 465
—— of his driving the Demons from the field ib. 505
—— of *Clorinda's* actions ib. 523

DESCRIPTIONS, of *Argillan* rushing to fight ib. 569
—— of *Lesbinus*, the Soldan's page ib. 606
—— of his death ib. 619
—— of the defeat of the *Pagans* ib. 705, *to the end*
—— of the Soldan tired with slaughter ib. 753
—— of his flight x. 1
—— of *Ismeno's* conveying him to *Jerusalem* in an enchanted chariot ib. 99
—— of the manner of their entering the city ib. 194
—— of the Soldan's breaking from a cloud ib. 342
—— of *Armida's* castle x. 436
—— of the metamorphosis of the *Christian* knights ib. 475
—— of a religious procession xi. 25
—— of the assault of the city ib. 168—278
—— of the use of wooden towers in the siege, and their operations ib. 317 *& seq.* xviii. 490
—— of *Godfrey's* being wounded xi. 370
—— of *Argantes* and *Solyman* issuing from a breach ib. 427
—— of the healing of *Godfrey's* wound by an Angel ib. 464
—— of the grief of a mother at parting from her infant xii. 191
—— of a tigress giving suck to an infant ib. 220
—— of *Argantes* and *Clorinda* issuing from the town, and setting fire to the *Christian* tower ib. 331

DESCRIPTIONS,

INDEX.

DESCRIPTIONS, of a single combat by night, between *Tancred* and *Clorinda* ib. 413—491
—— of *Clorinda's* death ib. 495
—— of *Tancred's* grief ib. 533, 509, 625
—— of *Clorinda's* appearance to *Tancred*, in a dream ib. 677
—— of the despair of *Arsetes* ib. 751
—— of a forest, supposed to be the resort of witches and evil spirits xiii. 9
—— of the incantations of *Ismeno* xiii. 33
—— of the enchanted wood ib. 149, 189, 241—337. xviii. 111—259
—— of *Alcastus* attempting it, and being put to flight xiii. 187
—— of *Tancred's* entering the wood ib. 227
—— of *Tancred's* retreat ib. 318
—— of a terrible drought that afflicts the *Christian* army ib. 378
—— of a shower that relieves them, and their joy on that occasion ib. 536
—— of a dream sent to *Godfrey* xiv. 1—142
—— of a magician walking on the water ib. 239
—— of a river dividing its water, of two knights entering into it, and of the wonders they saw in their passage xiv. 265
—— of the manner of *Armida's* ensnaring *Rinaldo* ib. 411
—— of a *Syren* ib. 439

DESCRIPTIONS, of *Armida's* falling in love with *Rinaldo* ib. 483
—— of the fountain of laughter ib. 535. xv. 415
—— of the miraculous Pilot that appears to convey the two knights to *Rinaldo* ib. 23
—— of their voyage through the *Mediterranean* ib. 63—172
—— of the *Egyptian* fleet and army ib. 75
—— of the *Fortunate Islands* ib. 257
—— of *Armida's* island ib. 311, 337
—— of the knights ascending the mountain ib. 355
—— of the summit of the mountain ib. 397
—— of two nymphs bathing ib. 431
—— of the gates of *Armida's* palace xvi. 9
—— of *Armida's* garden ib. 63
—— of the wanton dalliance of *Rinaldo* and *Armida* ib. 123
—— of *Armida's* cestus, ib. 175
—— of the two knights suddenly shewing themselves to *Rinaldo*, &c. ib. 195
—— of the confusion of *Armida* at *Rinaldo's* flight ib. 251
—— of her pursuing him ib. 273
—— of her despair and rage ib. 297, 445
—— of her destroying her enchanted palace, and her flight to *Gaza* ib. 486
—— of the situation of *Gaza* xvii. 1

DESCRIPTIONS,

INDEX.

DESCRIPTIONS, of the Caliph seated on his throne *ib*. 63
—— of the army passing in review before him *ib*. 89—233
—— of *Armida* in her chariot *ib*. 234
—— of *Emirenes*' receiving the command of the army from the Caliph *ib*. 264
—— of the return of *Rinaldo* and the two knights to *Palestine* *ib*. 380
—— of the knights landing, and discovering a suit of armour by moonlight *ib*. 398
—— of the figures on the shield *ib*. 463—561
—— of the arrival of the knights at the camp *ib*. 636
—— of *Rinaldo's* ascending mount *Olivet* at daybreak xviii. 69—110
—— of his entering the enchanted wood *ib*. 111
—— of nymphs coming out of the barks of trees *ib*. 169
—— of a nymph in the likeness of *Armida* *ib*. 197
—— of *Rinaldo's* cutting down the enchanted myrtle *ib*. 226
—— of nymphs assuming the form of *Cyclops* *ib*. 242
—— of the dissolution of the enchantment *ib*. 252
—— particular description of a moving tower used in the siege *ib*. 300
—— of a dove, that carried a letter from the *Egyptians*, intercepted by *Godfrey* xviii. 328
—— of *Vafrino's* departure for the *Egyptian* camp *ib*. 404
DESCRIPTIONS of the military operations on both sides *ib*. 416
—— of the attack of the town *ib*. 454
—— of the dreadful effects of the *Christians*' engines *ib*. 468
—— of *Rinaldo's* bravery *ib*. 494
—— of his scaling the walls *ib*. 510
—— of the fall of one of the *Pagans*' engines *ib*. 550
—— of the *Christian* tower, in danger of being destroyed by fire from the *Pagans* *ib*. 562
—— of *Ismeno's* death *ib*. 604
—— of the Celestial Army *ib*. 628
—— of *Godfrey's* gaining the walls, and planting his standard there *ib*. 666
—— of the victorious army entering the city *ib*. 692
—— of *Argantes*' intrepidity on the walls xix. 1
—— of *Argantes* and *Tancred* retiring together, to engage in a single combat *ib*. 41
—— of the combat between them *ib*. 69—181
—— of the miseries of a town taken by storm *ib*. 195
—— of *Rinaldo's* breaking open the gates of *Solomon's* temple *ib*. 238
—— of *Solyman's* defending *David's* tower *ib*. 284
—— of the *Egyptian* army encamped *ib*. 386
—— of *Armida* in her tent with her lovers *ib*. 452

DESCRIPTIONS,

INDEX.

DESCRIPTIONS, of the discovery of *Vafrino* to *Erminia* ib. 520
—— of *Vafrino* and *Erminia* finding *Tancred* wounded ib. 675
—— of *Erminia's* grief ib. 703
—— of the arrival of the *Egyptian* army xx. 1
—— of *Godfrey's* majestic figure ib. 45, 71, 127
—— of the order of the *Christian* and *Egyptian* armies ib. 51, 137
—— of the armies ready to engage xx. 171
—— of the onset ib. 195
—— of *Gildippe's* and *Edward's* actions ib. 201
—— of the actions of *Altamorus* ib. 241, 456
—— of the death of *Ormond* and his confederates ib. 281
—— of the field of battle ib. 328
—— of *Rinaldo's* exploits ib. 350
—— of *Rinaldo* passing by *Armida's* chariot, and her behaviour on the occasion ib. 404
—— of *Solyman's* rushing from the tower ib. 483
—— of *Tancred's* defending *Raymond* ib. 538
—— of the taking of *David's* tower ib. 599
—— of *Aladine's* death ib. 584
—— of the deaths of *Edward* and *Gildippe* ib. 618
—— of the deaths of *Adrastus* and *Solyman* ib. 666, & seq.
—— of *Emirenes'* bravery and death ib. 722

DESCRIPTIONS, of the combat between *Rinaldo* and *Tisopbernes* ib. 752
—— of *Armida's* flight ib. 779
—— of her despair ib. 825
—— of her interview with *Rinaldo* ib. 859—932
—— of *Altamorus* taken prisoner, and of *Godfrey* entering the temple in triumph ib. 957, to the end.
DOVE employed as a messenger xviii. 328
Dragutes kills *Henry* and *Holiphernes* ix. 314
DREAM sent to *Godfrey* to urge him to recall *Rinaldo* xiv. 1—142
DROUGHT, the *Christian* camp afflicted with a terrible one xiii. 378—455
Dudon, in the review, chief of the adventurers i. 402
—— his character by *Erminia* iii. 203
—— kills *Tigranes*, *Algazer*, *Corbano*, *Amurath*, *Mahomet* and *Almanzor* iii. 232
—— is killed by *Argantes* ib. 314
—— his funeral ib. 551
—— is seen by *Godfrey* to assist in the storming of *Jerusalem* xviii. 644

E.

EARTH, the vanities of it opposed to the glories of heaven xiv. 65
Eberard, in the review i. 421
—— one of the champions drawn by lot, to accompany *Armida* v. 539
—— demands to fight with *Argantes* vii. 492
(See *Champions*.)

VOL. II. A a *Edward*,

INDEX.

Edward, in the review   i. 423
—— described with *Gildippe*, by *Erminia*   iii. 328
—— demands to fight with *Argantes*   vii. 494
—— kills *Artaban* and *Alvantes*   xx. 235
—— is killed by *Solyman* ib. 638
  (See *Gildippe*.)
Emirenes, in the review, his character   xvii. 228
—— receives the command of the army from the Caliph   ib. 264
—— in discourse with *Ormond* in his tent   xviii. 414
—— draws up his army in order of battle   xx. 137
—— his speech to them   ib. 151
—— fights with one of the *Roberts*   ib. 319
—— wounds him   ib. 470
—— rebukes *Rimedon* for flying   ib. 722
—— rallies his troops   ib. 736
—— his valour   ib. 736, 933
—— fights with *Godfrey* ib. 941
—— is killed by him   ib. 953
Emmaüs, the *Christians* enter that city   ib. 427
ENCHANTED Wood (See *Wood*.)
Engerlan, in the review   i. 410
—— killed by *Algazeles* ix. 319
ENGINES, military, used by the *Christians* and *Pagans*   xi. 217, 256, 317, 349. xviii. 286—327, 538.
—— for casting darts and stones   ib. 299
—— their dreadful effects   ib. 468
Erminia, with *Aladine*, on the walls of *Jerusalem* iii. 91
—— points out the *Christian* commanders to *Aladine*   ib. 129, 284, 447

Erminia, her emotion at the sight of *Tancred*   vi. 137
—— her history   ib. 405
—— sees the combat of *Tancred* and *Argantes*   ib. 453
—— her fears for *Tancred*   ib. 467
—— her debate with herself   ib. 485, & seq.
—— resolves to leave the city   ib. 631
—— dresses herself in *Clorinda's* armour   ib. 646
—— goes out at the gate by night   ib. 673
—— sends a messenger to *Tancred*   ib. 699
—— her impatience and solicitude   ib. 723
—— is discovered by the light of the moon   ib. 755
—— is assailed by *Poliphernes*, and flies   ib. 762
—— arrives on the banks of the river *Jordan*   vii. 19
—— her speech to a shepherd   ib. 49
—— is entertained by him   ib. 119
—— her life among the shepherds   ib. 127
—— is in *Armida's* tent, and discovers *Vafrino*   xix. 530
—— leaves the *Pagan* camp with him   ib. 582
—— gives him an account of the design against *Godfrey's* life   ib. 588
—— relates the particulars of her early love for *Tancred*   ib. 617
—— finds *Tancred* wounded   ib. 685
—— her grief and lamentation   ib. 703

Erminia

INDEX.

Erminia recovers *Tancred* from his swoon *ib.* 758
—— undertakes the care of his wounds *ib.* 780
Erneſtus killed by *Albazar* ix. 318
Erotimus, the phyſician, his character xi. 474
—— endeavours, in vain, to relieve *Godfrey* when wounded *ib.* 484
—— acknowledges a divine power in healing of *Godfrey's* wound *ib.* 510
Eſtè, House of x. 541. xvii. 465
Euſtatius, *Godfrey's* brother, in the review i. 406
Euſtatius addreſſes *Armida* iv. 265
—— conducts her to *Godfrey's* tent *ib.* 297
—— is enamoured of her, and pleads with *Godfrey* in her behalf *ib.* 568
—— is fearful leſt *Rinaldo* ſhould accompany her v. 53
—— perſuades *Rinaldo* to accept the command of the adventurers v. 61
—— departs from the camp by night, to follow *Armida* v. 572
—— his conteſt with *Rambaldo* *ib.* 578
—— confined with the reſt of the knights in *Armida's* caſtle, and releaſed by *Rinaldo* x. 430—530
—— wounded in the ditch at the aſſault of the town xi. 413
—— is help'd by *Rinaldo* to mount the walls xviii. 534 (See *Champions*.)

F

Flemiſh chief, wounded by an arrow from *Clorinda* xi. 299

Fez xv. 155
FOREST, the felling of trees in a foreſt deſcribed iii. 575
—— description of one ſuppoſed to be the reſort of witches and evil ſpirits xiii. 9
FORTUNATE-ISLANDS, deſcribed xv. 257
FOUNTAIN of laughter, its dreadful effects xiv. 537
—— further deſcribed v. 415
FUNERAL of *Dudon* iii. 551
—— of *Clorinda* xii. 703

G

Gabriel, the Angel, ſent to *Godfrey* i. 81
—— his figure and deſcent deſcribed *ib.* 99
Gades xv. 174
Gallus, killed by *Clorinda* ix. 530
GARDENS of *Armida* deſcribed xvi. 3—120
Gardo, killed by *Clorinda* iii. 109
Gaſcons, led by *Raymond*, i. 427
—— appointed by *Godfrey* to block up *David's* tower xx. 43
—— are attacked by *Solyman* in a ſally from the fort *ib.* 513
—— retreat before the *Pagans* *ib.* 546
—— are rebuked by *Tancred* *ib.* 560
—— rally and make themſelves maſters of the tower *ib.* 578
Gaza, its ſituation xv. 71. xvii. 1
Gazel, in the review xvii. 121
Gentonio, in the review i. 412
—— killed by *Altamorus* xx. 255
Gernando, in the review i. 408
—— his character by *Erminia* iii. 304

A a 2 *Gernando*,

INDEX X.

Gernando, his character further illustrated v. 114
—— is jealous of Rinaldo's aspiring to the command of the adventurers ib. 126
—— his discontent increased by the influence of a Demon ib. 134
—— exasperates Rinaldo by his calumnies ib. 568
—— is killed by him ib. 221
Gernier, in the review i. 421
—— demands to fight with Argantes vii. 489
—— wounded by Clorinda ix. 531
—— killed by Tisaphernes xx. 747
Gerrards, two, in the review i. 411
—— one of them is drawn by lot, to accompany Armida v. 559 (See Champions.)
—— one of them killed by Tisaphernes xx. 747
Gilbert, killed by Ariadenus ix. 316
Gildippe, in the review i. 423
—— described with Edward, by Erminia iii. 308
—— demands to fight with Argantes vii. 494
—— makes a great slaughter of the Pagans ix. 549
—— at the first encounter of the Christian and Egyptian armies, kills Hircanes xx. 203
—— kills Zopyrus, Alarcus, and Argantes ib. 209
—— is killed by Solyman ib. 628
Godfrey, characterised i. 61
—— receives a divine injunction by an Angel, to call a council of the Christian generals ib. 117
Godfrey, his speech to them ib. 161
—— is elected commander in chief of all the Christian forces ib. 247
—— orders a general review of the army ib. 265
—— sends a messenger to Greece ib. 511
—— marches with the army towards Jerusalem ib. 557
—— grants a peace to the King of Tripoly ib. 571
—— gives audience to Alethes and Argantes, embassadors from Egypt ii. 458
—— rejects their proposals ib. 604
—— dismisses the embassadors with presents ib. 697
—— takes a view of the city of Jerusalem, from a hill iii. 419
—— described by Erminia ib. 447
—— visits Dudon's body ib. 507
—— sends workmen to the forest, to fell the trees for making engines ib. 567
—— hears Armida relate the story of her pretended misfortunes iv. 301
—— refuses the succours she desires ib. 475
—— grants her request at the intercession of Eustatius ib. 600
—— recommends to the adventurers to choose a leader in Dudon's place v. 15
—— determines to call Rinaldo to account for Gernando's death ib. 270
—— is proof against the charms of Armida ib. 453

Godfrey

INDEX.

Godfrey causes ten champions to be chosen by lot, to assist *Armida* ib. 521
—— dismisses them ib. 555
—— receives ill news from the fleet ib. 617
—— endeavours to encourage his army ib. 641
—— accepts *Argantes*' challenge to the *Christians* vi. 139
—— appoints *Tancred* to fight *Argantes* ib. 192
—— hears *Argantes*' fresh challenge vii. 417
—— is provoked at the fear of the *Christian* leaders, and resolves himself to undertake the combat ib. 436
—— is dissuaded by *Raymond* ib. 452
—— causes the champion to be fixed by lot vii. 514
—— presents *Raymond* with a sword ib. 525
—— sees *Raymond* wounded by treachery, and urges the troops to revenge it ib. 746
—— has the advantage of the *Pagans* ib. 820
—— is obliged to retire to his entrenchments ib. 870
—— hears the relation of *Sweno*'s death from *Charles the Dane* viii. 29
—— enquires of *Aliprando* the particulars of his finding *Rinaldo*'s armour ib. 362
—— hears of the insurrection in the camp ib. 556
—— addresses the malecontents ib. 568
—— causes *Argillan* to be imprisoned ib. 604
—— marches to oppose *Soly*-

man's incursion ix. 322
Godfrey encounters him ib. 371
—— wounds *Corcutes* and *Rosteno* ib. 700
—— kills *Selim* and *Rosano* ib. 701
—— hears the adventure of the knights, who followed *Armida* x. 420
—— leads the army in solemn procession to invoke the assistance of Heaven xi. 39
—— his orders and dispositions for the assault of the town ib. 114, 217
—— endeavours to enter a breach ib. 355
—— is wounded by an arrow from *Clorinda* ib. 370
—— retires to his tent ib. 382
—— his wound is healed by an angel ib. 464
—— returns to the walls ib. 516
—— encounters *Argantes* ib. 534
—— gives over the attack, at the approach of night ib. 560
—— with the rest of the leaders, endeavours to comfort *Tancred* xii. 635
—— sends his workmen to cut down the tree xiii. 121
—— hears the account of the enchantments from *Tancred* ib. 333
—— has thoughts of attempting the adventure himself, but is dissuaded from it by *Peter* ib. 353
—— prays for rain, to relieve the camp ib. 500
—— is admonished in a dream to recall *Rinaldo* xiv. 21

INDEX.

Godfrey consents to *Guelpho's* request, that *Rinaldo* may return *ib.* 183
—— goes to meet *Rinaldo* xvii. 652. xviii. 1
—— intercepts a letter from the *Egyptian* general *ib.* 328
—— his preparations for storming the town *ib.* 422
—— brings his tower near the walls *ib.* 562. 612
—— his intrepidity *ib.* 576
—— sees the celestial army, and souls of the deceased warriors, fighting on his side xviii. 628
—— forces his way against *Solyman*, and fixes his standard on the walls *ib.* 666
—— exhorts his companions to tend the sick and wounded *ib.* 346
—— is with *Raymond* wounded, and hears *Vafrino's* account of his discoveries in the *Egyptian* camp xix. 817
—— draws up his army in order of battle xx. 37
—— his speech to them *ib.* 87
—— kills *Ormond* *ib.* 281
—— encounters *Altamorus* *ib.* 310
—— renews the attack *ib.* 475
—— kills *Rimedon* *ib.* 935
—— kills *Emirenes* *ib.* 949
—— takes *Altamorus* prisoner *ib.* 959
—— enters the temple in triumph with his generals, and pays his devotions at the tomb *ib.* 993 *to the end.*

Granada xv. 156
Greeks, in the review i. 378
—— revolt from the army xiii. 490
Guasco, in the review i. 419
—— one of the champions drawn by lot, to accompany *Armida* v. 336 (See *Champions.*)
—— killed by *Altamorus* xx. 255
Guelpho, in the review, his character i. 315
—— endeavours to excuse *Tancred* to *Godfrey* v. 417
—— demands to fight with *Argantes* vii. 487
—— goes to oppose the *Pagans* ix. 347
—— wounds *Clorinda* *ib.* 557
—— kills *Osmida* *ib.* 561
—— is wounded at the assault of the town xi. 408
—— pleads with *Godfrey* for *Rinaldo's* return xiv. 16
—— appoints *Ubald* and *Charles* the *Dane*, to be the messengers to recall him xiv. 203
Guidos, two, in the review i. 420
—— demand to fight with *Argantes* xii. 488
—— one of them is wounded by *Argantes* *ib.* 779
—— one killed by *Altamorus* xx. 255

H

HEAVEN, the condition of the blessed there ix. 433
—— the glories of it xiv. 25
—— the permanent happiness of its inhabitants opposed to the vanities of earth *ib.* 65

HELL,

INDEX.

HELL, description of it iv. 1
Henry (the Frank) one of the champions drawn by lot, to accompany Armida v. 539
(See Champions.)
Henry (the messenger) sent to Greece i. 511
Henry (of England) killed by Dragutes ix. 314
HERMIT, Christian, finds Charles the Dane among his slain companions, and miraculously heals his wounds viii. 182
—— gives him Sweno's sword, and enjoins him to deliver it to Rinaldo ib. 244
—— entertains him in his cell ib. 295
Hidraotes, king of Damascus, sends his niece Armida to the Christian camp, to employ her arts among the commanders iv. 155
Hircanes, Soldan of Ormus, in the review xvii. 179
—— killed by Gildippe xx. 203
Holiphernes, killed by Dragutes ix. 314
Hugo appears to Godfrey in a dream xiv. 31
—— his discourse with him ib. 47
—— advises him to recall Rinaldo ib. 91
—— is seen by Godfrey to assist in the storming of Jerusalem xviii. 644
HYMN sung by the Christians in the procession xi. 47

I

Jerusalem, governed by Aladine i. 623
—— fortified by him, upon the approach of the Christians i. 675
Jerusalem, its situation iii. 421
—— assaulted by the Christians xi. 223
—— bravely defended by Solyman and Argantes ib. 186, 341
—— attacked, and taken by storm xviii. 454 to the end.
Jordan iii. 436. vii. 19
Judea xv. 127
INSCRIPTION on Dudon's tomb iii. 566
—— on the bark of a cypress xiii. 281
—— on a marble pillar xiv. 420
Ishmael, wounded by Gildippe xx. 217
ISLAND, Rinaldo decoyed to one by Armida xiv. 412
Ismeno, his character ii. 1
—— persuades Aladine to convey the Image of the Virgin from the temple to the mosque ib. 17
—— accosts Solyman x. 47
—— heals his wounds ib. 91
—— conducts him in an enchanted chariot to Jerusalem, and conceals him in a cloud ib. 95
—— foretells the ruin of the Christian empire in Palestine ib. 130
—— leads Solyman, by a subterraneous passage, into the hall where Aladine sits in council ib. 229
—— removes the cloud, and discovers him to the assembly ib. 342
—— receives great honours from Aladine ib. 387
—— furnishes Argantes and Clorinda

INDEX.

rinda with fire to burn the *Christian* tower xii. 327
Ismeno raises the Demons, and appoints them to guard the wood xiii. 33
—— informs *Aladine* of what he has done, and foretells a drought that will afflict the *Christians* xiii. 85
—— prepares fiery engines for the defence of the town xviii. 322
—— stands on the walls, with two magicians, at the attack *ib.* 592
—— is killed by a stone from an engine *ib.* 604

K

King of *Tripoly* (in *Syria*) makes peace with the *Christians* i. 571
—— of *Tripoly* (in *Africa*) in the review xvii. 134
—— of *Zumara*, in the review *ib.* 133

L

Latinus, with his five sons, attacks *Solyman* ix. 209
—— is killed by him *ib.* 295
Laurentes (one of *Latinus*' sons) with his father and brothers, attacks *Solyman* *ib.* 233
—— is killed by him *ib.* 265
Lesbinus (the Soldan's page) his person described *ib.* 626
—— killed by *Argillan ib.* 646
Libanon i. 113
Lilybæum xv. 138
Lion opposes *Ubald* and *Charles*, in their ascent to *Armida*'s palace xv. 375
—— is put to flight *ib.* 380

Loves of *Rinaldo* and *Armida* xiv. 485. xvi. 121. xx. 825

M

Magician (See *Ismeno*.)
—— (*Christian*) addresses the two knights, who are sent to recall *Rinaldo* xiv. 253
—— causes a river to divide, and conducts them to his subterraneous palace *ib.* 265
—— relates to them the particulars of *Rinaldo*'s being ensnared by *Armida* *ib.* 369—514
—— instructs them how to release him from her enchantments *ib.* 515
—— meets them at their return to *Palestine* xvii. 416
—— welcomes *Rinaldo*, gives him a suit of armour, and explains to him the sculptures on the shield *ib.* 463—561
—— foretels the future glory of *Alphonso* of *Este*, conducts the warriors within sight of the camp, and then leaves them *ib.* 578
Mahomet, killed by *Dudon* iii. 330
Malta xv. 130
Marlabustes, in the review xvii. 217
Marmarique xv. 121
Mauritania ib. 153
Mediterranean Sea, voyage through it *ib* 69—157
Metamorphosis of *Christian* knights into fishes x. 473

Meta-

INDEX.

METAMORPHOSIS of Nymphs into *Cyclops* xviii. 238

Michael, the arch-angel, sent to drive the Demons from the field of battle ix. 453

—— his descent described ib. 465

—— addresses the Demons, and compels them to retire ib. 487

—— appears to *Godfrey*, and shews him the celestial army engaged on his side xviii. 628

MONSTERS guard the ascent to *Armida*'s palace xiv. 527. xv. 383

Morocco xv. 155

Mulasses and *Agricaltes*, in the review xvii. 166

Mulasses, his station in the Egyptian army xx. 141

Mulasses and *Agricaltes* killed by *Argillan* ix. 610

MYRTLE, in the enchanted wood, a nymph comes out of its bark xviii. 197

—— cut down by *Rinaldo* ib. 249

N

Numidia xv. 149

NYMPHS, two bathing, are seen by *Charles* and *Ubald* ib. 431

—— endeavour to ensnare them with their beauty ib. 441

O

Obizo, in the review i. 414

Odemarus, in the review xvii. 212

Olderico, one of the Champions drawn by lot, to accompany *Armida* v. 537 (See *Champions*.)

Olindo, his love to *Sophronia* ii. 107

Olindo sees her condemned to be burned ib. 200

—— desires to suffer in her stead ib. 208

—— is sentenced to die with her, and bound to the same stake ib. 236

—— bewails their misfortune ib. 248

—— is released at the intercession of *Clorinda*, and marries *Sophronia* ib. 404

—— is sent with her into exile ib. 412

(See *Sophronia*.)

Olivet mount, the *Christians* pay their devotions on it xi. 71

—— *Rinaldo* ascends it xviii. 81

Oradine, is incited by *Beelzebub* to wound *Raymond* vii. 718

Oran xv. 152

Orcanes, his character x. 271

—— his invidious speech in *Aladine*'s council ib. 277

—— is threatened by the soldan ib. 358

Orindus, in the review xvii. 219

Ormano opposes *Argantes* vii. 774

—— killed by him ib. 780

Ormond discourses with *Emirenes* in his tent concerning a design against *Godfrey* xix. 414

—— is killed by *Godfrey* xx. 281

Ormusses conveys the *Arabs* from the battle into the city, and brings provisions to the besieged x. 392

Orontes xiv. 413

Osmida, killed by *Guelpho* ix. 562

Otho, in the review i. 417

Otho

INDEX.

Osbo fights with *Argantes*, and is overcome vi. 216

P

PAGANS in *Jerusalem*, their consternation at the approach of the *Christian* army i. 615
—— prepare for their defence iii. 77
—— make a sally from the town ib. 95, 254
—— repulsed by the *Christians* ib. 324
—— encounter the *Christians* vii. 752
—— are assisted by the Demons ib. 828
—— compel the *Christians* to retire to their entrenchments ib. 856 *to the end*
—— sally from the town to assist the *Arabs* ix 331
—— are defeated, and forced to retreat within the walls ib. 719 *to the end*
—— see the *Christian* procession xi. 81
—— defend the city with great resolution xi. 180, 260, 327
—— their grief and consternation at *Clorinda*'s death xii. 745
—— their defensive operations at the second assault xviii. 480, 540, 564
—— are driven from the walls ib. 676
—— part of them retire to *Solomon*'s temple xix. 220
—— part of them fortify themselves in *David*'s tower ib. 260
—— the temple being forced open by *Rinaldo*, they are terribly slaughtered ib. 252

Pagans sally from *David*'s tower xx. 503
—— are entirely defeated ib. 580

Pagan matrons repair to the mosque xi. 205

PALACE of *Armida* entered by *Charles* and *Ubald* xvi. 1
—— destroyed by *Armida* ib. 486

Palamedes, in the review i. 416
—— killed by an arrow from *Clorinda* xi. 311

Paphia xv. 101

PASTORAL scene vii. 1—168

Peter, the hermit, in council with the *Christian* leaders i. 223
—— his speech to them ib. 227
—— foretells the glory of *Rinaldo*'s posterity x. 531
—— exhorts *Godfrey* to implore the assistance of Heaven xi. 1
—— reproves *Tancred* for his excess of grief at *Clorinda*'s death xii. 641
—— dissuades *Godfrey* from attempting the enchanted wood, and foretells *Rinaldo*'s speedy return xiii. 364
—— directs *Charles* and *Ubald* what course they are to take to find *Rinaldo* xiv. 221
—— his speech and counsel to *Rinaldo* at his return xviii. 39

Pharos xv. 115

Philip, killed by *Ariadenus* ix. 316

Prius (one of *Latinus*'s sons) with

INDEX.

with his father and brothers, attacks *Solyman*
  ib. 233
Prius killed by him *ib.* 265
PILOT, miraculous, appears to *Charles* and *Ubald*
  xv. 23
—— conveys them through the *Mediterranean* to the *Fortunate Islands*
  ib. 63—274
—— shews them the fleet and army of the Caliph *ib.* 75
—— foretells the discoveries of *Columbus* *ib.* 216
—— sets the knights on shore at *Armida's* island *ib.* 325
—— returns with them to *Palestine* xvii. 384
Pindorus and *Arideus* (heralds) part *Tancred* and *Argantes* vi. 368
Pirgas, in the review xvii. 219
Pluto, enraged at the success of the *Christians* iv. 1
—— calls a council of the infernal powers *ib.* 11
—— his person described *ib.* 43
—— his speech *ib.* 65
Poliphernes iii. 270
—— sees *Erminia* in *Clorinda's* armour by night, approaching the *Christian* camp vi. 762
—— attacks and pursues her *ib* 772
PRAYER of *Raymond* before his fight with *Argantes*
  vii. 568
—— of *Godfrey* at the insurrection in the camp
  viii. 562
—— of the same for rain
  xiii. 607
PROCESSION religious, made by the *Christians*, to implore the assistance of Heaven
  xi. 25
Ptolemais xv. 123
Pyrrhus demands to fight with *Argantes* vii. 489
—— killed by *Clorinda* *ib.* 865

Q

QUEEN of *Æthiopia*, confined by her husband's jealousy
  xii. 167
—— is delivered of *Clorinda*
  ib. 181
—— gives the infant to her eunuch to be brought up
  ib. 191
—— her grief at parting from it *ib.* 193

R

Rambaldo, in the review i. 411
—— one of the champions drawn by lot, to accompany *Armida* v. 540
—— arrives with the rest of the knights at *Armida's* castle x. 448
—— renounces his religion, and espouses the *Pagan* cause
  x. 503
—— stands at the entrance of *Armida's* castle, and defies *Tancred* vii. 230
—— fights with him *ib.* 276
—— is saved by the interposition of *Armida* *ib.* 325
RAMS, battering. (See *Engines*.)
Raymond, in the review i. 457
—— his character by *Erminia*
  iii. 477
—— approves *Godfrey's* design of calling *Rinaldo* to account for *Gernando's* death v. 286
—— dissuades *Godfrey* from fighting *Argantes*, and resolves to fight him himself vii. 448

Raymond

INDEX.

Raymond is chosen by lot for the combat ib. 516
— receives a sword from *Godfrey* ib. 525
— his prayer before the battle ib. 567
— protected by an angel ib. 603—670
— meets *Argantes* ib. 612
— their combat described ib. 634—709
— is treacherously wounded by an arrow ib. 736
— is felled by a stone xi. 411
— advises *Godfrey* to send a spy to the *Egyptian* camp xviii. 376
— his station during the assault ib. 434
— endeavours to gain the pass at *David's* tower xix. 292
— is felled by the Soldan ib. 296
— counsels *Godfrey* ib. 875
— is placed by him to block up *David's* tower xx. 39
— is again felled by the Soldan ib. 528
— is defended by *Tancred* xx. 550
— kills *Aladine* ib. 584
— plants the standard on *David's* tower ib. 600
Rhinocera xv. 104
Rhodes ib. 117
Ridolphus, in the review i. 419
— one of the champions drawn by lot, to accompany *Armida* v. 537
(See *Champions*.)
Ridolphus, killed by *Argantes* vii. 865
Rimedon, in the review xvii. 213
— flies with the *Egyptian* standard xx. 722

Rimedon is rebuked by *Emirenes* ib. 724
— returns to the battle ib. 734
— is killed by *Godfrey* ib. 935
Rinaldo, characterised i. 75
— his figure, in the review ib. 435
— his birth and education ib. 443
— described by *Erminia* iii. 281
— fells *Argantes* ib. 318
— exhorts the adventurers to revenge *Dudon's* death ib. 378
— retires from the walls at the command of *Godfrey* ib. 409
— discourses with *Eustatius*, concerning his succession to *Dudon*, in the command of the adventurers v. 85
— is exasperated at *Gernando's* calumnies v. 192
— kills him ib. 212
— arms, and determines not to surrender himself to *Godfrey* ib. 323
— is persuaded by *Tancred* and *Guelpho* to leave the camp ib. 331, 373
— rescues the *Christian* knights that were made prisoners by *Armida* x. 515
— is enticed by *Armida* into an island xiv. 413
— is lulled asleep by a *Syren's* song ib. 479
— is carried away by *Armida*, in her chariot, to an island in a remote part of the world ib. 499
— his wanton dalliance with *Armida* xvi. 145

Rinaldo

INDEX.

Rinaldo is rouzed at the appearance of *Charles* and *Ubald* ib. 195
—— leaves the gardens with his conductor ib. 249
—— is purfued by *Armida* ib. 273
—— endeavours, in vain, to pacify her ib. 365
—— leaves her, and sets sail for *Palestine* ib. 437 xvii. 382
—— lands in *Palestine* ib. 398
—— is welcomed by the Magician, who had entertained *Charles* and *Ubald*, and is prefented by him with a fuit of armour ib. 421
—— hears the account of the fculptures on his fhield xvii. 461—561
—— is conducted by the hermit within fight of the camp ib. 578
—— arrives at the camp, and is gracioufly received by *Godfrey* xviii. 1
—— is counfelled by *Peter*, and receives abfolution from him ib. 39
—— afcends mount *Olivet* ib. 69
—— his prayer ib. 97
—— enters the enhanted wood ib. 111
—— fees nymphs iffue from the barks of trees ib. 169
—— fees a nymph in the likenefs of *Armida* ib. 169
—— cuts down a myrtle, and diffolves the enchantment ib. 278
—— leads the adventurers to the affault of the town ib. 506
—— fcales the walls ib. 515

Rinaldo makes a dreadful flaughter of the *Pagans* in the city xix. 210
—— breaks open the gate of *Solomon's* temple with a vaft beam ib. 238
—— with *Godfrey*, compels *Solyman* to retreat into *David's* tower ib. 514
—— his ftation in the *Chriftian* army xx. 63
—— defeats the *Egyptians*, *Moors* and *Arabians*, &c. ib. 350
—— kills *Affimirus* ib. 356
—— paffes by *Armida's* chariot ib. 404
—— is attacked by her lovers ib. 412
—— is fhot at by *Armida* ib. 420
—— fights with, and kills *Adraftus* ib. 676
—— kills *Solyman* ib. 702
—— fights with, and kills *Tifaphernes* ib. 765
—— follows *Armida* ib. 813
—— prevents her from killing herfelf ib. 853
—— foothes her grief, and promifes to reftore her to her Father's throne ib. 911

Ripoldo, in the review xvii. 216
RIVER, divides its waters at the command of a Magician xiv. 265
Roberts, two, in the review i. 295—337
—— their ftation in the *Chriftian* army xx. 57
—— engage *Adraftus* and *Emirenes* ib. 319
—— one of them wounded by *Emirenes*, and one taken prifoner by *Adraftus* ib. 469

Rogero,

INDEX.

Rogero, in the review i. 410
—— demands to fight with *Argantes* vii. 487
—— opposes *Argantes* ib. 773
—— is overthrown by him ib. 780
—— killed by *Tisaphernes* xx. 747
Rosano killed by *Godfrey* ix. 702
Rosmondo, in the review i. 413
—— killed by *Altamorus* xx. 248
Rosteno, wounded by *Godfrey* ix. 700
Roussillon, one of the champions drawn by lot, to accompany *Armida* v. 38
(See *Champions*.)

S

Sabinus (one of *Latinus's* sons) with his father, and brothers, attacks *Solyman* ix. 233
—— killed by him ib. 257
Saladine killed by *Argillan* ib. 609
Samaria iii. 439
SIEGE, operations offensive and defensive, at the siege of *Jerusalem*, xi. 172 to the end. xviii. 314—326, 426 to the end
Sardinia xv. 148
Selim killed by *Godfrey* ix. 701
Senapus, King of *Ethiopia*, jealous of his Queen, confines her in a tower from the sight of men xii. 159
SERPENT, opposes *Ubald* and *Charles* in their ascent to *Armida's* palace xv. 359
Sforza, in the review i. 416
SHEPHERD, with his sons, feeding sheep, on the banks of the river *Jordan* vii. 39
—— is accosted by *Erminia* ib. 45

SHEPHERD relates to her the story of his life ib. 56
—— entertains her in his cottage, and receives her among the shepherds ib. 119
Sigero commands the *Christians*, in *Godfrey's* name, to retire from the field iii. 402
—— is in *Godfrey's* tent when he is wounded xi. 466
—— killed by *Argantes* ib. 550
SIMILES, instruction conveyed in verse— to physick sweetened to deceive children i. 21
—— *Rinaldo's* early virtues—to trees yielding fruit and blossoms at the same time ib. 439
—— his person—to *Mars* and *Cupid* ib. 441
—— the joy of the *Christian* army at the sound of drums and trumpets before their march—to that of husbandmen at the noise of thunder, which foreruns rain ib. 537
—— the march of the *Christian* army—to the inundation of a river ib. 567
—— *Aladine*—to a snake and a lion ib. 641
—— *Argantes* declaring war—to *Nimrod* ib. 689
—— the joy of the *Christian* army at the sight of *Jerusalem*—to that of sailors at the prospect of land iii. 25
—— the confused sounds heard among the soldiers—to the murmurs of the wind through the leaves of

INDEX.

of trees, or the noise of waves breaking upon the shore *ib*. 45
SIMILES, *Clorinda's* hair tinged with blood from her wound—to rubies set in gold *ib*. 230
—— *Clorinda* flying from the *Christians*—to a bull pursued by dogs *ib*. 142
—— *Pluto's* groaning—to the bellowing of a bull iv. 67
—— his stature—to mount *Atlas* *ib*. 45
—— his eyes—to a comet *ib*. 51
—— his mouth—to a whirlpool *ib*. 55
—— his speaking—to the eruptions of mount *Ætna* *ib* 57
—— the blast of the infernal trumpet—to the noise of thunder and earthquakes *ib*. 21
—— the Demons rushing from hell—to tempests bursting from their caves *ib*. 143
—— *Armida's* appearance in the *Christian* camp — to a blazing star *ib*. 225
—— her locks—to sun-beams *ib*. 234
—— her tears—to pearls in the sun *ib*. 547
—— to dews on flowers *ib*. 550
—— *Rinaldo* armed—to *Mars* attended by Rage and Terror v. 328
—— *Argantes* defying the *Christians* — to *Enceladus* or *Goliath* vi. 178
—— the inarticulate rage of *Argantes* — to the roaring of wild beasts, or the noise of thunder *ib*. 286
SIMILES, *Argantes* wounded— to a wild boar *ib*. 331
—— *Erminia* flying from the *Christians*—to a hind flying from the hounds vi. 766
—— the *Christian* knights returning from the pursuit of *Erminia*—to dogs quitting the field when they have lost scent of the game vii. 7
—— *Tancred* taken prisoner in *Armida's* castle—to fishes caught in a net *ib*. 337
—— *Argantes* armed for the battle—to a comet *ib*. 581
—— to a bull *ib*. 599
—— *Raymond*—to a snake casting his skin *ib*. 523
—— *Argantes*, worsted in the fight—to a ship shattered by storms *ib*. 706
—— an insurrection of the army —to liquor boiling over in a vessel viii. 544
—— the rebels laying down their arms, and submitting to *Godfrey*—to a lion yielding to his keeper *ib*. 616
—— *Solyman's* fury in attacking the *Christian* camp—to storms, floods, lightening and earthquakes ix. 169
—— *Solyman* seen by night in battle—to a tempestuous sea seen by the flashes of lightening *ib*. 201
—— *Latinus* encouraging his sons to attack *Solyman*— to a lioness leading her whelps against the hunters ix. 225

SIMILES,

INDEX.

SIMILES, *Solyman* unmoved amidst the weapons of the enemy—to a rock amidst the waves *ib.* 241
—— the fall of *Latinus*—to that of an oak *ib.* 302
—— *Godfrey's* troops increasing in their march—to the river *Po* overflowing its banks *ib.* 355
—— the battle in suspense—to the billows of the sea driven to and fro by contrary winds *ib.* 403
—— the splendor of the Archangel *Michael*—to a rainbow *ib.* 483
—— his descent—to a falling star. *ib.* 485
—— *Garnier's* hand cut off—to a serpent divided *ib.* 535
—— *Argillan* rushing from his prison to battle—to a horse breaking from his stall and flying to the pastures *ib.* 577
—— *Lesbinus* killed—to a withered flower *ib.* 664
—— *Solyman* insulting *Argillan* dead—to a dog venting his rage on a stone *ib.* 683
—— flying from the field—to a wolf driven from the fold x. 9
—— *Argantes*—to a lion *ib.* 400
—— *Clorinda* on the battlements—to *Diana* xi. 197
—— *Solyman* and *Argantes* armed with fire-brands—to furies *ib.* 452
—— the *Christians'* tower battered and broken—to a ship damaged in a storm xi. 573

SIMILES, *Clorinda* retiring from the field—to a wolf xii. 391
—— the rage of *Argantes* and *Clorinda*—to the waves of the *Egean* sea *ib.* 481
—— *Tancred's* grief being increased by admonition—to a wound receiving fresh pain from being probed by the surgeon *ib.* 639
—— *Tancred* mourning for *Clorinda*—to a nightingale lamenting the loss of her young *ib.* 673
—— the terror of the *Christians* at entering the enchanted wood—to that of children at the approach of night xiii. 129
—— *Tancred's* amazement at hearing a voice from the cypress—to the emotions of one terrified in a dream *ib.* 318
—— the joy of the *Christians* at a seasonable shower of rain—to that of water-fowl *ib.* 546
—— a Magician walking on the water—to peasants skaiting on the ice xiv. 249
—— a glimmering light seen in a gloomy passage—to the new moon shining thro' the trees *ib.* 272
—— a Syren coming out of a river—to figures rising from a stage *ib.* 441
—— *Armida* hanging over *Rinaldo*—to *Narcissus* admiring himself in the fountain *ib.* 482
—— the two knights lifted up by the tide—to leaves rising with the stream xv. 21

SIMILES,

INDEX.

SIMILES, The pilot's changeable vest—to the colours of a dove's feathers *ib.* 35
—— the miraculous bark passing through the *Egyptian* fleet—to an eagle flying above other birds *ib.* 95
—— a nymph rising out of the water—to *Venus* and the morning star *ib.* 449
—— *Armida's* labyrinth—to the windings of the river *Meander* xvi. 56
—— *Rinaldo*, at the sudden appearance of *Charles* and *Ubald*—to a war horse at the sight of arms *ib.* 199
—— his confusion—to the surprise of a person waking from a lethargy *ib.* 221
—— *Armida* preparing to address *Rinaldo*—to musicians preluding to a concert *ib.* 305
—— the disappearance of her palace—to the vanishing of clouds or dreams *ib.* 503
—— the sands of the desart—to the waves of the sea xvii. 6
—— the Caliph on his throne—to a figure of *Jupiter* by *Phidias* or *Apelles* xvii. 75
—— *Armida's* chariot—to the sun's *ib.* 242
—— *Armida* in her chariot—to the *Phœnix* *ib.* 250
—— *Rinaldo's* vest assuming a fresh lustre—to a serpent casting his slough, or a flower reviving with the dew xviii. 109

SIMILES, A nymph issuing from the trunk of a tree—to the goddesses of the woods xviii. 177
—— the fall of an engine—to a fragment tumbling from a mountain *ib.* 554
—— *Ismeno*, on the walls—to *Dis* or *Charon* *ib.* 599
—— the combat of *Tancred* and *Argantes*—to the engagement of two ships xix. 83
—— their grappling—to *Hercules* grasping *Antæus* *ib.* 109
—— *Argantes* rising again from the ground—to a pine *ib.* 121
—— his last rage—to a torch's blaze when near extinguished *ib.* 143
—— *Rinaldo* endeavouring to enter a fort—to a wolf attempting to leap a fold *ib.* 232
—— *Solyman* retreating with his men into the fort—to a shepherd retiring with his flock from the field, at the approach of a storm *ib.* 318
—— the shout of the *Pagans*—to the noise of cranes xx. 11
—— the force of *Godfrey's* elocution—to the fall of torrents *ib.* 83
—— *Gildippe*—to an *Amazon* *ib.* 263
—— *Ormond* and his confederates—to wolves lurking among the dogs *ib.* 285
—— the swift motion of *Rinaldo's* sword—to a serpent's tongue *ib.* 364

Vol. II. B b SIMILES,

INDEX.

SIMILES, Rinaldo's fury decreasing as the enemy flies—to winds that blow gently when not opposed *ib.* 384
—— his rage—to a storm tearing up the corn *ib.* 398
—— Armida fearful of being made prisoner—to a swan threatened by an eagle xx. 452
—— Solyman, slaughtering the Christians—to a wolf *ib.* 516
—— to a bird of prey *ib.* 518
—— his sudden rushing into the field—to lightening *ib.* 612
—— the fall of Edward and Gildippe—to that of an elm and vine *ib.* 650
—— Solyman's efforts at the approach of Rinaldo—to those of men in sleep *ib.* 692
—— Tisaphernes encountering Rinaldo—to a lion *ib.* 761
—— attempting to follow Armida—to Marc Anthony *ib.* 791
—— Armida fainting—to a flower *ib.* 863
—— recovering from her swoon—to a rose revived with the dew *ib.* 869
—— her anger mollified by Rinaldo's words—to snows melting in the sun *ib.* 923

Solomon's temple, the Pagans take shelter in it xix. 220
—— the gate forced open by Rinaldo *ib.* 242

Solyman, late Sovereign of the Turks, his character and former dominions ix. 19
—— levies a body of Arabians *ib.* 41

Solyman is incited by Alecto to attack the Christians by night *ib.* 57
—— marches towards their camp *ib.* 97
—— animates the troops *ib.* 127
—— begins the assault *ib.* 169
—— his dreadful appearance *ib.* 193
—— is assailed by Latinus and his five sons *ib.* 233
—— kills his eldest son *ib.* 247
—— kills Aramantes, Sabinus, Picus and Laurentes *ib.* 249. *ib.* 257. *ib.* 263
—— is wounded by Latinus *ib.* 289
—— kills Latinus *ib.* 293
—— encounters Godfrey *ib.* 381
—— his grief for the death of Lesbinus *ib.* 657
—— kills Argillan *ib.* 677
—— is compelled to fly from the field *ib.* 753. x. 1
—— is accosted in his way to Gaza by Ismeno *ib.* 45
—— is conducted by him in an enchanted chariot to Jerusalem x. 95
—— their conversation on the way *ib.* 118
—— is led by him through a subterraneous passage into the council hall, where he stands concealed in a cloud, and hears the debates *ib.* 200
—— is discovered by the removal of the cloud, and addresses the assembly *ib.* 344
—— is welcomed by Aladine *ib.* 376
—— defends the city xi. 186, 340

Solyman

INDEX.

Solyman stands in the breach with *Argantes* *ib.* 431
—— sallies on the *Christians* with *Argantes* *ib.* 437
—— returns again to the breach *ib.* 456
—— takes his post against *Godfrey*, at the last attack of the town xviii. 460
—— opposes *Godfrey* in his attempt to gain the walls *ib.* 668
—— retreats, with part of the *Pagans*, to *David's* tower xix. 260
—— defends the pass with great intrepidity *ib.* 284
—— fells *Raymond* *ib.* 296
—— retires into the fort at the appearance of *Godfrey* and *Rinaldo* *ib.* 326
—— encourages the *Pagans* *ib.* 362
—— from the summit of the tower, sees the *Christian* and *Egyptian* armies engaged xx. 483
—— sallies on the *Christians* that surround the tower, and makes a great slaughter *ib.* 499
—— fells *Raymond* again *ib.* 524
—— rushes into the main battle *ib.* 604
—— kills *Edward* and *Gildippe* *ib.* 628
—— is assailed by *Rinaldo* *ib.* 684
—— is killed by him *ib.* 702
Song of a *Syren* to *Rinaldo* xiv. 454
—— of a nymph to *Charles* and *Ubald* xv. 467
—— of a wonderful bird in *Armida's* garden xvi. 99
—— of nymphs in the enchanted wood to *Rinaldo* xviii. 189
Sophronia, her character ii. 99
—— hears of the intended massacre of the *Christians* in *Jerusalem* *ib.* 120
—— goes to the King, and accuses herself of having stolen the image of the Virgin *Mary* from the mosque *ib.* 156
—— is condemned to die *ib.* 192
—— endeavours to dissuade *Olindo* from his purpose of suffering with her *ib.* 222
—— counsels him at the stake *ib.* 268
—— her fortitude *ib.* 320
—— is released at the intercession of *Clorinda*, and marries *Olindo* *ib.* 404
—— is sent with him into exile ii. 412
SPEECH of the Angel *Gabriel* to *Godfrey* i. 123
—— of *Godfrey* to the council *ib.* 161
—— of *Peter*, persuading them to elect a General *ib.* 227
—— of *Ismeno*, to induce *Aladine* to take away the image of the Virgin *Mary* from the *Christian* temple *ib.* 17
—— of *Aladine* ii. 83
—— of *Olindo*, desiring to suffer in *Sophronia's* stead *ib.* 208
—— of *Olindo* and *Sophronia* at the stake *ib.* 250, *& seq.*
—— of *Clorinda* and *Aladine* *ib.* 350
—— of *Clorinda* interceding for *Olindo* and *Sophronia* *ib.* 574

INDEX.

SPEECH of *Alethes* to *Godfrey*, persuading him to give over his design against *Jerusalem* ib. 472
—— *Godfrey*'s answer ib. 608
—— of *Erminia*, describing the *Christian* commanders iii. 145, 287, 449
—— of *Godfrey* over *Dudon*'s body ib. 519
—— of *Pluto* to the infernal Council iv. 65
—— of *Armida* to *Godfrey*, relating her pretended misfortunes, and desiring his assistance ib. 305—474
—— *Godfrey*'s answer ib. 496
—— of *Armida* on *Godfrey*'s refusal ib. 516
—— of *Eustatius* to *Godfrey*, pleading in her behalf ib. 572
—— *Godfrey*'s answer ib. 604
—— of *Godfrey*, *Eustatius*, and *Rinaldo* v. 15, & seq.
—— of *Godfrey*, *Tancred*, *Arnaldo*, and *Raymond*, on *Rinaldo*'s killing *Gernando* ib. 238, & seq.
—— of *Rinaldo*, on hearing *Godfrey*'s design to call him to account ib. 309
—— of *Tancred*, persuading *Rinaldo* to leave the camp ib. 332
—— of *Godfrey* and *Guelpho* ib. 395
—— of *Godfrey*, to encourage his army ib. 645
—— of *Argantes* to *Aladine*, desiring a single combat with one of the *Christians* vi. 17
—— *Aladine*'s answer ib. 65
—— *Erminia*'s soliloquies on her love for *Tancred* ib. 513, 585
SPEECH of *Erminia* on sight of the *Christian* camp ib. 740
—— of the shepherd to *Erminia* vii. 56
—— of *Raymond*, dissuading *Godfrey* from undertaking the combat with *Argantes* vii. 452
—— of *Argantes* defying the whole *Christian* army ib. 537
—— of *Charles* the *Dane* to *Godfrey*, relating the death of *Sweno* viii. 35—311
—— of *Sweno* before the battle ib. 99
—— of the Hermit, to *Charles* the *Dane* viii. 207, 246
—— *Godfrey*'s answer to *Charles* the *Dane* ib. 352
—— of *Argillan* inciting the *Italians* to revolt ib. 462
—— of *Godfrey* to the rebels ib. 584
—— of *Alecto* to *Solyman*, inciting him to attack the *Christian* camp ix. 65
—— of *Solyman* to his troops ib. 129
—— of the Arch-angel *Michael* to the Demons ib. 491
—— of *Ismeno* and *Solyman* x. 47, & seq.
—— of *Aladine* to his council ib. 245
—— of *Argantes*, in answer ib. 257
—— of *Orcanes* ib. 277
—— of *Solyman*, breaking from a cloud ib. 350
—— of *William*, relating the adventures of the champions

INDEX.

pions that followed *Armida* ib. 430—530
SPEECH of *Peter*, prophesying the glory of *Rinaldo*'s posterity ib. 541
—— of *Argantes*, insulting the *Christians* xi. 419
—— of *Argantes* and *Clorinda*, on a design to burn the *Christian* tower xii. 15, & *seq.*
—— of *Aladine* and *Solyman*, on the same ib. 77
—— of *Arsetes* to *Clorinda*, relating to her the story of her birth ib. 159—312
—— of an Apparition, commanding *Arsetes* to baptize *Clorinda* ib. 276
—— of the same, foretelling her death xii. 300
—— *Clorinda*'s answer to *Arsetes* ib. 316
—— of *Tancred* and *Clorinda* during their combat ib. 457
—— of *Clorinda* at her death, desiring baptism ib. 501
—— of *Tancred*, lamenting her death ib. 569, 613, 721
—— of *Peter* to *Tancred*, rebuking him for his excessive grief ib. 645
—— of *Clorinda*, appearing to *Tancred* in a dream ib. 683
—— of *Argantes*, vowing to revenge *Clorinda*'s death ib. 759
—— of *Ismeno*, invoking the Demons xiii. 45, 69
—— of the same to *Aladine* ib. 93
—— of *Tancred* to *Godfrey*, giving an account of the enchanted wood ib. 340

SPEECH of *Peter*, foretelling the return of *Rinaldo* ib. 366
—— of *Hugo*, in a dream to *Godfrey* xiv. 55
—— of the same, advising him to recall *Rinaldo* ib. 91, & *seq.*
—— of *Guelpho*, pleading for *Rinaldo*'s return xiv. 154
—— *Godfrey*'s answer ib. 167
—— of the *Christian* Magician to *Charles* and *Ubald* ib. 302
—— of the same, relating the manner of *Rinaldo*'s being ensnared by *Armida*, &c. ib. 369—578
—— of *Ubald* to *Rinaldo*, reproaching his effeminacy xvi. 227
—— of *Armida* to *Rinaldo*, to prevail on him to suffer her to accompany him ib. 313
—— *Rinaldo*'s answer ib. 367
—— her furious reply ib. 399
—— her soliloquy on his leaving her ib. 447
—— of the Caliph of *Egypt* to *Emirenes*, on giving him the command of the army xvii. 274
—— *Emirenes*' answer ib. 284
—— of *Armida* to the Caliph, offering her hand in marriage to him who shall kill *Rinaldo* ib. 308
—— of the *Christian* Magician to *Rinaldo* ib. 423
—— of the Magician, prophesying the future glory of *Alphonso* of *Est.* ib. 588
—— of *Rinaldo* and *Godfrey*, at their meeting xviii. 1, & *seq.*
—— of *Peter* to *Rinaldo* ib. 41, 60

INDEX.

SPEECH of the Demon in *Armida*'s likeness, to *Rinaldo* ib. 208, 232
—— of *Godfrey* to his commanders ib. 358
—— of *Michael* the Arch-angel, to *Godfrey* ib. 632
—— of *Tancred* and *Argantes*, before their last combat xix. 13, & seq.
—— of *Tancred* to *Argantes*, offering him peace xix. 133
—— *Argantes*' answer ib. 137
—— of *Solyman* and *Aladine* xix. 270, & seq.
—— of *Godfrey* to his troops ib. 347
—— of *Solyman*, to encourage the *Pagans* ib. 364
—— of *Armida*, *Adrastus*, and *Tisaphernes* ib. 476, & seq.
—— of *Erminia*, discovering herself to *Vafrino* ib. 546, & seq.
—— of the same, relating the design of the *Pagans* against *Godfrey*'s life ib. 588
—— of the same, relating her love to *Tancred*, &c. ib. 617
—— of *Tancred*, recovering from his swoon ib. 792, 805
—— of *Vafrino* to *Godfrey*, giving an account of his discoveries in the *Egyptian* camp ib. 825
—— of *Raymond* and *Godfrey* thereupon ib. 877
—— of *Godfrey*, to his army before the battle xx. 87
—— of *Emirenes* to his army ib. 153

SPEECH of *Tancred*, rebuking the *Gascons* for flying ib. 560
—— of *Emirenes*, rebuking *Rimedon* for flying ib. 724
—— *Armida*'s soliloquy on attempting to kill herself ib. 831
—— her speech to *Rinaldo*, on seeing him ib. 883
—— *Rinaldo*'s answer ib. 912
—— of *Altamorus*, on surrendering himself to *Godfrey* ib. 974
—— *Godfrey*'s answer ib. 979
Stephen, earl of *Amboise*, in the review i. 465
—— killed by an arrow from *Clorinda* xi. 298
STORM, raised by the Demons in favour of the *Pagans* vii. 828
Sweno, prince of *Denmark*, his impatience to join *Godfrey* viii. 39
—— marches with a select body of friends, from his father's court ib. 54
—— encamps near *Palestine* ib. 89
—— hears of a numerous army of *Arabians* advancing towards him ib. 91
—— his behaviour and speech to his companions thereupon ib. 95
—— his camp is attacked in the night ib. 112
—— his intrepidity ib. 117
—— makes great slaughter of the *Pagans* ib. 132
—— his last actions ib. 156
—— his death ib. 166
—— his body is miraculously enclosed in a tomb ib. 229

Syphantes,

INDEX.

Syphantes, in the review xvii. 221
Syphax, in the review ib. 156
SYREN, rises out of a river xiv. 439
—— her song to *Rinaldo* ib. 455

T.

Tancred characterised i. 67
—— in the review ib. 344
—— the particulars of his falling in love with *Clorinda* ib. 532
—— encounters *Clorinda* iii. 159
—— his interview with her ib. 192
—— pursues a soldier that wounds her ib. 222
—— supports his troops, and overthrows the *Pagans* ib. 272
—— pleads with *Godfrey* in *Rinaldo's* excuse v. 262
—— persuades *Rinaldo* to retire from the camp ib. 331
—— is proof against the charms of *Armida* ib. 469
—— is named by *Godfrey* to fight with *Argantes* vi. 190
—— sees *Clorinda* ib. 196
—— fights with *Argantes* ib. 289
—— they are parted by the heralds ib. 364
—— the combat deferred to the sixth day following ib. 393
—— hears of *Erminia's* approach to the *Christian* camp, and goes in search of her, supposing her to be *Clorinda* ib. 807. vii. 169
—— is conducted to *Armida's* castle vii. 206
—— fights with *Rambaldo* ib. 272

Tancred is made prisoner by enchantment ib. 333
—— returns to the camp with the rest of the *Christian* Knights ix. 713
—— pursues *Clorinda*, not knowing her xii. 395
—— fights with her ib. 413
—— desires to know her name ib. 457
—— mortally wounds her ib. 485
—— gives her baptism ib. 511
—— his distraction at knowing her ib. 517, 534
—— falls in a swoon by her side ib. 537
—— is carried with her to his tent ib. 551
—— laments her death ib. 567, 612
—— is rebuked by *Peter* for his excessive grief ib. 642
—— is comforted by *Clorinda*, who appears to him in a dream ib. 677
—— causes her to be buried ib. 703
—— his speech at her tomb ib. 721
—— undertakes the adventure of the Enchanted Wood xiii. 227
—— enters the Wood ib. 241
—— sees an inscription on a cypress ib. 272
—— attempts to cut down the tree ib. 294
—— sees blood issue, and hears a voice from the trunk ib. 296
—— returns to the camp without dissolving the enchantment ib. 318
—— relates his adventure to *Godfrey* xiii. 340

Tancred

INDEX.

Tancred offers his squire to be sent as a spy to the *Egyptian* camp xviii. 384
—— plants his standard on the walls of *Jerusalem* ib. 696
—— is reproached by *Argantes* with breach of faith xix. 9
—— defies him, and retires with him from the walls, to engage in single combat ib. 21
—— their combat described ib. 69
—— makes offers of peace to *Argantes* ib. 133
—— kills him ib. 176
—— faints away with the loss of blood ib. 184
—— is found by *Erminia* and *Vafrino* ib. 687
—— is recovered from his swoon by *Erminia* ib. 768
—— desires *Argantes*' body may be buried, and that himself may be carried to *Jerusalem* ib. 792
—— hears the tumult of the battle from the place where he lies ill of his wounds, sallies forth, and defends *Raymond* xx. 548
Tatinus, leader of the *Greeks*, in the review i. 386
—— murmurs against *Godfrey* xiii. 582
—— revolts from the army ib. 490
Tigranes, killed by *Dudon* iii. 332
Tigress gives suck to an infant xii. 222
Tisaphernus, in the review xvii. 224

Tisaphernus, his contention with *Adrastus* concerning *Armida* ib. 344. xix. 452
—— his station in the *Egyptian* army xx. 145
—— his valour ib. 324
—— disperses the *Normans* and *Flemings* ib. 745
—— kills *Gernier*, *Gerrard*, and *Rogero* ib. 747
—— attacks *Rinaldo* ib. 752
—— sees *Armida* fly from the field ib. 799
—— is killed by *Rinaldo* ib. 807
Tortosa i. 47
Towers, wooden, used by the *Christians* in the siege xi. 317. xviii. 434
Tower, battered by the *Pagans* xi. 326, 570
—— burnt by *Argantes* and *Clorinda* xii. 347
—— particular description of one xviii. 300
(See *Engines*.)
Tripoly xv. 129
Tunis ib. 133

U. V.

Ubald, in the review i. 412
—— is appointed with *Charles* the *Dane* to go in search of *Rinaldo* xiv. 203
—— his character ib. 206
—— meets with a Magician, who conducts him and *Charles* to his subterraneous dwelling ib. 243
—— hears from the Magician, the manner of *Rinaldo's* being ensnared by *Armida*, and receives instructions for his deliverance xiv. 400
—— enters into the miraculous bark with *Charles* xv. 21

INDEX.

Ubald converses with the pilot
  ib. 202, 212
—— ascends *Armida's* mountain, and puts the monsters to flight with an enchanted wand *ib.* 373
—— enters the palace, and reproaches *Rinaldo* with effeminacy xvi. 227
  (See *Charles*.)
Vafrino, Tancred's squire, his character xviii. 384
—— is sent as a spy to the *Egyptian* camp *ib.* 392
—— arrives at the *Egyptian* camp xix. 380
—— overhears a conversation between *Emirenes* and *Ormond* *ib.* 406
—— sees *Armida* with her lovers in her tent *ib.* 452
—— is known by *Erminia*
  ib. 530
—— departs with her from the camp *ib.* 576
—— hears from her the design of the *Pagans* against *Godfrey* *ib.* 588
—— finds *Tancred* wounded
  ib. 687
—— causes him to be carried to the city *ib.* 783
—— gives *Godfrey* an account of his discoveries in the *Egyptian* camp *ib.* 825
Vincislaus, one of the champions drawn by lot to accompany *Armida* v. 529
  (See *Champions*.)
VOICE heard by *Tancred*, when taken prisoner in *Armida's* castle vii. 345
—— heard by *Tancred* from the trunk of a tree
  xiii. 301

VOYAGE of the two knights through the *Mediterranean* to the *Fortunate Islands* xv. 69—280
W.
William, of *England*, in the review i. 338
—— described by *Erminia*
  iii. 483
—— relates the adventure of the *Christian* knights in *Armida's* castle x. 430
—— wounded by *Clorinda*
  xi. 287
William (the Bishop) in the review i. 297
—— in the procession xi. 73
William, of *Liguria*, sends advice from the fleet to *Godfrey* v. 617
—— leaves the ships, and joins the land forces xviii. 290
—— his skill in mechanics
  ib. 294
—— gives directions for making military engines
  ib. 296
WOOD (enchanted)
—— the *Christians* attempt, in vain, to enter it
  xiii. 121, 187
—— guarded by dreadful apparitions, and surrounded with fiery walls
  ib. 193
—— entered by *Tancred ib.* 227
—— further described *ib.* 260
—— entered by *Rinaldo*
  xviii. 111
—— fine description of it
  ib. 111—160
—— the enchantment is dissolved by *Rinaldo ib.* 238
  (See *Demons, Forest,* &c.)

FINIS.

www.ingramcontent.com/pod-product-compliance
Lightning Source LLC
Chambersburg PA
CBHW030403230426
43664CB00007BB/725